SPIRITUAL WARFARE HANDBOOK

From a Biblical, Evangelical Perspective

"For we are not ignorant of Satan's devices." II Cor. 2:5-11

EDWARD JOHNSON

Copyright Ó2024

QUICK REFERENCE GUIDE

Armor of God 64-70

Bible verses to use 70-72, 95-100

How Do We Know Bible Is True? 82-86

How Do We Know God Exists? 79-81

How Do We Know Jesus is God? 87-91

Listening to God 101-112

Openings for Demonizing 33, 37-37

Prayer, spiritual warfare 75

Prayer, for the armor 69-70

Steps to Deliverance 49-54

Symptoms of Demonizing 20 Topical Index 95-100

PRAYERS

Prayer for forgiveness of anger 30 Prayer for forgiveness of sin 29

Prayer for Freemasonry 41-42 Prayer for generational bondage 24

Prayer for idolatry sins 30

Prayer for marriage 59

Prayer for Masonic bondage 41-42 Prayer for occult involvement 41

Prayer for occult or New Age 45 Prayer for recovery from sin 36

Prayer for secret societies 41-42 Prayer for sexual sins 31

Prayer for son or daughter 58

Prayer for spiritual warfare in general 75-76 Prayer for the armor 69-70

Prayer for victory over fear 18

Prayer for victory over self-destruction, suicide, etc. 19

Prayer to break ungodly soul ties 27 Prayer to cleanse room or home 23

Prayer to forgive others 30, 51

Table Of Contents

SO YOU'RE IN A WAR! 1

I. **COMMANDERS BEHIND DEMONIZING** 3

    A. **THE GOOD GUYS** 3

    B. **THE BAD GUYS** 7

        1) SATAN - THE ENEMY COMMANDER 7

        2) DEMONS - ENEMY SOLDIERS 13

        3) DEATH, DARKNESS & SPIRITUAL BLINDNESS 17

II. **CHARACTERISTICS OF DEMONIZING** 24

    A. **DEMONIZING DEFINED** 24

    B. **DEMONIZING DEFENDED** 25

        CAN A BELIEVER BE DEMONIZED? 25

    C. **DEMONIZING DESCRIBED** 26

        THOUGHTS IN, THOUGHTS OUT 26

        LET YOUR MIND EXPLAIN REALITY TO YOUR EMOTIONS 27

        WHAT THE BIBLE SAYS ABOUT THE MIND 27

        HOW CAN WE BE DECEIVED IF WE KNOW THE TRUTH? 30

        RECOGNIZING TRUTH 31

        COMPULSIVE & OBSESSIVE THOUGHTS 31

        MENTAL ILLNESS 32

        SCHIZOPHRENIA 32

        FEAR 33

        ANGER 35

        CUTTING, SELF MUTILATION, SUICIDE 36

        OTHER CHARACTERISTICS OF DEMONIZING 37

        HOW RESPONSIBLE ARE THE DEMONIZED? 37

	EVIDENCE OF DEMONIZING 38

III. CAUSES FOR DEMONIZING 41

- A. **PHYSICAL ATTACK** 42
- B. **HISTORICAL ATTACK** 46
- C. **RELATIONAL ATTACK** 55
- D. **SPIRITUAL ATTACK** 56
    - REMEMBER, GOD PROMISES VICTORY! 57
    - ANGER BASED SINS 58
    - IDOLATRY BASED SINS 59
    - IMMORALITY BASED SINS 60
    - WRONG SELF IMAGE BASED SINS 62
    - LIST OF COMMON SINS 63
    - PATTACHING THE CRACKS 67
    - CONFESSION OF SIN 68
    - RECOVERY FROM SIN 73
    - WHO MAY BE DEMONIZED? 74
    - OCCULT & NEW AGE 78
    - OCCULT IN GENERAL 79
    - THE OCCULT AND DEMONIZING 81
    - SECRET SOCIETIES 84
    - SATANISM 87
    - NEW AGE 88
    - THE SOLUTION FOR MAN - AS NEW AGE SEES IT 91
    - THE DANGERS OF NEW AGE THOUGHT 91
    - CURE FOR THOSE INVOLVED IN OCCULT OR NEW AGE 95
    - MARTIAL ARTS AND THE BELIEVER 96
    - CONCLUSION TO SECTION ON CAUSES OF DEMONIZING 97

- **IV. CURE FROM DEMONIZING** 98
  - **A. THE SOURCE OF DELIVERANCE** 98
    - NO COMPROMISE WITH DEMONS 99
  - **B. STEPS TO DELIVERANCE** 100
    - AS JESUS DID IT 100
    - AS THE DISCIPLES DID IT 101
    - AS WE ARE TO DO IT TODAY 101
  - **C. SPECIFICS ABOUT DELIVERANCE** 114
    - PHYSICAL HEALING 114
    - FASTING 117
    - CHILDREN 118
    - HUSBAND AND WIFE 122
    - PARENT AND CHILD 124
    - THE CHURCH'S ROLE 125
- **V. CONTINUING BEYOND DEMONIZING** 128
  - **A. PROBLEM: ONGOING BATTLE** 128
    - WHY DOES GOD ALLOW THE BATTLE TO CONTINUE? 129
  - **B. SOLUTION: ONGOING BATTLE** 130
    - GROW SPIRITUALLY 131
    - SUBMIT TO HOLY SPIRIT 132
    - WEAR THE ARMOR 133
    - USE THE WORD OF GOD 144
    - RESIST, STAND FIRM 147
    - PRAY 149
    - HELPING OTHERS 156
    - OUR ROLE IN HELPING OTHERS (What God Expects) 157
    - WHAT YOU CAN DO TO HELP THOSE STRUGGLING: 158

IN CLOSING	**159**
APPENDIX 1	**161**
HOW DO WE KNOW GOD EXISTS	161
APPENDIX 2	**167**
HOW DO WE KNOW THE BIBLE IS GOD"S WORD?	167
APPENDIX 3	**180**
HOW DO WE KNOW JESUS IS GOD?	180
APPENDIX 4	**192**
HOW CAN I BE SURE I AM A CHRISTIAN?	192
APPENDIX 5	**194**
HOW CAN I BE SURE I STILL AM A CHRISTIAN?	194
APPENDIX 6	**197**
TOPICAL INDEX	197
APPENDIX 7	**208**
LISTENING TO GOD; What Does He Sounds Like?	208
APPENDIX 8	**222**
LISTENING TO GOD Telling God's Voice From Satan?	222
APPENDIX 9	**229**
DOES GOD WANT US TO SPEAK IN TONGUES TODAY?	229
APPENDIX 10	**234**
IS IT GOD"S WILL FOR EVERYONE TO BE HEALED TODAY?	234

SO YOU'RE IN A WAR!

One day a young man was out for a walk. As he went along the street, he saw a sign that invited him to sign up to see the world for free. Food, lodging, everything would be provided. He would be paid a salary, too. It sounded fine, too fine to pass up. So, he went in and signed his name. To his surprise, he was handed a rifle and military equipment. He soon discovered a whole army of soldiers who now were his enemy and whose sworn purpose was to destroy him. It wasn't what he expected.

There are many Christians today who, when they accepted Jesus as Savior, were surprised to find they, too had an enemy. Perhaps they expected life to be perfect and fine, all settled with no more problems. Salvation, though, doesn't end the battle. In many ways, it is just the start of it!

You see, when you accept Jesus as your Savior you also acknowledge Satan as your enemy! You deserted Satan's army to join his enemy's army, God's army. He opposes God, but can only get at God by attacking His people -- you and me!

So now you find yourself in the middle of a war you didn't want, don't like, can't understand, and seem unable to win. What do you do? Where can you find a quick training program for spiritual warfare? Read on, this information is for YOU...

This idea of war following salvation is nothing new. We see the same thing happening to the Jews in the Old Testament. Satan has been opposing God from the beginning, but getting nowhere. He made much more progress when he started attacking God through His creatures. First, Adam and Eve were in Eden, followed by Abraham, Isaac, Jacob, and Joseph. God's people ended up in Egyptian slavery for 400 years until God delivered them. He did it all: provided the innocent blood and the power to protect them from the angel of death as well as deliver them unharmed through the Red Sea. They did nothing but accept His salvation. Then the battles started for them: the Amalekites attacked, then the Canaanites, and on it went. The Jews had to learn to fight. When they learned to fight behind their leader Joshua ("Jesus" in Greek) they conquered and settled the land God had meant all along for them to have. When we learn to fight behind our general, Jesus, we, too, can have victory in life.

First of all, what are the weapons this enemy uses against you? The Bible says they are three-fold, "the world the flesh, and the devil." The world refers to the organized system of ideas, people, activities, purposes, goals, motives, priorities, and values that are based on Satan's system (I John 2:15; John 15:19). The "world" does not refer to nature, but to Satan's substitute for God's way. Peer pressure, rejection, persecution, problems getting along with people, pride, desire for popularity and success, etc., all these things are ways Satan attacks us through the world (Matthew 4:8-10; 12:26).

While these attacks are from without, we also have an enemy within -- our flesh. By 'flesh' we mean our old sinful nature, that tendency in us to be naturally self-centered, sinful, prideful, willful, and immature (Romans 7:15-25; Galatians 5:19-20). Even the 'good' we do in the flesh is like filthy rags (Isaiah 64:6). This results in our sinning. Sin is thinking or doing wrong things, doing good things for the wrong reason/motive, or not doing good things that should be done. Temptations to worry, fear, get angry, be greedy, fulfill our lusts, think only of ourselves, feel self-sufficient or self-righteous, be jealous, gossip or criticize, etc. come from or through the flesh (Ephesians 4:22-27).

This booklet is designed to help you in spiritual warfare. It will summarize your battle with the enemy and how to have victory in Jesus.

I. COMMANDERS BEHIND DEMONIZING

A. THE GOOD GUYS

1) GOD - OUR COMMANDER

Everything starts with God. Everything came from Him. If you are unsure of the existence of God this must be settled in your mind to continue. Please read Appendix 1 pages 79-81. The Bible is our final authority in all areas and reveals God's truths for us today. If you aren't convinced of the inspiration and total accuracy of the Bible please read Appendix 2 page 82-86. This must be completely settled in your mind to continue. Finally, you must believe beyond a shadow of a doubt that Jesus is God Himself come to earth. If unsure read Appendix 3 page 87-91. God is our commander in spiritual warfare as well as in every area of life.

2) ANGELS - OUR HELPERS

CREATION God created the angels before the world was created (Job 38:6-7), the same time He planned to create each one of us (and already knew us in His mind). He created an "innumerable" number of angels (Heb. 12:22; Rev 5:11). No angels have been created or destroyed since then. The number is exactly the same. People who die do NOT become angels; in eternity we have a position greater than the angels will have (I Cor. 6:3).

PERSONALITY God created angels and humans in His image in that we all have a mind to rationally think and reason (I Peter 1:12), emotions to feel and experience (Luke 2:13), and a free will to choose our destiny (Jude 6). Soon after creation, the top angel (Lucifer, now called Satan Ezekiel 28:12-15) used his free will to rebel against God (II Thes 2:4) and as a result was kicked out of heaven (Isa 14:12-15, Ezek 28:15-17; Luke 10:18). The angels then had a one- time choice to follow Satan or God. About one-third (Rev. 12:4) followed Satan in his rebellion and also lost their first position, now being called demons. This was the only time angels ever had an opportunity to exercise their free will. They are now „locked in" and cannot change their state (angels cannot fall to becoming demons, demons cannot move up to being angels).

Angels do not know what it is to experience God's grace in their lives. That is why they are so interested in watching us as we talk and live (I Pet 1:12) for our lives show God's grace and love in operation in a way they don't personally experience. They are impressed with God and His undeserved mercy on us. They are amazed at His special love for us, unworthy as we are.

NATURE Angels are spirit beings. They are not like God in that they do not know everything. They are limited to being in one place at a time. They are not all-powerful or all-knowing (Ps 103:20; II Thes. 1:7). They have no physical body, but sometimes do appear in the form of a person (Heb 13:1). This is to help God's people in need. Some have wings to show power and glory, but not all have wings. While possessing all the traits we would call „masculine" and, feminine, " angels are always referred to as masculine. Male pronouns are always used. Angels are different, just like people are different: different abilities and functions in God's service, different traits and skills. Angels can't and don't reproduce (Mt 22:30; Mk 12:25) although it does seem that demons somehow impregnated women before the flood in Noah's day (Genesis 6:1-4). Angels never die (Luke 20:36).

ORGANIZATION Angels (and also demons) are organized in a military-like fashion with generals, colonels, lieutenants, sergeants, privates, etc. They are called archangels, princes, rulers, seraphim, etc. (Rom 8:38; Eph 3:10; 6:12; Col 1:16; 2:5). Some have leadership over geographical areas, others over groups of people (as Michael the archangel cares for Israel).

Apparently, there are different kinds of angels with different characteristics and roles: cherubim, seraphim, and archangels. Seraphim (Isaiah 6:2-3; Ezekiel 1:27) have a fiery appearance because they are usually associated with the Presence of God. Cherubim (Genesis 3:24; Exodus 25:18-22; Hebrews 9:5) are represented with wings, feet, hands and often more than one face (Ezekiel 41:18; 10:21). They guard sacred things (the tree of life in Genesis 3:24; the Ark of the Covenant in 1 Samuel 4:4). Archangels are the highest created beings, angels of the greatest power and majesty. Lucifer (Isaiah 14:12) was an archangel. Michael (1 Thessalonians 4:16; Jude 9) and Gabriel (Daniel 8:15-26; 9:21-27; Luke 1:11-38). Michael and Gabriel are warrior angels (Revelation 12:7) who do battle (Daniel 10:13, 21; 12:1). Gabriel seems to be in charge of the care of the Jews. Other angels exist in various levels of authority and function under these (Ephesians 6:12). God has angels organized in a military-like manner with a chain-of-command from 'generals' to 'privates.'

DUTIES The Greek word for „angel" („angelos") means "messenger." Actually, the word is just transliterated in our Bibles (English letters replace Greek letters but the word is the same). Were it translated into English we would have the word "messenger" every time „angel" appears. That is basically their function -- messengers (servants) of God. They are God's servants who help God's people (Heb 1:14). Individual angels seem assigned to children and believers (Acts 12:12) to help them in special ways.

God could use His sovereign power to do things such as prevent an automobile accident or have a child fall safely and not be hurt, or similar actions, but usually, He has His angels do that work. They protect God's people (Psalm 34:7; 91:12; Matthew 18:10). They bring answers to prayers (Acts 12:7), although sometimes demons oppose them, and the answers are delayed (Dan. 10:10-21). They minister to our physical, spiritual, and emotional needs (Hebrews 1:14). Angels watch and learn from believers (I Cor. 4:9; I Tim 5:2). They encourage us in danger (Acts 27:23-24). They even help in evangelism (Luke 15:10; Acts 8:26). They care for God's people when they die (Luke 16:22; Jude 9). They fight against demons (Revelation 12). They watch God's children to learn about God's grace (I Peter 1:12).

OUR RESPONSE TO ANGELS

Angels are not to be communicated with, ordered around, or in any way contacted by us. They do not steal any of God's glory. We aren't in any way to focus on them or worship them (Revelation 19:10). All the credit and glory go to Him (Revelation 4:11; 5:9-11). All the attention is His. In the Bible when someone tried to give them credit, they passed it on to God. We aren't to communicate with them, but we can ask God to send them to do various things that need doing. And yes, they do manifest at times. There are many cases in the Bible. Sometimes they manifest as spiritual beings. I think young children can see or sense them quite more readily than adults. They also manifest as people and help us without us knowing they are angels. Hebrews 13:2 talks about this. Angels are always present around us, especially when we gather with other believers in Jesus" name. However, we never can see them unless God opens our eyes in a special way (II Kings 6:17). It's quite likely you have seen angels, but in appearance as people (Heb

13:2) and therefore not recognized as an angel. That stranger who just happens to show up at the right time to provide help or assistance, whom we called an angel, "might well have been one!

B. THE BAD GUYS

1) SATAN - THE ENEMY COMMANDER

EXISTENCE OF SATAN Unfortunately we live in a time when more people believe in the Loch Ness Monster than in Satan! Some people who do believe in him tend to make him smaller than he really is. Your devil is too small if you see Satan as merely a personification of evil. The picture of a devil in a red suit with a tail and trident comes from ancient times when red stood for death, horns for power, and tails and cloven hoofs for bestiality. Satan is a real, live personality, not a symbol of evil.

Your devil is also too small if you consign him to long-ago times or faraway places. He is too small if you assume he leaves Christians alone (that's one of his biggest lies, which he uses to cover his tracks). He is too small if you don't think he is capable of performing miracles and other feats of power, or if you think you can recognize and defeat him on your own. He is powerful, even using forces of nature such as lightning (Job 1:16) and strong wind (Job 1:19) to do his will.

On the other hand, some see Satan as more powerful than he is. Your devil is too big if you see him as an evil god. He is not equal to God; he is limited to one place at a time and does not have all knowledge. You also see him as too big if you live in fear of him and avoid learning about how to fight him.

The truth about Satan is that he was created as an angel. He was the top ranking of all God's angels, the highest created being God ever made (Ezekiel 28:12-15). Known as Lucifer, he was the highest angelic creation and the closest to the throne of God. However, he didn't want to serve God but wanted to be worshipped in place of God (II Thessalonians 2:4). His sin was self-centeredness: pride (Isaiah 14:12-15) therefore God threw him out of heaven (Isaiah 14:12; Ezekiel 28:15-17; Luke 10:18). He lost all his position and privilege. With that rebellion of his sin, he entered the universe.

POWER Satan has great power (Ephesians 6:12; 1:21; Revelation 9:3,10; Acts 26:18; 1 Corinthians 15:24; Colossians 1:16; 2:10,15). He has the power of death (Hebrews 2:14; Luke 11:21-22) but can only use it as God permits (Job 1 and 2). He uses traps and schemes (Ephesians 6:11-12) and lies and deceives (John 8:44). He devours like a lion (1 Peter 5:8).

His power is inferior to Jesus" power, though (Colossians 1:16; 2:10,15). He can only be one place at a time (Daniel 9:21; 10:12-14, 20; Luke 8:33). He is not sovereign [total and absolute authority over everything and everyone] (2 Corinthians 12:7), not omnipotent [all powerful] (1 John 4:4), not omniscient [all knowing] (2 Peter 1:11-12) and not omnipresent [everywhere at once] (Daniel 9:21). He cannot act against us without God's permission. God limits what he can do (Job 1:12).

We must always remember that Satan is a defeated foe. He was cast out of his original position in heaven because of pride (Ezekiel 28:16; Luke 10:18; Isaiah 14:12). His judgment was pronounced in Eden (Genesis 3:14-15). He was defeated by the cross (John 12:31). He will be cast to the earth in the tribulation (Revelation 9:1; 12:7-12), bound during the Millennium (Revelation 20:1-3) and then cast into the lake of burning sulfur forever (Revelation 20:7-10; Isaiah 27:1; 40:23-24; 2 Thessalonians 2:8)

CHARACTER Looking at the various names of Satan help us understand his character and work better.

Satan (Job 1:6-9; Matt. 4:10) The title "Satan" occurs 53 times in 47 verses in the Bible. The primary idea is 'adversary, one who withstands.'

The Devil (Matt. 4:1, 5, 9; Eph. 4:27; Rev. 12:9; 20:2)"Devil" is the Greek word diabolos which means "slanderer, defamer." This accentuates his goal and work to impugn the character of God.

The Serpent (Rev. 12:9) This name for Satan looks back to Genesis 3 and the temptation in the Garden.

Lucifer (Isa. 14:12) The Hebrew word for Lucifer (KJV translation) is literally "the shining one." This name draws our attention to his pre-fall condition and to the nature of the cause of his fall - pride.

The Evil One (John 17:15; 1 John 5:9) The Greek poneros means "wicked, evil, bad, base, worthless, vicious, degenerate." It points to Satan's character as active and malignant.

The Dragon (Rev. 12:7) The Greek word is drakon (as in draconian) and refers to a "hideous monster, a dragon, or large serpent." This word stresses the cruel, vicious, and blood thirsty character and power of Satan.

The Prince or Ruler (John 12:31) The Greek literally means, "the ruler of this world system." This points to Satan as the head and energy behind the arrangements of things as they are in the world today.

The God of This World or Age (2 Cor. 4:4) The fact Satan is called, the god of this world (Greek, aionos, "age, course") may emphasize Satan's rulership over this final period or economy which is so marked by a growing increase in apostasy, deception, and moral decay.

The Prince of the Power of the Air (Eph. 2:2a) This points to Satan as the head of the demonic hosts which includes all the fallen angelic beings who operate night and day in our immediate spiritual atmosphere-an atmosphere of demonic influence controlled by Satan.

The Accuser of the Brethren (Rev. 12:10) The Greek word for "accuser" is kathgor, which refers to one who brings condemning accusations against others. In view of Job 1 and 2, this is also an attempt to malign the character of God and His plan. 2).

The Tempter (Matt. 4:3; 1 Thess. 3:5) This title reveals him in another of his primary activities as seen from the very beginning with Eve in the Garden of Eden (Gen. 3).

Belial (2 Cor. 6:15) This name means "worthless" or "hopeless ruin." The personification of worthlessness, hopeless ruin and the source of all idolatry and religion which is also hopeless or futile.

Beelzebul (Matt. 12:24; Mark 3:22) Three possible spellings of this word each have a different meaning: (1) Beelzebul means "lord of the dung," a name of reproach. (2) Beelzebub means "lord of the flies." Either one of these are names of reproach and of uncleanness applied to Satan, the prince of the demons and uncleanness. (3) Beelzeboul, means, "the lord of the dwelling." This would identify Satan as the god of demon possession. This spelling has the best manuscript evidence behind it.

Abaddon, Apollyon (Rev 9:11) Abaddon is the Greek form and Apollyon is the Hebrew equivalent. These words mean 'destroyer,' 'destruction.' This title stresses his work of destruction; he works to destroy the glory of God and God's purpose with man. He further works to destroy societies and mankind.

The Proud One The five **"I will"** in Isaiah 14:12-14.

The Father of Lies (John 8:44) Using his network of deception through demonic forces and duped people, he promotes false doctrines in the name of God.

A False Angel of Light (2 Corinthians 11:14) One of his purposes is to make men as much like God as he can, but always without God. So, he will copy as much of God and His plan as he can, but he will always either distort, pervert, substitute or leave out those key ingredients of truth that are vital to the plan of salvation and sanctification through Christ.

PURPOSE His goal is to rule the whole world instead of God. He was given authority over this world system by Adam when he sinned (2 Corinthians 4:4; Ephesians 2:2) and controls our world system (1 John 5:19). He rules over it (Matthew 4:8-9; John 12:31; Luke 4:5-7; John 14:30; 16:11). He is behind its values and world view (James 3:15). Presently he words to deceive the nations (Daniel 10:13,20; Matthew 4:8; Ephesians 6:12; Revelation 20:3,7-8; 16:14;
I Kings 22:6-7). He leads mankind into idolatry (Psalm 96:5; 106:36-38; Leviticus 17:7;
Deuteronomy 32:17). He especially wants to destroy God's special people: Israel (Revelation 12:13-17; 20:10; 2 Thessalonians 2:9) and the Church.

WORK AGAINST ALL PEOPLE He works against the gospel, hardening hearts to God's truth (Matthew 13:19-22). He blinds their minds (2 Corinthians 4:3-4; 2 Thessalonians 2:7-10; Luke 8:12;

Colossians 2:18). When they hear the truth Satan tries to snatch it from their minds (Mark 4:15; Matthew 13:19).

He denies the truth (Genesis 3:1; 2 Timothy 4:3-4) and promotes false teaching (1 Timothy 4:1-2; 2 Thessalonians 2:9). As is true of any good counterfeiter, he tries to make his deceptions as close to the truth as possible so as to deceive more. The authority of the Scriptures, the person and work of Jesus and salvation by grace are areas he especially tries to obscure so make sure anything you believe has these at its heart and core.

Satan brings oppression on all he can. His does this through sickness such as dumbness (Mark 9:17-29), blindness (Matthew 12:22), deformity (Luke 13:11-17), epilepsy (Luke 9:37-43) and other ways. He also uses the following to oppress: mental illness (Mark 5:1- 20; 9:14-29; Luke 9:39), sin (Genesis 3:13-24; Ephesians 2:2), lawlessness (2 Corinthians 6:15) and death (Revelation 18:2; 9:13-18).

WORK AGAINST BELIEVERS A primary objective of Satan is to oppose God's work and God's people. He oppresses and leads the persecution against the Jews (Revelation 12:13-17; 20:10; 2 Thessalonians 2:9). He works especially hard against believers, for we are the light in his darkness, the only threat on this work against his kingdom. Since he can no longer attack Jesus directly, he does so indirectly by attacking His children. He accuses us before God (Job 1:6-21; 2 Corinthians 2:11; Revelation 12:9-10; Zechariah 3:1-2) but Jesus is our defense attorney, our Advocate when accused (1 John 2:1).

Satan does all he can to oppose and hinder our service to God (2 Corinthians 4:4; 1Thessalonians 2:18; 2 Corinthians 112:7; Zechariah 3:1; Matthew 13:19). He tries to infiltrate
the church through false teaching (1 Timothy 4:1-2; 2 Thessalonians

2:9), false teachers (1 Timothy 4:1-3; 1 John 4:1; 2 Peter 2:1-2) and false „Christians" (Matthew 13:38-40).

While not all temptation comes from Satan and demons, he certainly does all he can to entice us into sin (2 Corinthians 2:11; 1 Timothy 3:7; 2 Timothy 2:26) as he did when tempting Jesus. He will use our sin nature (James 1:14-15), the world system (1 John 2:15-16) or attack directly through demons (1 Corinthians 7:5). He can cause and use anger (Ephesians 4:27), pride (1 Timothy 3:6; 1 Chronicles 21:1; 1 Timothy 3:6), immorality (1 Corinthians 7:5), lies (Acts 5:1-3), doubting God's Word and goodness (Genesis 3:1-5; Luke 4:9-12), „miracles" to deceive (Mark 4:8-9; 2 Corinthians 11:13-15; 2 Thessalonians 2:3,9-11), hypocrisy (John 8:44; Acts 17:22), self-sufficiency (1 Chronicles 212:1-7), worry and fear (1 Peter 5:7-9; Hebrews 2:14;

Psalm 23;4), lack of faith (Luke 22:31-32; 1 Peter 5:6-10), physical affliction (Job 1:6-22; 2:1-7;

John 8:44; 1 Corinthians 5:5; 1 Timothy 1:20) and sin of any kind (1 Thessalonians 3:5; Matthew

4:3; 1 Corinthians 10:19-21, 2 Corinthians 11:3,13-15; 1 John 3:8).

2) DEMONS - ENEMY SOLDIERS

CREATION When Satan rebelled and decided to oppose God instead of serving God, about a third of the angels joined him (Revelation 12:4). They, too, were case out of heaven and lost their position and privilege. They are now called "demons." They, as all angels, have personality (mind, will, emotions) but no body. They are limited to being one place at a time and do not have all knowledge or power.

CHARACTER "Demon" means "destroyer." They are also called evil or unclean spirits, referring to the fact they don't have a physical body. They spread their sin and uncleanness any way they can. They are spiritual terrorists, trying to destroy the work of God's kingdom. As with human terrorists, no one is safe from them, they are deadly serious and have no softness or mercy. They serve Satan, who is their commander, and carry out his orders. They receive the worship given to idols or anything other than God (I Corinthians 10:20).

ORGANIZATION Satan organizes his demons in the same manner God has angels organized - in a military-like structure. These are similar to generals, colonels, majors, lieutenants, sergeants, corporals, privates, etc. (Ephesians 6:12). Usually a "strong man" (or ruler) is assigned to a task, and he has lesser demons under his command to help in the work (Matthew 12:25-29; Daniel 10:2-6, 12-14). The names of these demons usually refer to their work ("Fear," "Anger," "Lust," "Pride," "Deception," etc.).

POWER Their power, too, though is limited for they are under Satan and he is under God (Job 1:12). They answer to God, as we see Satan do in the Book of Job. They are powerful but NOT omnipotent like God (John 10:21); they are exceedingly clever but NOT omniscient like God and know their eventual destiny (Matthew 8:29); and they are mobile but NOT omnipresent like God. Like Satan, they can only be one place at a time (Daniel 9:21; 10:12-14,20; Luke 8:33). They share the same fate as Satan. Some are already judged and are in chains awaiting coming judgment (2 Peter 2:4; Jude 6; Revelation 9:14-15). Other demons have already been confined to the Abyss (Luke 8:31; revelation 9:11). All will be sent to the lake of fire with Satan when he is sent there (Matthew 25:41). Satan and his forces are defeated foes, having given their all to destroy Jesus on the cross, but being beaten by Him instead

(Heb 2:14-15; I Pt 3:18- 22). When Jesus returns Satan and his demons will be cast into the lake of fire forever (Matthew 25:41; Rev 20:1-15).

DUTIES AGAINST ALL Demons carry out Satan's commands and wishes. After enticing Adam and Eve to sin and getting authority over the world from them, Satan and his forces have continued trying to keep worship from God and getting it for themselves. They blind the minds of unbelievers (II Cor 4:4) and snatch the Word from their hearts (Luke 8:12). They do all they can to oppose God's work (Rev 2:13). Since they can't attack God, they take their anger out on those who are God's -- His people (Jews and Christians today). Satan and his forces tempt Christians to lie (Acts 5:3), accuse and slander them before God (Rev 12:10), hinder our work (I Thes. 2:18), do anything possible to defeat us (Eph 6:11-12), tempt to immorality (I Cor 7:5) and incite persecution against us (Rev 2:10). They promote human wisdom (1 Corinthians 2:12; 2 Corinthians 11:4; 1 John 4:5-6). They influence and control the nations (Daniel 10:13,20; Ephesians 6:12) and mislead them so they can destroy them (Isaiah 9:14). It must always be kept in mind, however, that God is in sovereign control. They can do nothing without God's permission (Job 1:6-12).

Physically they can give superhuman strength (Mark 5:4); physically torment (Revelation 9:5,10), emotionally torment (1 Samuel 16:14-23); do miracles (Revelation 16:13-14; 13:12-15), inflict disease (Matthew 9:33; Luke 3:11,16), indwell people (Matthew 8:28-34) and indwell animals (Matthew 8:31-32).

Emotionally they torment (1 Samuel 16:14-23), cause fear (1 Samuel 18:12,15; 2 Corinthians 11:4; 2 Timothy 1:7; Romans 8:15; Job 4:14-15), cause anger (1 Samuel 18:10-11), cause jealousy (1 Samuel 18:10-15) and harden consciences (1 Timothy 4:2).

Sexually they cause immorality (Revelation 9:21-22; 2 Timothy 3:1-9; 1 Timothy 4:1-3) and cause all kinds of impurity (Zechariah 13:2).

Mentally they cause bondage (2 Corinthians 11:4), influence the mind (Genesis 3:15; Ephesians 6:10-20; 2 Corinthians 4:4; Colossians 1:13), control the mind (1 Corinthians 10:20; 2 Corinthians 4:4), and deceive, mislead and lie to people (1 Timothy 4:1,6; 1 Kings 22:22-23; 2 Chronicles 18:20-23).

Religiously they promote false doctrine (1 John 4:1-3; 1 Timothy 4:1; 1 Kings 22:22; Revelation 16:13), counterfeit the truth (2 Corinthians 10:20-21), promote hypocrisy (1 Timothy 4:2), promote legalism (1 Timothy 4:3), use false prophets and false teachers (1 John 4:1; 1 Kings 22:22-23; 2 Chronicles 18:20-23), use fortunetelling and occult practices (Acts 16:16-18) and promote idolatry while receiving the worship of idols (Leviticus 17:7; Deuteronomy 32:17; Psalm 106:37; Revelation 9:20; Hosea 4:10-12; 5:4; Acts 16:16; 1 Corinthians 10:20).

DUTIES ESPECIALLY AGAINST BELIEVERS They especially work against believers by frustrating and opposing God's perfect will (Acts 16:16-18), putting obstacles in the path of following God (1 Thessalonians 2:18; Romans 15:22), influencing believers to mislead other believers (Matthew 16:22-23.) and instigating things such as jealousy, pride and disunity (James 3:13-16). They seek to get believers to turn from God and living for Him (1 Timothy 4:1), they can cause physical torment (2 Corinthians 12:7), and they try to get us to operate by our own strength and ability (2 Timothy 3:5). All this work will intensify as the return of Jesus gets closer (1 Timothy 4:1).

3) DEATH, DARKNESS & SPIRITUAL BLINDNESS

Satan is a liar and the father of lies (John 8:44). Demons do this work for him (I Kings 22:22-23; II Chronicles 18:20-23). He is characterized by any kind of falsehood and deceit (I John 4:16) and is not above mixing in some truth to make the lies more quickly accepted. Like any good counterfeiter, he knows the importance of making his false product appear as much like God's original as possible. He is very good at lying and deception (Revelation 12:9) and even tries to make it seem like he is bringing light instead of darkness (II Corinthians 11:13-15).

In actuality all Satan's forces operate in the realm of darkness (fear, deception, blindness, confusion, hopelessness, depression, self-pity, anger, revenge, suicide, death, etc.) He blinds men to spiritual things (II Corinthians 4:4; I John 2:11). He hardens minds and hearts to spiritual things (II Corinthians 3:14; Ephesians 4:18; Romans 1:21). He does this to individuals as well as nations (i.e.: Israel Romans 11:7-10). His purpose is to keep men from God's light and salvation (II Corinthians 4:4). God's light is greater than Satan's darkness (Genesis 1:14-19; John 1:5-9; 3:19-20; 8:12; 9:5; Matthew 17:2; Ephesians 5:8; I John 1:5-7; Revelation 21:11,23-24; 22:5; Isaiah 60:1). Believers are in the light, not darkness (Acts 26:18; I Thessalonians 5:4-5; Colossians 1:12-13; John 8:12).

The epitome of darkness is death. Satan's plan for man is death, just as God's plan for man is life. Satan is a murderer from the beginning (John 8:44). His name, Abaddon or Apollyon means "Destroyer." He tries to destroy physical (John 8:44; Mark 9:20-22; I John 3:12) or spiritual (II Corinthians 4:4) life. Satan has power to bring death (Job 1:19; Luke 11:21-22; Hebrews 2:14; Revelation 9:14-16), but because the power of death was destroyed at the cross (Hebrews 2:14-15) he cannot use that power without God's permission (Job 2:6; Revelation 9:4). Satan cannot separate us from God, even by death (Romans 8:38).

OVERCOMING SATAN & HIS FORCES God is greater than Satan and his forces (I John 4:4), so we need not fear them (Luke 10:17-19). We must humble depend on God's strength, not our own (James 4:6-7; 5:16). Admit sin and open spots that Satan uses in your life (Psalm 32:5; 139:23-24), and confess any sin (I John 1:9). Accept God's forgiveness and, with His help, turn from the sin (Amos 3:3; Ezekiel 20:43). In prayer claim back any openings Satan is using in your life (Acts 19:18-19; Matt 3:7-8). Cover yourself with the armor of God each day (Eph 6:10-18). Stay in the Scriptures (Psalm 1:1-3). The Word is a mirror (James 1:22-25) a lamp (Psalm 119:105) a cleanser (Ephesians 5;25-26) a sword (Hebrews 4:12) and food (I Peter 2:2; Matthew 4:4). Use it for all these. Develop a life of continuous praise & prayer (I Thessalonians 5:17). Stay in close fellowship with other believers (Hebrews 13:5). Commit yourself to totally follow God (Ephesians 6:16).

THE BASIC REQUIREMENT: JOINING GOD'S ARMY Just as there are physical principles that govern the universe around us, so there are spiritual principles that govern our relationship with God. The first and most basic principle is that God loves us and has a wonderful plan for our lives (John 3:16), but when sin entered the world it separated man from our holy God (Romans 2:23). Being a just and righteous God, sin cannot be overlooked but must be paid for and since there is no way we can pay for our own sins God Himself, in His great love, became the payment for our sins. That first Christmas celebrates the fact that He voluntarily left heaven to come to earth as a human being.

Although we celebrate Jesus" birth on Christmas, we know that He wasn't born just to give us a holiday where we remember Him as a baby – He was born to die to pay the price for our sins. We worship Jesus as a baby, but the story doesn't end there. He Jesus grew up and went through all the things we go through in life.

He was rejected and crucified, but while dying on the cross He suffered the eternal punishment of every sin we would ever commit. In other words, He went through our hell so we wouldn't has to (Romans 5:8). Because He was man, He could represent us and take our place.

Because He was God, He could endure punishment way beyond anything we could ever experience. At the end of the crucifixion, Jesus said "It is finished" and His spirit returned to heaven. His body went into a grave but 3 days later came back to life, proving forever that sin and death had been conquered.

He is in Heaven today! There He has made a place for us if we only accept the gift and joy He has offered us. Salvation is freely available to every person (Ephesians 2:8-9), but it is a gift we must voluntarily receive by recognizing our need and asking Him to forgive us and live in us (John 1:12). He Himself then lives within us and gives us new meaning and ability in life. If you have "t received this wonderful free gift do so now by asking God for His gift of salvation.

While there are no special or magical words to use, here is the idea of a prayer to pray to accept God's free gift of salvation. It's not saying the words but meaning them that makes the difference. Here is a sample prayer you can use:

> "Dear Jesus, I recognize my need of you. I know I sin and am guilty in your sight. Thank you for leaving heaven to come to earth and die on the cross for my sins. I know you took my eternal condemnation on Yourself on the cross and paid for it all. Please forgive sin and fill me with Your Holy Spirit. I freely accept your gift of salvation. I want to live for you and only you. I put you first in my life and want to serve You. I reject any other forces or powers and forbid any them to have any influence on me. Dear Jesus, fill me and use me. Thank you for hearing and answering me. In Jesus' name I pray. Amen."

Know that if you have ever prayed this prayer or something similar to it you are born again into God's family and nothing can take your salvation away. One of Satan's first lies is to get us to doubt our salvation, to question it we are a child of God or not. If you have doubts about having done this in the past just pray it again now, write your name and the date below, and you'll know for sure that you are a child of God and in God's army.

_____   _____

        (name)   (date)

WHY SPIRITUAL WARFARE?

There are those today who say Christians aren't to get involved in spiritual warfare, but instead, we are to trust God and think only of Him. While God is always our only focus, He has given us tools to bring victory in this area. He has provided medical knowledge for us to use in the physical realm. He has also provided spiritual knowledge to help us in the spiritual realm. Paul tells us to ensure we aren't ignorant of Satan's devices (2 Corinthians 2:5-11). We are to understand and use the resources He has provided. I believe God commands us to be involved in spiritual warfare (I Timothy 6:12). Here are some reasons:

1. **THE BIBLE COMMANDS US TO USE SPIRITUAL WARFARE**

"Our struggle is not against flesh and blood but against principalities, etc." Ephesians 6:10-12

"We are not ignorant of Satan's devices" II Cor. 2:11

We are to understand our enemy before battling him (count the cost) Luke 14:31

Armor in Ephesians 5 - why would we be given armor if there wasn't a spiritual battle going on?

<u>IF GOD IS SOVEREIGN, WHY DO WE NEED TO FIGHT SATAN?</u> If God is sovereign, why do we need to witness, pray, believe, work for our money, drive carefully, go to a doctor, or do any of those things? If we trust in God, why lock doors at night? There are some things God expects us to do, in His strength. By doing these we learn to trust Him more. The Jews were given the land of Canaan but had to learn to fight to live in it. We praise Him more when we see His provision, might, and deliverance. We are better able to pray for and give guidance to others.

Also, we see the awfulness of sin and its consequences so we can better turn from it. We see His glory as He uses us for victory. Others see it and He is glorified in their sight.

2. **JESUS USED SPIRITUAL WARFARE** Jesus talked about Satan & demons more than anyone in the Bible. He cast out demons. He taught and commanded His disciples to fight Satan and cast out demons (Matthew 10:8; Luke 10:1, 17-20). He was disappointed when they were unable to deliver a demonized boy without Him (Mark 9:14-29). The religious rulers accused Jesus (Mark 3:22) and John the Baptist (Luke 7:33) of being demonized. He commanded His disciples to cast out demons, too

3. **EXAMPLES OF OTHERS WHO USED SPIRITUAL WARFARE** DANIEL prayed spiritual warfare prayer for three weeks (Daniel 10:2-6,12-14). JEREMIAH's whole ministry was one of spiritual warfare.

    PAUL was twice involved in casting out demons (Acts 13:6-12; 16:16-18) and wrote much about spiritual warfare (Ephesians 4:26-27; 6:10-13; Galatians 2:10, 13; etc.)
    MOSES was challenged by Satanic forces (Jannes & Jambres, Exodus 7:1-11, etc.).
    Many examples in church history show the involvement of God's people in spiritual warfare.

4. **PERSONAL EXPERIENCE SUPPORTS SPIRITUAL WARFARE** The testimony of many who have been involved in spiritual warfare supports and validates its importance as an important tool for Christians today. It is not our only tool, for different tools are needed for different jobs. Spiritual warfare is one tool among many (prayer, witnessing, counseling, praising, etc.) that God gives us to use at the proper time.

5. **LAST DAYS EMPHASIS OF SPIRITUAL WARFARE** The closer the rapture comes the more spiritual warfare will increase. There will be MUCH of it in the tribulation as Satan's forces are released.

II. CHARACTERISTICS OF DEMONIZING

A. DEMONIZING DEFINED

The Greek word doimonizomai ("demonizing") refers to one who is heavily impacted by demons. It is used 15 times in the New Testament. It does not differentiate between possession (demons within) or influence (demons without). If God doesn't make that clarification or distinction, I don't think it's something we need to make, either. In the spiritual realm there are no clear-cut divisions like we try to make (demons 'within' or 'without', etc.). There are, of course, degrees of demonizing depending on the person, the demons involved, the access, etc., but it isn't always possible or necessary to pinpoint these things. The common denominator is that the person being demonized usually doesn't separate their own consciousness from the demonic influence. The thoughts and feelings the demon feeds them they assume are their own. A person always has a free will to turn to God for help, but when followed these impulses bring one deeper and deeper into bondage.

Perhaps demonizing can be better understood by thinking of it as a kind of spiritual hypnotism from within. Hypnotism of any kind is something for God's people to avoid (Psalm 54:4-5; Joshua 1:8; Philippians 4:8).

We don't need to know the exact extent of demonizing, just that it is taking place. The cause is the same, and so is the cure. We will use the broad term 'demonizing' as the Bible does, referring to the whole spectrum of demonic influence/possession.

Other words the Bible uses for the same thing are "entered in" (as when Satan entered into Judas - John 13:27) and "filled" (the same word that is used of believers being filled with the Holy Spirit - Acts 5:5 about Ananias and Saphira).

B. DEMONIZING DEFENDED

CAN A BELIEVER BE DEMONIZED?

While all Christians agree that unbelievers can be demonized, some don't believe that can happen to believers. Demonizing speaks of influence, not ownership. A believer still has a free will to give soul access to demons, as do unbelievers. His spirit belongs only to God, but it is up to us to allow God's spirit to control or not.

The Bible makes no distinction between believers and unbelievers as far as demonizing is concerned. In fact, the Bible refers to many believers who were demonized: Paul's thorn in the flesh was a demon (II Corinthians 12:7), King Saul was a believer (I Samuel 11:6) and was obviously demonized (I Samuel 16:14-23), David was motivated by Satan to take a census of the people (I Chronicles 21:1ff; II Samuel 24:1ff), Ananias and Saphira were believers (Acts 4:32-35) but allowed Satan to "fill" them (Acts 5:3), and Peter was Satan's spokesman in tempting Jesus to not go to the cross (Matthew 16:23). Paul warns believers to not give Satan a "foothold" in their life (Ephesians 4:26-27), showing such a thing is possible. Jesus Himself called deliverance "the children's bread" (Matthew 15:22-28), meaning it was for His children. A Christian can receive another spirit (II Cor 11:2-4) and there are examples of believers being demonized (Luke 13:10-16; I Cor. 5:4,5). Christians are warned to guard against this (I Pt. 5:8- 9; Eph. 6:10-18).

A believer belongs to the Lord Jesus Christ. Satan cannot own him as he did before salvation (I John 4:4), but he can still demonize. When the words „possessed" or „oppressed" are used then the question can asked if a believer can be "possessed." To answer that then "possessed" must be defined. The Bible simply does not define it, not does it even talk about "possession" – just "demonizing" which means being influenced by a demon. No one would doubt this happens to believers.

As long as we are in this body, we still have a sin nature, a capacity to sin just the same as we did before salvation. Salvation creates a new spiritual nature within us. But the old capacity to sin still remains in us. It is in this area, this sin nature, this capacity to sin, that demons work. Our new nature is greater but doesn't take away our free will choice to still function in our sin nature. Paul's struggle as recorded in Romans 7 describes this well.

A Christian has every right and resource to be free from this demonizing, however, property which you own can be trespassed on by another person, but you have every right and resource to put him off your property. You just need to learn how to do it.

C. DEMONIZING DESCRIBED

THOUGHTS IN, THOUGHTS OUT

The majority of demonizing consists of demons putting thoughts into a person's mind or snatching thoughts out of a person's mind. While they don't have access to our minds and thoughts to the same extent that God does, the Bible makes it clear there is some access. Jesus said this in the Sower and the seed: *"Satan comes and takes away the word that was sown."* (Mark

4:15). David's thought to take a census was demonic (I Chronicles 21:1ff; II Samuel 24:1ff). So was Ananias & Saphira's greed (Acts 5:3) and Saul's jealousy/anger (I Samuel 16:14-23). That's why, when talking about spiritual warfare, Paul says we are to *"bring every <u>thought</u> into captivity to the obedience of Christ."* (II Corinthians 10:4-5). Not only can Satan's forces put wrong thoughts into our minds, they can snatch right thoughts out of our minds (Mark 4:15) so we forget them.

LET YOUR MIND EXPLAIN REALITY TO YOUR EMOTIONS

Feelings and emotions are fine, important and necessary. They are icing on the cake of life. They add color and enjoyment to life. God created them for this purpose. But He didn't create them to be the source of our decision-making. Our feelings should dependent on our rational thought. When our feelings get ahead of it or away from it then trouble comes. You know in your mind that you are an OK person, yet your emotions fear you will be rejected. When feelings aren't founded on the truth of the mind they go wrong. The truth is that you are a fine person, but your emotions reject that truth and try to do the „thinking" themselves.

I often tell people they need to let their mind explain reality to their emotions. When we feel our emotions are correct over our mind we err. One of the greatest needs of our emotions/feelings is security. This is closely related to love so we could say the core of our heart is love/security. Love must bring security but doesn't always do so. Other factors can tribute to our security as well.

WHAT THE BIBLE SAYS ABOUT THE MIND

The Bible distinguishes between the **heart** (seat of emotions, subjective reasoning) and the **mind** (seat of thought, objective reasoning). The emotions are to enjoy life, the mind is for decision-making. It is the rational control center of our beings, the center of decision-making (Luke 10:27; Psalm 26:1-3; Proverbs 23:7)

Demons can and do influence a person's mind (Mark 5:15-16). That person isn't aware Satan is doing it; it appears to be their own thoughts. We see Satan deceiving mankind in the very start of the Bible (Eden) and at the very end. (through the Antichrist). Man's mind can be deceived (Genesis 3:13; Rev 20:10). Therefore, God gives us 2 ways to victory over deception. One is the mind of Christ placed within us by God's Holy Spirit (1 Corinthians 2:16). The other is the Word of God which we must study and learn (2 Timothy 3:16-17; Hebrews 4:12).

The reason our mind is untrustworthy without the mind of Christ and the written Word is that it is influenced by out sinful nature (Romans 7:14-25). Paul clearly says his mind isn't in control of everything for what he wants to do in his mind he is often unable to do because of the pull of sin in him. This same tendency to sin can influence the mind and warp its perspective. Victory over the sin nature comes by submitting to God's power and presence and allowing Him to take complete control over every aspect of our lives (Romans 8:5-8; 12:1-2).

Our minds only find peace in God (Isaiah 26:3-4). God promises us steadfast minds (Isaiah 26:3). Steadfast means „firm, secure, fixed, settled" – our minds must be totally submissive to and dependent on God's control. Then He will give us peace. As the verse says, trust is a key factor. We can't trust and fear at the same time, we can have both but must choose to follow one or the other, not both. God knows our thoughts and intentions better than we do and, when we let Him, will work and guide us (Romans 8:26-27).

Those not in control of their minds are in a dangerous position. Giving up our mental control to anything or anyone opens us to the demonic seizing that access. Paul uses the example of speaking in tongues to make this point (1 Corinthians 14:13-16). When speaking in tongues the mind is doing things that the person is not in control of. The person lets the mind go on its own, out of their control. Paul warns that this is dangerous, that the mind needs to be involved in everything we are doing.

What you put in your mind has an effect on what you think. Remember those scary movies you watched as a kid, and then had nightmares? It didn't take long to realize that the way to avoid the nightmares was to stop watching that kind of movie. God has provided a way to overcome unhealthy thoughts and behaviors, and gain the self-control you seek. It's a matter of taking charge of your life - His way.

In order for us to take our thoughts captive (Romans 12:21) we must first accept responsibility for our thoughts. God gave us a free will choice and the ultimate responsibility is ours. If we have unwelcome thoughts, we are responsible to resist them and get to the root cause so they can be removed. Thoughts are the key to actions (James 4:1) so we aren't to just try to change actions (that is hypocrisy) but the thoughts behind them (Romans 12:2).

When we take our thoughts captive, we reject any lies or deception they may bring and turn them over to God. We can best defeat unwanted thoughts and temptations by quoting Scripture. When Jesus was tempted, He quoted Scripture to have victory over Satan's temptations. Paul says our only offensive weapon is the sword of the Spirit, the Word of God. Psalm 119:9,11 tell us that it's through God's Word that we have victory. When you have these thoughts and attacks use Scripture to have victory. Ask God to give you some verses that will help against these things, write them down and memorize them. Say them over and over when these thoughts attack you. That is the only way to victory, and God guarantees it will work!

In addition, we are required to make every effort to think about things that are true, noble, right, pure, lovely and admirable (Philippians 4:8).

HOW CAN WE BE DECEIVED IF WE KNOW THE TRUTH?

Do you remember the children's story about the emperor's new clothes? Some crooks convinced him they were making fine garments which only the enlightened could see so he pretended to see them. Everyone else did also. Then in a parade a little boy spoke the truth and everyone realized they had been believing a lie and deceiving themselves. Satan deceives us into believing a lie. But how can we be deceived if we know the truth?

1. We can be demonized. Like a drunk is influenced by alcohol so we can be by demons.

2. We can prefer to be deceived because we don't want to face the truth or don't like the truth, so we convince ourselves that a lie is true. We start to really believe it because we want to.

3. We let our emotions run the show instead of our mind. When we let our feelings explain reality to our emotions (reacting out of fear for example) we replace the truth with deception.

4. Our mind can be deceived, too, when we use it as the final determining factor and think absolute truth comes from it. Without the anchor of God's Word to form our mind and correct our errors we can truly believe something based on the facts as we interpret them. But we may not be interpreting them correctly. However, only God has all the facts and perfect insight, seeing the future as clearly as the past, so when we reject His truth, we are open to any kind of deception.

5. Satan and demons tempt us to deception. Of course, they don't „sell" their product as a black lie, but make it look as appealing and good as possible. We sometimes fall for the bait.

6. Even aside from the enemy, our natural tendency to sin (sin nature) causes us to prefer sin for we are often more interested in what is easiest and most enjoyable now instead of what is best in the long run. Our „flesh" desires instant gratification and we can „want" something so much that we leave all reason and balance behind.

RECOGNIZING TRUTH

How does your heart know truth? How do you know when your mate is telling the truth? It's not something you can explain or put into words. It's not something others who don't know your mate can tell, either. But you know them well enough to be able to read the subtleties and know what they are communicating. That takes time as a relationship grows. The more time one spends listening to God the better he knows what God is saying. The more you listen to and follow the truth, the better your heart will recognize it. Really it is His Holy Spirit in us that speaks to our thoughts (and emotions as well). He promises to reveal His truth to us (John 16:13-15). For more information on listening to God read Appendix 7 & 8, pages 101-108.

COMPULSIVE & OBSESSIVE THOUGHTS

Thoughts we don't have captive (aren't in control of) fall into two categories: compulsions and obsessions. A compulsion is a force that causes us to act against our inclinations. It comes from within but is not under our control and drives us to unpleasant behavior. These often take the form of a 'ritual' or tradition to be superstitiously followed. It can be an extremely detailed preoccupation with minor, every-day tasks or be a besetting sin we are unable to conquer. It feels like a force greater than self is driving the person.

An obsession is a thought which forces itself into conscious thought against our will (usually something unpleasant and/or sinful) and can't be dismissed by ones our free will.

MENTAL ILLNESS

Demons can and do cause mental illness: they can make a person be not in his 'right mind' (Mark 15:15), they can cause screaming and convulsions, foaming at the mouth (Luke 9:39), they can cause self-destructive thoughts and actions (Mark 9:22), they can make a person appear to be 'raving mad' (John 10:20), and they can cause immoral, anti-social behavior that makes the person seem not right mentally (Mark 5:15; Luke 8:35).

It cannot be said that all mental illness is demonic. Other factors are involved such as chemical imbalances, birth defects, damage from injury or drug usage, etc. However, demonizing must always be considered until completely ruled out. One way to tell if it is demonic or not is the person's willingness to listen or talk about Jesus. If they fall asleep, change the subject constantly, don't seem to be hearing you, get violent, want to leave in a hurry, etc., you have good reason to suspect demons are involved.

SCHIZOPHRENIA

One of the most severe psychological disorders is schizophrenia. In general, it is characterized by a loss of interest in life, withdrawal and varying degrees of thought disorders. Among the symptoms most frequently observed are: secluding one's self and withdrawal from society, irritability, excessive daydreaming or preoccupation with thoughts and fantasies, delusive thinking characterized by self-pity and feelings of persecution, bizarre behavior and/or language, and over-sensitivity to criticism and comments of others. I am no expert in these things, but in every case, I have seen this has been demonic (Mark 5:6-7).

FEAR

Fear is one of Satan's biggest weapons. Demons are often behind and use fear (Romans 8:15). If it takes the form of insecurity, anxiety, worry, preoccupation with problems, or whatever, it is still fear. Demons put fear of David into Saul (I Samuel 18:10-15) and put fear and terror into Eliaphaz by gliding by his face (Job 4:15). Anything not of faith is sin (Romans 14:23). God does not give us fear (II Timothy 1:7; Romans 8:15), so if you experience fear realize it is not from God but from Satan. This doesn't mean it is always through demonizing, for you can be attacked with fear without being demonized.

Fear takes root when we choose to focus on circumstances instead of God. Peter walking on water is a good example. When his eyes were on Jesus his faith was strong, but when he looked at the waves, they grew in his mind to be greater than Jesus" power and he started sinking. He did the right thing, though, and put his eyes back on Jesus.

Dream with me for a minute. Suppose as a young child you had a father who loved you more than anything and constantly showed it. He was always there for you, always showing his love, enjoying you and laughing with you. Whatever you needed he was there to help and supply. How would that make you feel? What difference would it have made? There is something down deep inside all of us that would love to have someone we could trust, someone to take care of us, someone to always be there no matter what. Then we wouldn't need to be in control so we wouldn't fear. Control is a poor but often necessary substitute for love and trust.

It may have been necessary in your past but isn't necessary anymore!

TRUST, THE ANTIDOTE TO FEAR How can we understand trust, what it means and how it works? I think understanding how a family should work is the best answer. God established a family relationship to answer all those questions. He is the Father; we are the children. Do your children trust you? What do they have to do? What do you expect of them? It's exactly the same. Jesus says we are to be like little children in order to learn faith and trust. Let your children teach you. Put yourself in their position - with a Perfect Father.

PRAYER TO HAVE VICTORY OVER FEAR

Dear Heavenly Father, I come to You as Your child. I voluntarily place myself under your protective care. I acknowledge that You are the only legitimate fear object in my life. I confess that I have been fearful and anxious because of my lack of trust, my unbelief and believing the lies of the enemy. I have not always trusted You. Too often I have lived in fear and relied on my own strength and resources. I confess that as sin and thank You for Your forgiveness.

I know that you have not given me a spirit of fear, but of power, love and a sound mind (2 Timothy 1:7). Therefore, I renounce any fear in my life. I ask You to reveal to me all the areas where the sin of fear as affected me. Show me the lies I have believed and help me to believe Your truth instead. I desire to live in faith by the power of Your Holy Spirit. Fill me with Your presence and Your Spirit so I can follow You by faith. In Jesus" name. Amen.

ANGER

Anger comes from mishandling hurt and pain. Instead of feeling it as hurt we turn it into anger. Demons are behind and use anger, too. They made Saul angry at David, so much so that he tried to kill David (I Samuel 18:10-11; 19:9-10). Paul says there is a very close connection between anger and demonizing (Ephesians 4:27).

As I said before, anger comes from pain and hurt that is buried inside. You can't bury something alive and think you are getting rid of it. The hurt must be dead - faced, admitted, healed, removed, forgiven. When a person buries hurt alive it keeps poising everything until it is dug out and destroyed.

While there is a legitimate use for anger („righteous indignation") most of what we face is not right. Anger is a secondary emotion, unlike fear which is a basic emotion. Wrong anger is always the result of mishandling another, deeper emotional like fear or pain. Let's take pain, first of all. When a person hits their finger with a hammer what do they do? Usually, they get angry. What they feel is pain, but it comes out as anger because anger is a much easier emotion to handle than pain. When someone says something critical or threatening it hurts, but the natural response in many is to get angry. That way they don't have to face the pain – but it stays and causes more and more anger. That's where fear comes in. It's not just pain that causes anger, but fear of pain. Fear is at the root of anger in other ways as well. To seek to manage our fears we try to control our lives and circumstances (thus the control emphasis part grows). We feel that is necessary to prevent pain and other things we fear. We use anger as a control tool. The adrenalin rush makes us feel in charge instead of a victim. We learn that people can be manipulated and controlled by our anger (or the threat of it) and we use that to control as well. This is another reason why it's important to deal with and get victory over the fears down inside. When they go the anger and control issues will become much more manageable. A person can't stop their anger as long as what causes it is still inside pushing it out. They must get the root cause out, and that is where dealing with the fear comes in.

CUTTING, SELF MUTILATION, SUICIDE

Some today explain cutting and other self-mutilation activities as purely psychological. They say it is a way of refocusing pain, of using physical pain to alleviate emotional pain. While that may be true, I believe there is a deeper cause to these things. From my experience and the Bible, I am convinced that self-mutilation is contrary to our natural desire to „love" ourselves and the natural drive to protect self and survive at every cost. Mark 5 talks about a demonized man who was continually cutting himself (Mark 5:5). Then there is the demonized boy who keeps throwing himself in the fire to burn or water to drown (Matthew 17:15). Satan loves pain and death. They are his tools of trade. He would have all of us dead if God would not forbid it. So, the best he can do it to try and get us to harm ourselves. The ultimate of this is suicide. The prophets of Baal regularly used to cut as a means of appeasing their demonic gods, as seen in their encounter with Elijah on Mt. Carmel (1 Kings 18:28). Accounts of suicide in the Bible also show close association with demonization. Saul killed himself after his encounter with the witch of Endor. Judas" suicide came after being indwelt by Satan and betraying Jesus.

> **PRAYER FOR THOSE WITH SELF DESTRUCTIVE OR SUICIDAL TENDENCIES**
>
> In Jesus' name I renounce all suicidal thoughts and any attempts I've made to take my own life or in any way injure myself. I confess _(name each sin of self-destruction that comes to mind) and put it under the blood of Jesus. I renounce the lie that life is hopeless and that I can find peace and freedom by taking my own life. Satan is a thief and comes to steal, kill and destroy. I put any access any demons claim to my life or to my family under the blood of Jesus. In Jesus' name I cover all that with the blood of Jesus. I choose life in Christ Who came to give me life and give it abundantly. Thank You for Your forgiveness that allows me to forgive myself. I choose to believe that there is always hope in Christ. In Jesus name I pray. Amen

OTHER CHARACTERISTICS OF DEMONIZING

Luke 8:26-39, the account of the Gadarene demoniac, clearly describes various symptoms of demonizing. There is nakedness (immodesty, immorality), self-destructive tendencies (even to suicide and death), supernatural strength, animalistic behavior, schizophrenia, mental illness, preoccupation with darkness and death (living in a graveyard), fits of rage, resistance to spiritual things, etc. The strong man (ruler) was "Legion", meaning he had many demons under his authority that are doing these various works.

HOW RESPONSIBLE ARE THE DEMONIZED?

How could a person be responsible and at the same time have demons affect the mind? While we aren't responsible for everything that happens when demonized we are responsible for letting it happen and not being in control. Think of it this way. Someone gets drunk and kills another family in the car. They didn't want to kill them, probably didn't even realize they were doing it until it happened. Does that mean they aren't responsible and can walk away free? No. They are responsible for their actions. They are certainly responsible for getting drunk and allowing themselves to be in a situation that could cause death. Just because sometimes they drive without killing anyone doesn't mean they are any less guilty then, too. The same is done with demonizing. Allowing another power to influence us makes us accountable for all that happens while under that influence.

But if someone is demonized from childhood and isn't aware of it, are they responsible? Yes and no. Yes, they are responsible, but no, for God covers it with His grace and His work on the cross. Just like a little child is guilty of sin but God doesn't hold him accountable until he is old enough to know the difference between right and wrong, so the person demonized that way isn't accountable until they start to realize what is going on. The option then is to turn to Jesus for help over it.

EVIDENCE OF DEMONIZING

III. COMPULSIVE THOUGHTS

_____Extremely low self-image (feel unworthy, unclean, no good, etc.) Luke 8:2

_____Constant confusion in thinking (especially about spiritual things), restlessness

_____Inability to believe spiritual truths which you hear or read

_____Mocking and blasphemous thoughts (esp. when hearing spiritual truths)

_____Perceptual distortions (thinking others are angry at you when they are not)

_____Repetitious dreams or nightmares (sexual, horror-filled, fearful, etc.)

_____Violent thoughts (of suicide, rape, murder, self-abuse, cutting, etc.)

IV. COMPULSIVE FEELINGS

_____Hatred and bitterness toward others for no justifiable reason
_____Tremendous hostility, fear, restlessness when challenged about demonizing
_____Deep depression and despondence (frequent and long)
_____Irrational fears, panic, and phobias (Rom. 8:15 Luke 9:39)
_____Irrational anger or rage (Mt. 8:28)
_____Irrational guilt and extreme self-condemnation, not forgiving self

V. COMPULSIVE BEHAVIOR

_____Desire to do right but inability to carry it out
_____Sudden personality & attitude changes (like, and then hate someone)
_____Strong aversion to Scripture reading & prayer
_____Lying compulsively, then often wondering why (Acts 5:3)
_____Stealing compulsively, if you need the thing or not
_____Drinking or using drugs (prescription or not) compulsively, if you really desire to or not
_____Eating compulsively (or reverse, bulimia or anorexia nervosa)
_____Sexual sins that are compulsive (especially perversions) Matthew 15:5 Luke 8:27
_____Irrational, inappropriate laughter
_____Irrational violence (compulsion to hurt self or someone else) Mt. 17:15; Mk. 5:5; Lk 9:39
_____Sudden speaking of a language not previously known
_____Reactions to the name and blood of Jesus (uncomfortable, move away, etc.)

_____Uncontrollable cutting and mocking tongue and language
_____Vulgar language and actions (Luke. 4:33-34)
_____Uncontrollable greed, which drives you on (Acts 5:3)

VI. CONSCIOUSNESS PROBLEMS

_____Loss of time (little or a lot, not knowing how you got someplace what you did)

_____Extreme sleepiness around spiritual things (Bible study, prayer, etc.)

_____Demonstration of extraordinary abilities (ESP, telekinesis, out of body, disassociating)

_____Voices heard in the mind (mock, intimidate, accuse, threaten, bargaining

_____A voice speaking from you refers to you in the third person ("he" "she")

_____Supernatural experiences (haunting, movement or disappearance of objects, etc.)

VII. ABNORMAL MEDICAL PROBLEMS

_____Seizures (Mk. 1:26 Mk. 7:24-30 Mk. 17:15) (may or may not be demonic)

_____Pain without justifiable explanation, problem doctors can't cure

_____Physical ailments alleviated by a spiritual command (epileptic seizure, asthma attack, headache, nausea, etc., which stops when commanded in Jesus' name to be gone)

_____Sudden interference with bodily functions (buzzing in ears, irritability to speak or hear, increased hypersensitivity in hearing or touch, sudden chills, etc.)

III. CAUSES FOR DEMONIZING

Having looked at what demonizing is and some characteristics of it, the next step is to find out what allows demons to do this work in/against us. These openings are like cracks in a wall which allow the enemy to slip in. When you have these openings, it could be that demons are using this to demonize you. Demons are like rats that feed on garbage. To get rid of the rats one must get rid of the garbage, then the rats will be gone.

The most common avenue to demonic entrance is through a family line. One person opens themselves to demonic influence and the demons claim them and all they have, including children. Then the same traits and influences pass on to the children and their children. Occult and Satanic involvement by activities, drugs, acid rock music, Ouija boards, etc. is another opening. Cult involvement in the family, especially Masons, opens one. The Bible says that when 2 people have sex the two become one flesh and that allows demons to claim the other person. Abuse of any kind or any form of trauma, especially when young, open one to the demonic. Strong soul ties with someone involved can cause an opening. Being unwanted when in the womb or young is a definite opening. These are some of the main avenue's demons use to gain entrance and attack people.

BECAUSE OF OUR PROPERTY

Past use of the location Personal objects

BECAUSE OF OUR RELATIONSHIP WITH JESUS

BECAUSE OF OUR ANCESTORS

Ancestors past actions Our past actions

BECAUSE OF SIN IN OUR LIFE

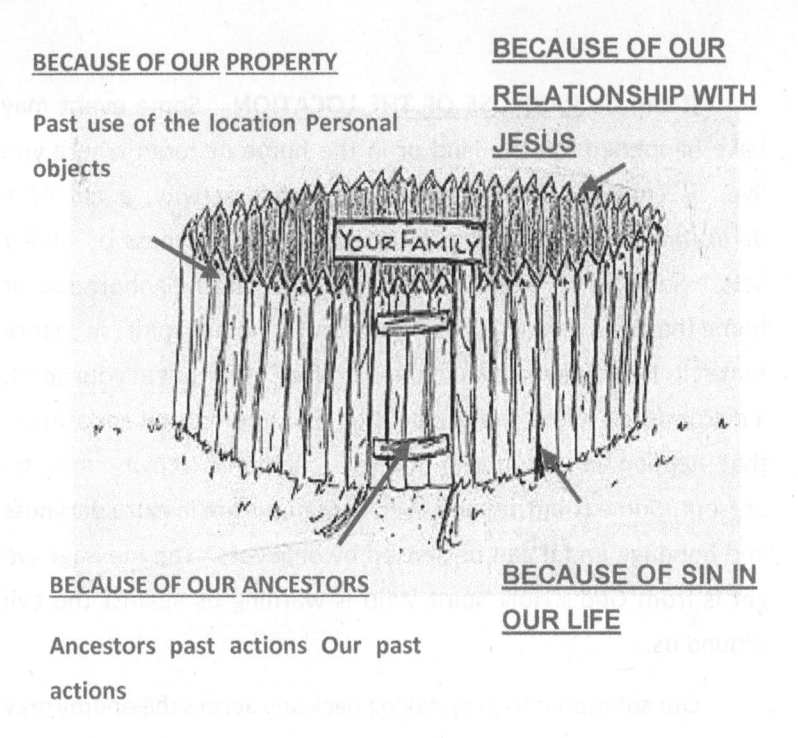

In order to have victory over the attacks of the enemy it is important to understand where those attacks come from – what is the cause of them. This is very important in being able to defend against them. If we know the direction from which our enemy will attack, we can better defend ourselves and defeat those attacks. If you think of your life as a fort you can better understand what is happening. Think of a frontier fort such as were built for protection in the early days of the USA. An enemy can 1) claim access through an open door, 2) enter through a weak spot in the wall, 3) claim the land on which the fort is built, or 4) attack us because of our commitment to Jesus. Let's look at these four avenues of attack.

A. PHYSICAL ATTACK

We can be attacked because of access given through what has happened on the land or to the property in the past.

It can be **PAST USE OF THE LOCATION.** Some event may have happened on the land or in the home or room where you live. It could be a violent act, an occult activity, a curse, a dedicating of the property to the powers of darkness or similar acts. Sometimes when we go into a certain neighborhood or home there is a „sense" of evil, a discomfort in our spirit. In a store that sells New Age materials you may „feel" different in your spirit, a discomfort. This is the explanation for supernatural apparitions that happen in „haunted" homes – demonic activity may be present. Some countries and even continents are in extra darkness and bondage and it can be sensed by believers. The message we get is from God's Holy Spirit Who is warning us against the evil around us.

Our solution is to pray, taking back any access the enemy may claim to the property and asserting our right as children of God to claim and use it. Put any other claims under the blood of Jesus and dedicate it to Him for His honor and glory. A sign, picture or cross on the wall can be a good visual reminder to all of the ownership of the property by the Lord Jesus Christ.

Pray, anoint the house and property, etc. Walk around your boundaries praying out loud, claiming your property for God and forbidding any demons to have any access to it. Dedicate it to God and invite His presence through all of it. Take back any access any demons may claim to the property and put the access under the blood of Jesus. Break it in Jesus" name. Ask God to put an angelic hedge of protection around it. Do the same in all the rooms of the house, especially the basement (if you have one). Anoint each room with oil by dipping your finger in the oil and putting a cross on the door, walls, etc. Pray as you did when you walked around the property. If there is one particular part of the house that seems worse put a night light there so there is always light in to room. You could do that to all the rooms. Demons hate light, and they hate hearing Jesus praised, so you can play praise music in various places 24 hours a day. It can be really soft – they will hear it!

In addition, it can be from **PERSONAL PROPERTY ON THE LOCATION**. When the Jews took possession of Canaan under Joshua, they were told to not keep any of the objects they captured. Even animals and children were to be destroyed.

They had been dedicated to Satan and were claimed by him. Those who used these things would be opening themselves up to the demonic powers they had been dedicated to. That's why Paul had the people in Ephesus burn all their occult books. Today we must watch for things like literature from other cults and religions, Ouija boards and other occult paraphernalia, pagan objects from primitive cultures, objects from Masonic or other secret societies, some Native American artifacts or the like. Pornography, drug or alcoholic supplies, music with a black or evil dimension

The solution is to remove and destroy such objects as God convicts you or as being openings for demonic access. Ask for forgiveness for having them, cleanse the room from their presence, take back any access the enemy may claim and dedicate the space as well as yourself to Jesus. Ask Him to reveal to you anything else that may need to be dealt with.

When a room or object is under the control of an evil spirit for whatever reason they claim, painting crosses by dipping a finger in oil and making them on a wall claims the place for Jesus. Playing Christian music and leaving a small light on also are offensive to the forces of darkness. Of course, praying and quoting scripture while making the crosses is important, too. I know I, as a Christian, have great power in blessing people, especially my own family and other Christians. 'God bless you' is more than a slang or shallow comment. There's real power in it when one means it that way. It's a privilege I use and repeat often to people. Distance doesn't seem to affect it at all. Of course, there is something even more special about touching a person when I pray or ask God to bless them, but when at a distance it carries just as well. The power is in God who is everywhere (omnipresent). Satan and demons are limited to one place at a time so they are at a distinct disadvantage in this, too.

The promise God gives us to claim and use is: ***The One who is in you is greater than the one who is in the world.*** *I John 4:4*

PRAYER TO CLEANSE A ROOM OR HOME

Remove and destroy all objects of false worship, then pray this aloud in every room. Using your finger to print small crosses of oil on the doors and walls is good to do. Also, leaving a light on (against darkness) and/or music praising Jesus playing in the room is also good. Demons don't like light or hearing Jesus praised.

"Heavenly Father, I acknowledge that You are the Lord of heaven and earth. In Your sovereign power and love, You have entrusted us with this place to live and we thank You for it. I dedicate this place to You for Your honor and glory. I pray this would be a place of spiritual, emotional and physical safety and blessing for me and my family and ask for Your protection from all the attacks of the enemy. As a child of God, I command every evil spirit claiming ground in this place to be gone. We put under the blood of the Lord Jesus Christ any access you may claim. Any sin that has been committed here, any spirits invited here in any way and anything that may have happened on this location we put under the blood of Jesus and we forbid you to take any access to this place or do any work against us or anyone in this place."

B. HISTORICAL ATTACK

This attack comes through our or our ancestors" sins. It is the same as leaving the front door open while building a secure fortress. It may be because of our **ANCESTOR"S/PARENT"S PAST ACTIONS.** When one person opens themselves up to demonic influence, that person's descendants are also at risk of demonizing. When a demon has access to a person, he also claims right to all that person has, including their children. The Bible says God "punishes the children for the sin of the fathers to the third and fourth generation" (Exodus 20:4-5; Deuteronomy 5:8-9; Exodus 34:6-7). The Bible says that children are affected by their parents' sins (Ezekiel 18;2) and this is one of the ways. In fact, this is one of the most common reasons people are demonized. This is especially true of first-born males, for Satan seeks to claim them just as God does (Exodus 34:20).

Generational bondage is often discerned by the sin patterns that repeat from generation to generation. It is not uncommon to observe generations of abuse, addiction, hatred, superstition and fear, pride, control and manipulation, rejection, sexual sins and perversions, aberrant religious beliefs, witchcraft, and rebellion etc.

If you notice some of the same problems in your life as in your siblings, parents, aunts, uncles, or grandparents it could very well be ancestral demonizing. The same demons have access to those in the family and do the same work in various members (not all members, that would be too obvious). They claim the blood line and use that as access. If you see some patterns in the symptoms or characteristics of demonizing that were covered previously in others in your family that could show ancestral access. That is why so often a boy who hates his father for beating his mother grows up to beat his own wife, or a child of an alcoholic becomes an alcoholic themselves.

A very, very common pattern is for the **first-born male** to be affect first and most by generational attacks. The first-born Jews were dedicated to God and so Satan tries to attack and claim them first, too. Often it is the first-born male in a family that is attacked spiritually.

Generational bondage can be broken by personally repenting of and confessing the sins of past generations. Claim the blood of Christ as stronger than your blood line and put that access under the blood of Jesus (Romans 5:15). Claim that you are a "new creation, old things have passed away, all things have become new" (II Corinthians 5:17). Ask God to turn curses into blessing (Deut. 23:5).

PRAYER FOR DELIVERANCE FROM GENERATIONAL BONDAGE

"Gracious Father over all, I acknowledge before you the sins of my parents and ancestors. I know that they have sinned because all men and women are sinners. And so, I openly confess the sins of my parents and ancestors. I know I cannot do what only they could have done in attaining forgiveness of their sins, but I am sorry for their sins against you and I ask that you cover their sins with the blood of Jesus and not hold their consequences against me or my descendants. I claim the finished work of Jesus Christ, Who bore all my sin upon Himself. In faith I accept that work on the basis of your holy Word. I reclaim any consent given to Satan's forces by my parents" sin. Dear Jesus, please set me free from all evil influences coming from my parents and ancestors in the name of Jesus. I know I am a new creation in Christ. Old things have gone and all things have become new. I here and now reject and disown all the sins of my ancestors. As one who has been delivered from the power of darkness and translated into the kingdom of God's dear Son, I cancel out all demonic working that has been passed on to me from my ancestors. As one who has been crucified and raised with Christ and who sits with him in heavenly places, I reject any and every way in which Satan may claim ownership of me. I declare myself and my descendants to be eternally and completely signed over and committed to the Lord Jesus Christ. I now command every evil spirit and every enemy of the Lord Jesus Christ that is in or around me to flee my presence and never to return. I now ask You, heavenly Father, to fill me with Your Holy Spirit. I submit my body as an instrument of righteousness, a living sacrifice, that I may glorify You in my body. All this I do in the name & authority of the Lord Jesus Christ. Amen."

The sin that opens the door for demonic attack doesn't have to be done by others, though. It could be **OUR OWN PAST ACTIONS.** The lists of sins that are especially prone to allowing demonic access are listed in this handbook on pages 20, 32-33. This refers specifically to things that happened early in life, often in childhood, which gave demons access to work against us. Present acts of sin will be considered separately.

This can include occult, New Age, Ouija Board or other involvements in the past. Having become a Mason, Shriner or member of any secret society, have had a traumatic experience, rape, molestation or abuse experience, been involved in drugs, alcohol or immoral behavior, having someone lay hands on you to pray and they had demonic issues themselves or having a curse put on you or your family.

God clearly states that **SEXUAL UNION** means two become one flesh, even if it is sex with a prostitute (1 Corinthians 6:16). Therefore, sexual activity with anyone before or outside marriage can be a direct opening to demonization. Any demons that have access to the person you are involved with will have immediate and instant access to you as well. It is like a spiritual AIDS infection, but there is no prevention, no „safe sex" application. Those sexual involvements of the past must be confessed and put under the blood of Jesus. Any access given to any demons through them must be broken in Jesus' name. Ask to be filled with His Presence instead, and thank Him for His mercy!

It may be someone has put a **CURSE** on you or your family by asking that something bad happen to you. That is really a prayer that Satan really loves to answer! Parents can curse their children by saying they wish they hadn't had them, they hate them, don't want them they are no good and will never amount to anything, and so forth. Finally, we can curse ourselves (Proverbs 6:2) by saying we hope we die, that we aren't good enough, that we'll never be happy or any of many such things about ourselves.

The area of curses is a less common but still a strong opening to demonic access. To curse someone is to ask for evil to happen to them. Those requests (really prayers) are heard by Satan and his forces and 'answered' when possible. This includes everything from occult and witchcraft curses to one individual 'wishing' harm on another. Balaam was paid to curse Israel, but God wouldn't allow it (Numbers 22 - 24). These curses, when in effect, can also be passed on from generation to generation. The Bible says that speaking evil of someone is the same as cursing them (Romans 12:14). Things like: "I hope you die…" "Since he/she won't love me, I wish they'd …." "You're no good, you'll never amount to anything…" "I hope she gets some of her own medicine…" "I hope your children do …. to you when you grow up." You can even curse yourself by what you say (Proverbs 6:2). Our words are powerful and important. They aren't something to be taken lightly. Using profanity ("curse" words) also falls into this category. When someone "damns" someone to "hell" that is an awful, awful thing to say! Demons love to hear it; they use the power of the hate in the speaker and will latch onto any authority or justification to do their evil!

Balaam tried to curse the Jews (Dt 23:4). The Bible says we can curse others (Ps 109:17). Demons use this as an excuse to work against the person, as a „prayer" to gain access. Old Testament men (Abraham, Isaac, Jacob, etc. Gen 27:23, 38) would bless or curse their children (Genesis 48:20). Sometimes they even put a curse on them, as Abraham did with Ishmael and Isaac cursed Esau. The Levites were used to pronounce blessings (Dt 10:8; 21:5). When Naomi came back to Israel, she said she was to be called „mara" because things had turned „bitter" for her. A father is to bless his children by his words and send them into life with his and God's blessing. What you have done is the opposite.

If you feel this may have happened to you remember to *"Bless them that curse you"* (Matthew 5:44). Treat the person with love and kindness, for when you return good for evil the *"undeserved curse does not come to rest"* (Proverbs 6:2). Break that curse against you in Jesus' name, claiming Galatians 3:10,13 which says *"Christ redeemed us from the curse of the law by becoming a curse for us, for it is written: 'Cursed is everyone who is hung on a tree.'"* Ask God to turn the curse to a blessing (Deuteronomy 23:5).

ADOPTED CHILDREN are quite often attacked because of openings in their past: rejection, illegitimacy, rape (mother or them), abuse or many other things. There are often many generational demons at work. Deliverance should be sought early for adopted children who show signs of difficulties adjusting and adapting to their new family. Any child who has experienced a traumatic experience when young can have demonic openings from it. A car or other kind of accident or any situation that causes terror can be the reason. So can abuse, rape, molestation or any form of rejection.

In order to bring deliverance to adopted children first of all the bond with the natural mother must be broken. It's like cutting an invisible spiritual umbilical cord. Pray to break any claim by sprits of abandonment, resentment, anger, lust, low self-esteem, self-centeredness, jealousy, rejection, self-rejection, etc., and pray for them to be free from any generational spirits who would be claiming them. Pray against any family curses, spirits of occultism or anything that had access to the family through the ancestors. For more information about children and deliverance see pages 57-58, 60.

Rejection If, before birth, one or both of the parents reject the pregnancy and the baby is unwanted, demons can step in and claim the baby. Also, if there is a difficult birth or the parents are disappointed because of the sex or a physical feature (or handicap) of the baby then demons can claim it. Sometimes even extreme sibling rejection can cause this. Rejection can come later too, especially if a baby cries a lot or causes problems for the parents, or if it interferes in their life or career.

If you felt rejection in your childhood, what can you now do about it? First, make a free will decision to forgive the person/parent. In Jesus' name break anything they said/felt against you (as with curses above). Freely accept God's love to fill and heal you. In Jesus name forbid any demons of rejection to do any work against you. From then on take every thought captive (II Corinthians 10:4-5) and don't let negative thoughts about your past rejection dominate (Philippians 4:8). Claim your new relationship to God (II Corinthians 5:17).

Abuse This includes any form of incest or physical abuse (physical or emotional). As seen before, sexual union gives demons access (I Corinthians 6:16). The trauma of abuse creates openings that demons often use in the child's life from then on.

Rebellion Rebellion is often seen as "natural," but can be as much an invitation for demonizing as direct occult involvement (I Samuel 15:23 says so!). There is a difference between normal "trying to find one's self" and real rebellion. In Israel older children who rebelled were stoned to death. How can we tell normal rebellion from abnormal?

It is normal for a child to want his curfew extended to that of his friends but abnormal to ignore their curfew and sometimes stay out all night. It is normal for a child to exhibit mood swings (without violence of destruction) but abnormal when they become more and more irrational and violent. Showing less interest in family activities as they grow older is normal for children, but becoming so withdrawn they only use the home for a bed and breakfast is abnormal. Showing some impatience with rules and restrictions is normal, but purposefully disobeying and speaking disrespectfully are not. A gradual change in interests and friends as a child grows in normal, but suddenly dropping all former interests and activities is not. It is normal that a child will not confide in a parent as much as they used to as they mature, but abnormal for them to be sneaky and secretive, even dishonest and manipulative. Children may want to stretch the dress code you lay down, but it is abnormal to purposely dress in a way that will shock and offend you. The Bible says this abnormal rebellion will grow in the last days (II Timothy 3:1-5) and it certainly has been.

If you sense this in your child please pray specifically and regularly for them. Confront them in love. Reestablish the relationship so grounds of communication can be opened. Counseling can be helpful, too. Try to distinguish between their attitude and their action. Sometimes one must be addressed first, other times the other. Ask God for wisdom (James 1).

SOUL TIES in our past can be another opening for demons. Just like they can transfer from one person to another through a physical union like sex, so they can transfer through an emotional union as well. Souls can bond as well as bodies. When one gives their trust, their heart to another a bonding is formed. Bonds between mates, parents and children, godly friends, etc., are good and necessary. But when we bond with someone who is demonized then those demons can use that as access to the other person. Souls become bonded, or tied together. If you have any of these in your past that you feel may not have been godly and healthy, confess them as sin and break the bond in Jesus" name.

> **PRAYER TO BREAK UNGODLY SOUL TIES**
>
> In the name of the Father, the Son and the Holy Spirit, I ask God to break all ungodly spirit, soul and body ties that have been established between me and (name person). I sever that linking supernaturally and ask God to remove from you all influence of the other person (name them) and draw back to myself every part that has been wrongfully tied in bondage to another person. I now speak directly to every evil spirit that has taken advantage of this ungodly soul tie. You no longer have any rights here and I order you to leave now without hurting or harming me or any other person and without going into any other member of the family. In Jesus" name. Amen

BREAKING ACCESS GIVEN IN CHILDHOOD

FROM YOUR OWN CHILDHOOD Confess (admit) what happened as sin and put it under the blood of Jesus (I John 1:9). Even if it isn't your sin, you must label what happened as sin and break its power over you by Jesus' blood. Forgive anyone that has been influential or guilty in any of these areas. In Jesus' name take back any access demons can try to use. Ask to be filled by the Holy Spirit and healed from the results of any of these. Claim II Corinthians 5:17, that you are now a new creation in Jesus and all those old things are gone and passed away.

IN YOUR OWN CHILDREN Confess the sin and especially your part in it, putting it under the blood of Jesus (I John 1:9). Forgive anyone involved (others or yourself). In Jesus' name take back any access demons can try to use from it. Ask to be filled by the Holy Spirit and healed from the results of any of these. Pray for them regularly and specifically. Claim II Corinthians 5:17 for them if they are believers (they are a new creation and all these things in the past are gone). If they aren't a believer pray for their salvation.

God's promise to us in this area is: ***Therefore, if anyone is in Christ, He is a new creation; the old has gone, the new has come! II Corinthians 5:17***

C. RELATIONAL ATTACK

One of the most common reasons for our attacks is because of our commitment to Jesus. The fort is attacked just because it is there and represents a threat to those who don't want it there.

We don't have to have done anything – just our stand with Jesus will draw attacks for Satan is committed to opposing God's kingdom in any and every way he can. Satan can't attack Jesus directly so he takes his hate and anger out on God's children. That's why the Jews have experienced such persecution through the years. While we were in Satan's army, or even when we were neutral and ineffective for God, demons didn't need to waste time and effort on us. But when we become committed to serving Jesus and building His Kingdom, we find we have spiritual enemies sworn to do anything they can to destroy us. Sometimes these attacks are direct, other times they take an indirect approach. Our marriage, finances, children or health may be attacked to discourage us and cause us to cease to actively participate in the cause of Christ. These attacks can also take the form of opposition from others. There may be a person who does what he can to make life difficult for you. This is why Satan attacked Job – because he was effective in his faith and Satan wanted to stop that. That seems to be the cause of Paul's demonic „thorn in the flesh" attack as well (2 Corinthians 12).

How can we tell what is a normal problem of the flesh or life in a fallen world from what is an attack of the enemy? If it brings a long, ongoing battle, and especially if you are having trouble having victory over it, you should seek for deeper causes. Or if it is a very new, very sudden attack that threatens to overwhelm and defeat you. If it is something large that comes from nowhere, like a gigantic wave that threatens to wash you away. Then suspect spiritual causes as well.

Pray for a hedge of protection around yourself, your property and your family, as Job did (Job 1:45, 10-11). Turn to God's Word for guidance:

God opposes the proud but gives grace to the humble. Submit yourselves, then, to God. Resist the devil, and he will flee from you. Come near to God and He will come near to you. James 4:6-8

All things work together for the good of those who love God. Rom 8:28

There is no testing taken you but such as is common to man. God will not allow you to be tested beyond what you can bear, but with the testing will make a way of escape so you can bear it. I Cor 10:13

D. SPIRITUAL ATTACK

The major cause for most of our battles, especially if we are struggling with sins that defeat us. These are like having cracks and rotten spaces in our defense. They are a sure invitation for attack and defeat.

For children such sins as self-centeredness, pride, rebellion, anger and unforgiveness are especially damaging in this area. Rebellion (1 Samuel 15:23), immorality, substance abuse, pride and self-rejection are sins teens commit which open them to the enemy. For adults any ongoing sin patter, pride, greed, anger, lust, etc., can be an opening for demonic attack. The lists of sins that are especially prone to allowing demonic access are listed in this handbook on page 20, 32-33. Demons love to piggy-back on human sins, so watch out! Demons are like rats attracted to garbage. To get rid of the rats you must get rid of the garbage. For us that would be sin.

Ask God to show you any sin in your life so that you can effectively deal with it. ***Ps 139:23-24 Search me, O God, and know my heart; test me and know my anxious thoughts. See if there is any offensive way in me, and lead me in the way everlasting.***

Sin must be confessed (I John 1:9). That means to see the sin as God sees it. It includes thoughts, actions, motives and sins of omission. Fasting can be a way of showing humility and seeking victory over sin (Ps 169:10 Dt 8:2-3, 11-14; Isa 58:3). For more information on fasting see page 56-57.

REMEMBER, GOD PROMISES VICTORY!

"Thanks be to God, He gives us the victory through our Lord Jesus Christ." I Cor. 15:57

"But thanks be to God, who always leads us in triumphal procession in Christ." II Cor. 2:14

"Who is He that overcomes the world? Only he who believes Jesus Christ is the Son of God." I John 5:5

So let's define sin. Sin is anything we do, anything we think or anything we feel that is not what Jesus would do, think or feel. It is anything we could do, think or feel that is right and He wants us to do but we don't do, think or feel it. Or it could be something good we do, think or feel but do, think or feel it motivated by our own selfish reasons. Sin is more motive than action.

> **PRAYER FOR FORGIVENESS FOR SIN AND DELIVERANCE**
>
> "Dear heavenly Father, You have told us to put on the Lord Jesus Christ and make no provision for the flesh in regard to its lusts (Romans 13:14). I acknowledge that I have given in to fleshly lusts which wage war against my soul (I Peter 2:11). I thank You that in Christ my sins are forgiven, but I have transgressed Your holy law and given the enemy an opportunity to wage war in my members (Ephesians 4:27; James 4:1; I Peter 5:8). I come before Your presence to acknowledge these sins and to seek Your cleansing (I John 1:9) that I may be freed from the bondage of sin (Galatians 5:1). I now ask You to reveal to my mind the ways that I have transgressed Your moral law and grieved the Holy Spirit. (Then confess each sin that comes
>
> to mind one by one.) I now confess these sins to You and claim through the blood of the Lord Jesus Christ my forgiveness and cleansing. I cancel all ground that evil spirits have gained through my willful involvement in sin. I ask this in the wonderful name of my Lord and Savior Jesus Christ. Amen."

Let's look a little more specifically at some of the sin areas that are especially related to demonizing, either by cause or by effect.

ANGER BASED SINS

One of the leading causes of demonizing is unconfessed anger. Anger includes any form of unforgiveness, bitterness, hate, jealousy, gossip, criticism, etc. Paul says these can *"give the devil a foothold"* (Ephesians 4:26-27). He tells the Corinthians that if they don't forgive each other Satan will use that to *"outwit"* them (II Corinthians 2:10-11). Jesus Himself said that those who don't forgive others will be turned over to tormenting demons to bring them to repentance (Matthew 18:34). This anger includes anger toward others, parents' self, or God. There can be no removing demons using this access until all anger is truly confessed and put under the blood of Jesus. This is one of the first things that usually comes up when we counsel people and pray for their deliverance. Do NOT take this lightly!

> **PRAYER FOR FORGIVENESS OF ANGER & UNFORGIVENESS**
>
> "Dear heavenly Father, I thank You for the riches of Your kindness, forbearance, and patience, knowing that Your kindness has led me to repentance (Romans 2:4). I confess that I have not extended that same patience and kindness toward others who have offended me, but instead I have harbored bitterness and resentment. I pray that during this time of self-examination You would bring to mind only those people that I have not forgiven in order that I may do so (Matthew 18:35). I also pray that if I have offended others you would bring to mind only those people from whom I need to seek forgiveness and the extent to which I need to seek it (Matthew 5:23-24). I ask this in the precious name of Jesus. Amen.
>
> **PRAYER TO FORGIVE OTHERS**
>
> Thank You, Jesus, for dying that I might be forgiven. By an act of my will, I now choose to express the desire of my heart and forgive those who have hurt me. (name the people) I release each and every one of these people into the freedom of my forgiveness. In Jesus" name. Amen

IDOLATRY BASED SINS

Sins which specifically put something or someone before God also give openings to demons. Putting anything before God is idolatry, and is forbidden by God (Exodus 20:3,4,23; 23:24). These sins include greed, envy, jealousy, materialism, or putting anything (career, possessions, etc.) or anyone (mate, child, parent, self, etc.) before God. Demons receive the worship we give anything other than God (Zechariah 10:2; I Corinthians 10:19-21). Ananias and

Saphira were guilty of this (Acts 5:3). Spiritual adultery is something God hates (Jeremiah 3:8- 10; Ezekiel 16:23-43; 23:24-30; Revelation 17:1-5). This starts in the mind (Judges 2:10-13; Ezekiel 14:7).

PRAYER FOR FORGIVENESS FROM IDOLATRY BASED SINS

"Dear heavenly Father, You have said the pride goes before destruction and an arrogant spirit before stumbling (Proverbs 16:18). I confess that I have not denied myself, picked up my cross daily, and followed You (Matthew 16:24). In so doing I have given ground to the enemy in my life. I have believed that I could be successful and live victoriously by my own strength and resources. I now confess that I have sinned against You by placing my will before Yours and by centering my life around self instead of You. I now renounce the self-life and by so doing cancel all the ground that has been gained in my members by the enemies of the Lord Jesus Christ. I pray that You will guide me so that I will do nothing from selfishness or empty conceit, but that with humility of mind I will regard others as more important than myself (Philippians 2:3). Enable me through love to serve others and in honor prefer others (Romans 12:10). I ask this in the name of Christ Jesus my Lord. Amen. "

IMMORALITY BASED SINS

God created sex to show the great oneness of believers and Christ (Ephesians 5). Therefore, Satan tries hard to pervert and destroy this model. Any sex outside marriage is sinful (Ephesians 5:3, 5-6). This includes thoughts (Matthew 5:27-30).

Sexual sin has an element that other sins don't have. When you unite yourself with another person that also opens you to being demonized by any demons that are demonizing the person you are united to. This is true even if it is simply sexual lust with a prostitute (I Corinthians 6:16). Sex creates a special union, a spiritual oneness, an opening of total sharing between two people. Often demons will claim this as access from one person to another. It is like a spiritual AIDS disease, but much more contagious and with far worse consequences.

It is important for each believer to confess all their past immorality and put it under the blood of Jesus, as well as taking back any access given to Satan's forces by that act. Ask God to heal and cleanse you spiritually. Of course, a good spiritual life (connecting with God in devotions each morning, reading your Bible, etc.) is a must.

When a person first gets tempted, when the first thought pops into their mind, they must get victory over the thought and not allow it to stay and grow. Victory only happens by quoting scripture. Jesus had victory over Satan by quoting scripture and that is our sword of the Spirit. Her are some passages you can use. Start quoting or reading them when tempted and don't stop until well beyond the temptation" 2 Corinthians 5:17; Psalm 51:10-12; Romans 12:1;

James 4:6-8; I John 4:4; Philippians 4:19; Matthew 16:23; Psalm 139:23-24; 2 Corinthians 5:17;

2 Corinthians 12:9-10; 1 Peter 5:8-9; Job 31:1; Matthew 5:27-28. These verses can be your sword for victory. Make sure you have an accountability partner who will check on you and be there for you as well!

PRAYER FOR FORGIVENESS FROM SEXUAL SINS

Father, I confess that at various times in my life I have been powerless against the continuing agree with Your verdict on my sin. I renounce all pleasure associated with these sins. I ask You to cleanse my memories, heal the hurts and forgive me. In Jesus" name. Amen

ANOTHER PRAYER FOR SEXUAL SIN

Loving Heavenly Father, I thank you for the gift of human sexuality and the high and holy purpose for which you created it. In the name of the Lord Jesus Christ and by the power of His blood, I resist all strongholds of sexual pervertedness assigned to manipulate and rule over

_____ I specifically resist demons and strongholds of _____ (name the areas of sexuality where they are being defeated), I command all of Satan's forces to cease all activity and leave and go to where the Lord Jesus Christ sends them. In Jesus" name I pray. Amen.

WRONG SELF IMAGE BASED SINS

While there is often too much focus on self today under the guise of "developing a good self-image," it is true we are to accept ourselves as God made us (Psalm 139). We are to accept ourselves as we accept others (Luke 10:27) - accepting both strengths and weaknesses without over-emphasizing one or the other. Overemphasizing our strengths is pride, and that is the sin that caused Satan's downfall. He tries to use it today as much as possible. The other extreme (under-emphasizing our strengths) is to dislike or not accept ourselves as God made us. Self-love and self-hate are both from pride. Both focus on self and are preoccupation with self. In one we see ourselves as better than others in the other you see yourself as worse. Both are definite cracks to demonizing, sins which must be confessed.

King Saul is a fine example of someone with a poor self-image, someone who was insecure and thought he was inferior to others (I Samuel 10:22). This was a crack that opened him to demonizing (I Samuel 16:14, 23).

It's as important to forgive yourself as it is to forgive others! Satan tries to bring up past sins to have us feel defeated, unworthy, etc. Don't let this tactic work! The next time the devil reminds you of your past, remind him of his future.

<u>LIST OF COMMON SINS</u>

The following sins are examples of those which can allow Satan and his demons to have access to "demonize" you. If you are now doing these you must confess them and take back any access you gave Satan through them. If you no longer do them, still make sure they are confessed and then renounce them. If a close relative does or has done them seek God's guidance as to if Satan has used that to attack you through the relative. This list is not complete, but will give you an idea of things:

When these are confessed and renounced, claim back for God the ground that Satan may have claimed for his through these sins. Then make sure you ask and invite God's Holy Spirit to fill those areas. If they aren't replaced with the Holy Spirit, Satan will re-enter in stronger fashion (Mt. 12:43-45; Lk. 11:24-26). If there is a particular fruit of the Holy Spirit (love, joy, peace, patience, kindness, goodness, faithfulness, gentleness and self-control, Gal. 5:22-23), that you need to counteract what you have confessed, ask God for His Spirit to produce that in you., Be specific when you pray.

SEXUAL SINS

_____Fornication

_____Adultery

_____Pornography

_____Bestiality

_____Incest

_____Lust (fantasies)

_____Masturbation

_____Homosexuality

_____Rape

_____Exhibitionism

DRUGS

_____Illegal (name the drug):

_____Legal (name the drug):

_____Alcohol

_____Nicotine

IDOLATRY

_____Eastern religions (name):

_____Meditation - Chanting, Mantras, Invocations

_____Cults (name them):

_____Catholicism

_____Secret Orders (name):

_____Material things (name):

_____People (name):

OCCULT PRACTICES

_____Astrology

_____Fortune telling

_____Ouija Board

_____ESP

_____Séances

_____Hypnotism

_____Pow Wows

_____Witchcraft

_____Mind Control

_____Psychic healing

_____Dungeons and Dragons

_____Other (name):

FEAR
_____Worry

_____Anxiety

_____Depression

_____Hopelessness

UNBELIEF
_____Doubts

_____Lack of trust

ANGER
_____Towards God

_____Towards Self

_____Towards Parents

_____Towards others (name):

_____ Bitterness

_____ Hatred

_____ Revenge

_____ Unforgiveness

ENVY
_____ Covetousness

_____ Jealousy

_____ Rebellion - towards authority

PRIDE
_____ Self-centeredness

_____ Poor self-image

_____ Self-sufficiency

LIES
_____ Believing Satan's lies

_____ Lack of honesty

_____ Deceitfulness

STEALING
_____ Gambling

CURSING
_____ Blasphemy

_____ Slander

_____ Gossip

VIOLENT ACTS
_____ Attempted suicide

_____ Abortion

_____Rape

_____Fighting

_____Beating others up

_____Planning how to harm others

UNSCRIPTURAL SEEKING OF GIFTS

_____Tongues (seeking, laying on hands)

_____Visions

_____Healing (seeking ability to heal all)

_____Other (name):

SATANISM

_____Bargain with Satan

_____Worship of Satan

MUSIC

_____Occultist

_____Satanic

_____NonChristian Hard Rock music

SPELLS & CURSES

_____Anything else you feel guilty of (Name):

_____Anything else that came to mind as you went through this list:

PATTACHING THE CRACKS

The only cure for sin is the blood of Jesus. Any sin you recognize in your life must be confessed (admit it is sin - I John 1:9). There is no other way of deliverance from demonizing caused by sin. Demons are like rats that feed on garbage. Remove the garbage and the rats will be gone!

Prayerfully and carefully read the Scriptures listed below and meditate on the questions about each verse (Psalm 139:23-24). Every time God's Spirit pricks your heart pray and admit/confess your sin. Put it under the blood of Jesus, and take back any access this sin has given to Satan's forces.

CONFESSION OF SIN

"Search me, O God, and know my heart; try me and know my thoughts; and see if there is any wicked way in me, and lead me in the way everlasting." Psalm 139:23-24

1. MATTHEW 6:12,14

Is there anyone against whom you hold a grudge?

Is there anyone you hate? Is there anyone you do not love? Are there any misunderstandings you are unwilling to forget?

Is there any person against whom you are harboring bitterness, resentment, or jealousy? Is there anyone you dislike to hear praised or spoken well of?

Do you justify a wrong attitude toward another?

2. MATTHEW 6:33

Is there anything in which you have failed to put God first?

Have your decisions been made after your wisdom and desires instead of by seeking and following God's will?

Do any of the following in any way interfere with your surrender and service to God: ambition, pleasures, loved ones, friendships, desire for recognition, money, plans?

3. MARK 16:15

Have you failed to seek the lost for Christ?

Have you failed to witness consistently with your mouth for the Lord Jesus Christ?

4. JOHN 13:35

Are you secretly pleased over the misfortunes of another?

Are you secretly annoyed over the accomplishments or advancements of another? Are you guilty of any contention, division or strife? Do you quarrel or argue?

Are there people whom you deliberately slight?

5. ACTS 20:35

Have you robbed God by withholding His due of time, talents, or treasure? Have you given less than He wants you to give to God's work?

Have you failed to support mission work in prayer or offerings?

6. I CORINTHIANS 4:2

Are you undependable so that you cannot be trusted with responsibilities in God's work?

Are you allowing your emotions to be stirred for things of the Lord but not following through?

7. I CORINTHIANS 6:19-20

Are you in any way careless with your body?

Do you fail to care for it as the temple of the Holy Spirit? Are you guilty of intemperance in eating or drinking?

Do you have any habits which are defiling to the body?

8. I CORINTHIANS 10:31

Do you take the slightest credit for anything good about you, rather than giving all the glory to God? Do you talk of what you have done rather than of what Christ has done?

Are your statements mostly about "I"? Are your feelings easily hurt?

Have you made a pretense of being something that you aren't?

9. EPHESIANS 3:20

Are you self-conscious rather than Christ-conscious?

Do you allow feelings of inferiority to keep you from attempting things you should do in serving God?

10. EPHESIANS 4:28

Do you do little in your work?

Have you been careless in the payment of debts?

Do you waste time? Do you waste other people's time?

11. EPHESIANS 4:32

Do you complain?

Do you find fault with others?

Do you have a critical attitude toward any person or things? Are you irritable or cranky?

Do you get angry? Do you become impatient with others? Are you ever unkind or harsh?

12. EPHESIANS 5:16

Do you listen to unedifying radio or TV programs? Do you read unworthy material?

Do you find it necessary to seek satisfaction form any questionable source?

Are you doing certain things that show you are not satisfied in the Lord Jesus Christ?

13. EPHESIANS 5:20

Have you neglected to thank Him for all things, the seemingly bad as well as the good? Have you virtually called God a liar by doubting His Word?

Do you worry?

Is your spiritual temperature based on your feelings instead of on the facts of God's Word?

14. PHILIPPIANS 1:21

Are you taken up with the cares of this life?

Is your conversation or heart joy over things rather than the Lord and His work? Does anything mean more to you than living for & pleasing God?

15. PHILIPPIANS 2:14

Do you ever, by word or deed, seek to hurt someone? Do you gossip?

Do you speak unkindly concerning people not present?

Do you carry prejudice against true Christians because they are of a different group or church? Do you think less of people who do not see everything exactly like you?

16. PHILIPPIANS 4:4

Have you neglected to seek to be pleasing to Him in all things? Do you carry any bitterness toward God?

Have you complained against God in any way?

Have you been dissatisfied with His provision for you?

Is there in your heart any unwillingness to obey God fully?

Do you have reservations as to what you would or wouldn't do about anything that might be His will? Have you disobeyed some direct leading from God?

17. COLOSSIANS 3:9

Do you engage in empty and unprofitable conversation? Do you ever lie? Do you ever exaggerate?

Do you ever cheat? Do you ever steal?

18. II TIMOTHY 2:22

Do you have any personal habits that are not pure?

Do you allow impure thoughts to stay in your mind?

Do you read that which is impure or suggest unholy things?

19. HEBREWS 10:25

Do you think about other things while God's Word is taught? Are you as faithful in your attendance as God wants you to be? Have you neglected or slighted daily private times of worship? Does your family have regular family worship together?

Are you neglecting studying the Bible as you should?

20. HEBREWS 13:17

Do you hesitate to submit to leaders in the church? Are you lazy?

Do you in any way have a stubborn or unteachable spirit?

21. JAMES 1:27

Is your manner of dress pleasing to God?

Do you spend beyond what is pleasing to God on anything? Do you neglect to pray about things that you buy?

22. JAMES 4:6

Do you feel that you are doing quite well as a Christian? Do you feel that you are not so bad as others?

Do you feel you are good enough for God?

Are you stubborn? Do you insist on having your own way? Do you insist on your "rights"?

23. JAMES 4:11

Have you dishonored Him and hindered His work by criticizing God's servants? Have you failed to pray regularly for your pastor and leaders?

Do you find it hard to be corrected?

RECOVERY FROM SIN

Psalm 51 (David's confession after his sin with Bathsheba and Uriah) is a model for recovery from sin.

1. Admit the failure to yourself (v. 3), don't blame others or make excuses.

2. Admit the failure to God (v. 4). Recognize sin is basically against God.

3. Claim God's faithfulness and forgiveness (v. 1).

4. Come to terms with your sinful humanity (v. 5). Face up to and admit your sinful nature.

5. Ask God to put your together again (v. 10). Take hold of God's pleasure in restoring sinners.

6. Turn to the task at hand (v. 13). Get on with life. Accept God's forgiveness, forgive yourself.

PRAYER FOR RECOVERY FROM SIN

"Dear heavenly Father, You have told us to put on the Lord Jesus Christ and make no provision for the flesh in regard to its lusts (Romans 13:14). I acknowledge that I have given in to fleshly lusts which wage war against my soul (I Peter 2:11). I thank You that in Christ my sins are forgiven, but I have transgressed Your holy law and given the enemy an opportunity to wage war in my members (Ephesians 4:27; James 4:1; I Peter 5:8). I come before Your presence to acknowledge these sins and to seek Your cleansing (I John 1:9) that I may be freed from the bondage of sin (Galatians 5:1). I now ask You to reveal to my mind the ways that I have transgressed Your moral law and grieved the Holy Spirit. (Then confess each sin that comes to mind one by one.) I now confess these sins to You and claim through the blood of the Lord Jesus Christ my forgiveness and cleansing. I cancel all ground that evil spirits have gained through my willful involvement in sin. I ask this in the wonderful name of my Lord and Savior Jesus Christ. Amen."

WHO MAY BE DEMONIZED?

Those who experience any of the following may be demonized:

1. If you were conceived in fornication or adultery.
2. If you were not wanted at the moment of conception or while your mother was pregnant.
3. If your mother had a difficult pregnancy.
4. If your mother had a long or hard delivery.
5. If your mother was depressed a lot throughout her pregnancy with you.
6. If your mother died giving birth to you or if your father or mother died in your first few years.

7. If you severely lacked oxygen or were delivered with forceps on the head.

8. If your parents separated or divorced before you were an adult.

9. If you have some childhood handicap or infirmity.

10. If you are an orphan or your father and mother left you.

11. If you were treated cruelly or were molested, raped or fondled.

12. If you have a very painful memory.

13. If you wish that you had never been born.

14. If you wish that you were dead.

15. If there is a history of sickness in your blood line, such as cancer, diabetes, learning disability or mental illness.

16. If you have been cursed or have curses in your blood-line.

17. If you have an uncontrollable habit and you have tried prayers, fasting and a firm effort of your will but with little success.

18. If you have a persistent or uncontrollable fear of any kind.

19. If you have strong rejection, depression, loneliness, despair, hopelessness, thoughts of suicide, etc.

20. If you have a constant desire to be held.

21. If you don't want to be touched.

22. If you're obsessed with sexual desire or are abnormally frigid.

23. If you dislike the opposite sex or your own sex.

24. If you have guilt or condemnation for another person or yourself.

25. If you find it very difficult to forgive a certain person.

26. If you have resentment against God, for example, blaming Him: "God, why did you let this happen?"
27. If you lived in a war zone or were in combat.
28. If someone very close to you died, especially a sudden, tragic death.
29. If you saw someone killed or murdered, watched an accident occur, or were in an accident.
30. If you are constantly angry, or shy, or embarrassed, or timid.
31. If you are afraid of demons or of deliverance.
32. If you every waed to operate as a witch or warlock.
33. If you are or have been engaged in an adulterous relationship.
34. If you or your family were ever involved with the occult: Satan worship, playing with a Ouija board, tarot cards, witchcraft, mind control, séances, out of body experiences, spirit guides, astrology, etc.
35. If you ever had an abortion or were a party to one.
36. If you were ever in any religious or para-religious cult or false religion.
37. If you have watched movies or TV which opened you to fears, lust or the occult.
38. If you compulsively indulge in fleshly sins that you detest but cannot live in freedom from sexual sins, lying, desire to curse God, alcoholism or drug addiction, smoking, desire to tear up Bibles, intense overwhelming anger or rage, rock music, desire to commit suicide.
39. If you are unable to progress beyond a certain point of spirituality, have trouble reading your Bible, or often fall asleep during spiritual meetings or events.

40. If your life has been much worse since becoming a Christian.

41. If you resist or have constant distractions while trying to read the Word or pray, even when there is a desire to do so, of if Scripture seems to always condemn you as you read it.

42. If you ever feel the presence of evil around you.

43. If you sometimes feel there is some force of power controlling you from within, or if you sometimes feel you are a different (strange) person.

44. If you ever hear voices speaking to your mind.

45. If you have repeated unwanted thoughts, you don't seem able to get rid of permanently.

46. If you have ever observed yourself from some vantage point somewhere outside your own body (an out-of-body experience).

47. If someone has ever laid hands on you or prayed for you to receive a certain spiritual gift.

48. If you have recurring dreams or nightmares that are of a horrible nature, or if you have clairvoyant dreams.

49. If you have a compulsive desire to curse the Father, the Lord Jesus Christ, or the Holy Spirit.

50. If you have compulsive murderous or suicidal thoughts or sudden surges of violent rage, uncontrollable anger, or seething feelings of hostility.

51. If you have deep feeling of bitterness and hatred toward a person or group of people for no logical reason (Jews, church, strong Christian leaders).

52. If you experience compulsive temptations which week to force you to thoughts or behavior which you truly do not want to think or do.

53. If you have compulsive desires to tear other people down even if it means lying to do so, or if you speak with a vicious cutting tongue.

54. If you experience overwhelming feelings of guilt and worthlessness, even after honestly confessing your sin and failure to the Lord.

55. If certain physical symptoms suddenly appear and pass quickly for which there can be found no medical reason (choking sensations, unexpected pains which seem to move around, feelings of tightness about the head or eyes, dizziness, blackouts, fainting spells, ringing in the ears, etc.

56. If you are frequently in deep depression and despondency.

57. If you have terrifying seizures of panic or abnormal fears.

58. If you have persistent doubt of your salvation even though you once knew the joy of your salvation.

59. If you get thoughts like "Grab that knife and kill that person/yourself," " Jump over the edge" (when up high), etc.

These will be covered in more detail in coming pages. We'll group these openings into five main areas: 1) sin in life, 2) ancestral access, 3) curses, 4) childhood experiences and 5) occult & new age involvement. First, sin in life.

OCCULT & NEW AGE

On the banks of the Amazon River live a species of large, colorful spiders. When they spread themselves out, they look exactly like the blossoms of a brilliant flower. When bees and insects land on one to find pollen, they find instead a spider that poisons and kills them. Satan does the same thing with the occult and New Age movement today.

OCCULT IN GENERAL

Many, many Bible verses clearly forbid God's people to get involved in any occult activity. The power behind the occult is always demonic (Acts 8:9-24; 16:16-18). While sins of the flesh give opening to Satan's forces, involvement in the occult gives MUCH more access. It is direct involvement with demons, and voluntarily asking them to work in your life. Deuteronomy 18:9- 13 gives a list of some of the main occult activities which are forbidden.

> *9. When you enter the land the LORD your God is giving you, do not learn to imitate the detestable ways of the nations there. 10. Let no one be found among you who sacrifices his son or daughter in the fire, who practices divination, or sorcery, interprets omens, engages in witchcraft, 11. or casts spells, or who is a medium or spiritist or who consults the dead. 12. Anyone who does these things is detestable to the LORD, and because of these detestable practices the LORD your God will drive out those nations before you. 13. You must be blameless before the LORD your God.* Deuteronomy 18:9-13

sacrifices on or daughter in the fire **Worship** of Molech (includes worship of stars, sorcery, divination, etc.) Manasseh did this (II Kings 2:1-17)

divination *kosem kesamim* Foretell future or discover hidden knowledge by supernatural powers. Ezekiel 21:21 used arrows (picked one with label that they like), or livers (color and configuration).

sorcery *money* Predict future based on planets, etc. Drugs usually part of this (*pharmakeia* - Greek Gal 5:20) This is referred to in Acts 8:9-24

omens *menachesh* Inspect entrails of beasts, flight of birds, especially they used snakes back then. To find hidden, secret info, knowledge

witchcraft *mechashsheph* Literally to reveal truth, uncover mysteries, usually by magic or witchcraft (drugs, herbs, perfumes to call demons, etc.). The Jews learned it in Egypt & from pagans. It is associated with idolatry (turn from God) and is strongly forbidden (II Kings 9:22; II Chronicles 33:6; Micah 5:12; Nahum 3:4). God gave the death penalty for doing this (Exodus 22:18; Leviticus 20:27)

cast spells *chober chaber* A charmer, hypnotism, spells, curses

medium *shoel ob* 'engastromuthoi' or 'ventriloquist' - demon speaking through man (Isaiah 8:19, Leviticus 19:31; 20:27). This is the same as Phythona spirit in Acts 16:16,18. This is the name of the dragon/snake Apollo killed at Delphi who guarded the priestess there and gave her oracles. Thus, this Apollo spirit became the one by which the god spoke to the person who had it, enabling them to pronounce oracles. This can be misinterpreted as 'speaking in tongues'.

spiritist *yiddeoni* A wizard (male witch) who would contact demons trying to get information God doesn't give out

consults the dead *doresh el hammethim* Necromancy, contact the dead, is forbidden (Leviticus 19:31; 20:6,27; II Kings 23:24; I Chronicles 10:13-14). Saul went to the witch of Endor to do this (I Samuel 28:7- 25).

THE OCCULT AND DEMONIZING

Listed below are many forms of the occult today. While not all-inclusive, it does give an idea of sins that need to be confessed and things to be avoided in this area.

Acupuncture

Amulets (good luck charms)

Apparitions (things move untouched)

Automatic Writing (hand writes while person sleeps or is in a trance)

Astrology (not astronomy)

Astral Projection (out-of-body travel)

Black or White Magic

Clairvoyance (discerning things beyond the 5 senses)

Coffee Grounds reading

Color Therapy (threads or light used to heal or get information)

Charming (spells, „healing", etc.)

Candles burning to invite spirits

Crystal ball readings

Divination (to foretell the future, find something lost, etc.

Drugs, especially illegal

Extra Sensory Perception

Eye Diagnosis (Iridology) (reading spots in the eye to tell info.)

Fetishes and related paraphernalia

Fire Walking

Fortune Telling

Graphology (some forms, not all)

Herbology

Horoscopes

Hypnotism

Letters of Protection

Levitation (raising objects, tables)

Magic of any kind

Materializations (things appear or disappear without being touched)

Mind Reading

Necromancy (talk to the dead)

Numerology (numbers foretell things)

Occult Healing

Occult Games (Dungeons & Dragons, I Ching, Kreskin, etc.)

Omens (occurrence to tell future)

Ouija Board

Pendulum

Palm Reading

Pyramidoloty

Psychedelic Lights or Music

Psychometry (personal objects tell information)

Reflexology

Ring or Needle on a Thread

Rock Music (nonChristian)

Scientology

Séances

Sorcery

Screening (Protection from a 'hex')

Satanism

Soothsaying (to tell future)

Speaking in a Trance

Spells (give or receive) & Curses

Spiritistic Visions

Table Tapping or Raising

Tarot Cards

Tea Leaves - reading

Telepathy (communication by unusual ways)
Tongues (seeking it, hands laid on)
Transcendental Meditation (Eastern Rel.)
Vitagenics (health appeal)
Water witching (depending on how it is done)
Wizardry
Yoga of any form
Zodiac signs, going by them

It can be that some of these, in proper conditions, may not have anything to do with demonizing, and I'm sure other activities and beliefs could be added to the list. My purpose is not to make a conclusive list, but to give an idea of the types of things that open us to demonic involvement. The point is that sins of these kinds MUST be admitted, confessed, renounced, and all access taken back from Satan. Then any demons who are working through these areas must be cast out in Jesus' name.

Prayerfully and honestly read the list and check anything you have ever been involved in, then confess, renounce, and take back all access. Command the demons to be gone, too.

> **PRAYER FOR DELIVERANCE FROM OCCULT INVOLVEMENT**
>
> I unreservedly forgive all my ancestors for all the things they have done that have affected me and my life. I specifically renounce the consequences of their sins in Jesus" name. As a child of God, I now claim that the power of the blood of Jesus is setting me free from the consequences of generational sins. I claim my freedom from the consequences of all occult activity on either my father or my mother's family lines (name specifically), from curses and pronouncements that have had an effect on my life, from hereditary diseases and from the effects of any of their sins that have influenced me. I put any and all sins of an occult nature that I may have committed under the blood of Jesus and ask for Your forgiveness for each of them (specifically name as many of them as you can). I take back any access I have given to any of Satan's forces through these sins. I pray this in the name of Jesus, who became curse for me on Calvary and died that I might be set free. Amen

SECRET SOCIETIES

While often quite popular today, even in Christian circles, secret societies have definite occult connections. These are not so obvious from a distance, but are there. In Scottsdale, Arizona, hotels and motels paint their grass green to lure tourists. You can't tell the difference until you get up close. So, with these societies. Secret societies include groups like the Masons, Shriners, Elks, Moose, Odd Fellows and Klu Klux Klan. They are counterfeit religions for they talk about God and being good, have chaplains, pray, quote Scripture and often meet in "temples." They appeal today because of their WASP policies and pride in belonging.

However, as the name implies, there are 'secrets' those without (and often the majority within, too) don't know. An oath is taken to join, with a curse that comes if the secrecy oath is broken. These secrecy oaths are commitments which open a person to demonizing. Jesus and the Bible are against this secrecy (Matthew 5:33-37; James 5:12; Exodus 20:7; John 18:20; Ephesians 5:11-12). In these societies believers are unequally yoked to unbelievers. Their view of God is wrong (they have a secret name for Him, which some say is Lucifer, and equate God with Allah and all other gods). Jesus is dethroned and made equal to Buddha, Mohammed, etc. Prayer is not "in Jesus' name." Salvation is promised through doing the good works of the group, and that is wrong (Ephesians 2:8-9). These groups usually see themselves as superior to the church and Christian fellowship. Titles for their leaders like "Worshipful Master" are pure blasphemy.

The power and appeal behind these things are demonic. They receive the worship and instill the pride (I Corinthians 10:19-21; Zechariah 10:2). Joining one of these groups give a clear opening to demonizing. Once in a family these usually pass down ancestrally, even if the next generation doesn't join a secret society.

The cure is to leave, confess the involvement as sin (I John 1:9), and put any access given under the blood of Jesus. Often these are powerful demons and this renouncement must be made over and over while depending on God's deliverance.

PRAYER FOR DELIVERANCE FROM FREEMASONRY BONDAGE

"Father God, creator of heaven and earth, I come to you in the name of Jesus Christ your Son. I come as a sinner seeking forgiveness and cleansing from all sins committed against you, and others made in your image. I honor my earthly father and mother and all of my ancestors of flesh and blood, and of the spirit by adoption and godparents, but I utterly turn away from and renounce all their sins. I forgive all my ancestors for the effects of their sins on me and my children. I confess and renounce all of my own sins, known and unknown. I renounce and rebuke Satan and every spiritual power of his affecting me and my family, in the name of Jesus Christ. I renounce and annul every covenant made with Death by my ancestors or myself, including every agreement made with Sheol, and I renounce the refuge of lies and falsehoods which they have been hidden behind.

In the name of the Lord Jesus Christ, I renounce and forsake all involvement in Freemasonry or any other lodge, craft or occultism by my ancestors and myself. I also renounce and break the code of silence enforced by Freemasonry and the Occult on my family and myself. I renounce and repent of all pride and arrogance which opened the door for the slavery and bondage of Freemasonry to afflict my family and me. I now shut every door of witchcraft and deception operating in my life and seal it closed with the blood of the Lord Jesus Christ. I renounce every covenant, every blood covenant and every alliance with Freemasonry or the spiritual powers behind it made by my family or me.

I renounce every position held in the lodge by any of my ancestors or myself, including "Master," "Worshipful Master," or any other occult title. I renounce the calling of any man "Master," for Jesus Christ is my only master and Lord, and He forbids anyone else having that title. I renounce the entrapping of others into Masonry, and observing the helplessness of others during the rituals. I renounce the effects of Masonry passed on to me through any female ancestor who felt distrusted and rejected by her husband as he entered and attended any lodge and refused to tell her of his secret activities. I also renounce all obligations, oaths and curses enacted by every female member of my family through any direct membership of all Women's Orders of Freemasonry, the Order of the Eastern Star, or any other Masonic or occult organization. In the name of Jesus Christ, I renounce the oaths taken and the curses and iniquities involved in any aspect of Freemasonry, by myself or my ancestors.

Holy Spirit, I ask that you show me anything else which I need to do or to pray so that I and my family may be totally free from the consequences of the sins of Masonry, Witchcraft, Mormonism and all related Paganism and Occultism.

(Pause, while listening to God, and pray as the Holy Spirit leads you.)

Now, dear Father God, I ask humbly for the blood of Jesus Christ, your Son and my Savior, to cleanse me from all these sins I have confessed and renounced, to cleanse my spirit, my soul, my mind, my emotions and every part of my body which has been affected by these sins, in the name of Jesus Christ. I also command every cell in my body to come into divine order now, and to be healed and made whole as they were designed to by my loving Creator.

I ask you, Lord, to fill me with your Holy Spirit now according to the promises in your Word. I take to myself the whole armor of God in accordance with Ephesians Chapter Six, and rejoice in its protection as Jesus surrounds me and fills me with His Holy Spirit. I enthrone you, Lord Jesus, in my heart, for you are my Lord and my Savior, the source of eternal life. Thank you, Father God, for your mercy, your forgiveness and your love, in the name of Jesus Christ, Amen."

SATANISM

Satanism is one of the fastest growing religions today. The dark nature of it has a strong appeal to those already demonized, and of course any involvement in it opens a person to deep demonizing. Children and teens are more and more drawn into this through drugs, sex, rock music, movies and other avenues. Satanists believe Satan represents indulgence (instead of abstinence), vengeance (instead of turning the other cheek), and meeting your sensual desires (instead of spiritual pipe dreams). Man is just another animal free to indulge any desire he wants. Satan represents power and immediate gratification instead of Jesus' seeming weakness and living for the future. Satan seems near and concerned, willing to quickly do whatever a person wants. Involvement in Satanism is usually the end result of a path that starts very subtly by allowing other openings to demonizing. Of course, God is greater and it can be broken, but even dabbling with it in curiosity is very serious business.

There are many good Christian books in Christian bookstores that can give much more detailed information about this subject than we can here. If necessary, please avail yourself of them.

NEW AGE

Definition Of The New Age Movement

New Age Movement: A loosely knit group of individuals and organizations that fundamentally believe that persons will all evolve into God and achieve a global unity that will transcend religious, racial, cultural and political ideologies. New Age Magazine, "What is the New Age?" defines it as: "A form of utopianism thinking, the desire to create a better society, a 'new age' in which humanity lives in harmony with itself, nature, and the cosmos. Various names are used: New Age, Aquarian conspiracy, Holistic Health Movement, Cosmic Consciousness, etc. Buzz words include awakening, centering, consciousness, cosmic energy, enlightenment, force of life, global village, holistic, human potential, networking, world unity, planetary vision, spaceship earth, synergistic, transcendental, transformational and transpersonal. Symbols include the rainbow, triangle, Pegasus, rays of light, unicorn, yin & yang, pyramid, and crystals.

Development Of The New Age Movement

New Age beliefs are not new. They are as old as man. In the current form they go back to Humanism and Unitarianism with a lot of spiritism sugar-coated and thrown in. In the current religious vacuum, it has moved in as Satan's lie of the last days, to set up his world empire.

Basic Principles Of New Age Belief

A. **MONISM (ALL IS ONE)** *"In J. D. Salinger's short story, 'Teddy,' a spiritually precocious youngster recalls his experience of immanent God while watching his little sister drink her milk. 'All of a sudden I saw that she was God and the MILK was God. I mean, all she was doing was pouring God into God.'"* Marilyn Ferguson, 'The Aquarian Conspiracy' Therefore all mankind is one big brotherhood. "We are one!" they say (as mankind did at the Tower of Babel, too). "We" here refers to man, animals, rocks, nature, etc.

B. **PANTHEISM (ALL IS GOD)** *"All boundaries and dualism have been transcended and all individuality dissolves into universal, undifferentiated oneness."* Fritjof Capra, 'The Turning Point' Trees, snails, books, people are all of one divine essence -- all are 'God'. This is pure Hinduism. Thus, today we worship "Mother Earth."

C. **HUMANISM (MAN IS GOD)** *"Each soul is its own God. You must never worship anyone or anything other than self. For YOU are God. To love self is to love God."* Shirley MacLaine, 'Dancing in the Light' This is what Satan promised Eve: "You will be like God" (Genesis 3:5). Reincarnation part of this (remember past lives - really is demon speaking, remembering). New Age teaches that Lucifer is light and the one who brings unity & wholeness into life. He is actually superior to Christ.

D. **A NEW WORLD ORDER** A coming one-world government (Age of Aquarius) will bring world peace. This is Satan's counterfeit to the Millennial kingdom of Jesus.

E. **MAYA - ALL IS ILLUSION (MAN CREATES HIS OWN REALITY)** *"If I created my own reality, then -- on some level and dimension I didn't understand -- I had created everything I saw, heard, touched, smelled, tasted; everything I loved, hated, revered, abhorred.... I was my own universe."* Shirley MacLaine, 'It's All in the Playing' They say we determine reality by our mind, so each mind can determine what is real and what isn't, what is absolute and what isn't, what is good and what is evil. Thus, abortion and homosexuality aren't 'wrong.' Consciousness-raising & positive thinking seminars are popular.

F. **CONTACT WITH KINGDOM OF DARKNESS SOUGHT** *"My own out of body experience...served to validate the answers to many questions -- the surest knowledge being derived from experience."* Shirley MacLaine, 'Dancing in the Light' Out of body experiences and altered states of consciousness are done by demons. It is opening one's self up to be demonized. Channeling by spirit guides is the same thing.

WHAT THE BIBLE SAYS ABOUT THIS *Let no one be found among you ... who practices divination, or sorcery, interprets omens, engages in witchcraft, or one who casts spells, or who is a medium, or spiritist, or who consults the dead. Anyone who does these things is detestable to the Lord..."* Duet 18:9-12 *The Spirit clearly* *says that in later times some will abandon the faith and follow deceiving spirits and things taught by demons. I Timothy 4:1 The Devil ... is a liar and the father of lies. John 8:44 For Satan himself masquerades as an angel of light. II Cor 11:1*

THE SOLUTION FOR MAN - AS NEW AGE SEES IT

A. **SEEK HIGHER CONSCIOUSNESS** *"spiritual disciplines are designed to attune the brain to ... a wider sensory realm and the mystical dimension by altering the brain's biochemistry. Meditation, breathing exercises, and fasting are among the common technologies for shifting brain function."* Marilyn Ferguson, 'Aquarian Conspiracy' The powers one tunes into in this are all demonic!

B. **AWAKEN THE GOD IN US** *"The goal is to awaken the god who sleeps at the root of the human being."* Theodore Roszak, 'Unfinished Animal'

C. **CULTIVATE QUESTIONS** *"A teacher in the traditions of direct knowing encourages questions, even doubts. This spirituality asks the seeker to drop beliefs, not add to them."* Marilyn Ferguson, 'The Aquarian Conspiracy'

D. **USE SPIRIT GUIDES** *"In my own far-out experiences...I have come upon two guides. They may be entities in other spaces They may be representatives of an esoteric hidden school They may be members of a civilization a hundred thousand years or so ahead of ours."* John Lilly, "Center of the Cyclone'

THE DANGERS OF NEW AGE THOUGHT

A. **AN IMPERSONAL, FINITE GOD** New Age turns God into a mere impersonal energy source and crowns mankind with deity.

This is a lie (Romans 1:25), God is distinct from the universe (Genesis 1:3 - 2:3), He is an independent person who communicates with man (Exodus 3:13-14).

B. **DEIFIED HUMANS** The Bible condemns men thinking of themselves as God (Genesis 3:2-7; Daniel 11:36-37; Acts 12:21-23). God, not man is in control (Colossians 1:15-17).

C. **NO SIN** The Bible clearly says that man is dead in sin (Romans 1:18-32; 3:10-24; Ecclesiastes 7:20; Ephesians 2:1-3).

D. **LOSS OF INDIVIDUAL UNIQUENESS** Man will never merge into blissful cosmos oneness for man is a distinct individual from the rest of creation (Jeremiah 1:5; Psalm 139:13-16)

E. **NO TEST FOR EXPERIENCES** When the person himself is the final authority there are no absolutes. God warns against Satan's deception (Revelation 12:9; 20:7-10; II Corinthians 11:14).

F. **ETHICAL STANDARDS ABANDONED** When there are no moral absolutes anarchy reigns. History has proven that (Nazism, etc.). God has given moral absolutes in the Ten Commandments (Exodus 20) and Sermon on the mount (Matthew 5-7).

G. **FAILURE IMPORTED** India has practiced this same thing for 2,000 years and it is destitute

	BIBLICAL CHRISTIANITY	**NEW AGE PANTHEISM**
God	Father (Personal) Created all things	Force (Impersonal) Are all things
World	Created out of nothing Temporal, finite - will be redone by God	Emanated out of 'god' Eternal, will always remain just as it is
Man	Made like God, sinned & became evil Resurrection after death	Is God and totally good Reincarnation after death
Jesus Christ	God-Man Died and resurrected	Jesus just a historical man Christ is the god-force in all of us alike Died and reincarnated
problem	Sin against a holy God	Ignorance of innate divinity
Sin	Rebellion against holy God	Ignorance of personal divinity
Evil	Free choice in this life	Free choices in past lives
Solution	Trust in finished work of Christ in cross	Become conscious of innate divinity
Salvation	From moral guilt by grace	From disharmony by human effort
Faith	Put it in Jesus	Put it in man
Power	Resides in Almighty God, uses it for man	Resides in man

Cross	Provides deliverance from sin	Example of man perfectly united w/God
End of evil	Removed by God	Reabsorbed into God, eliminating distinction between good & evil
Holy Spirit	God, 3rd person of the Trinity, personal being	Energy that can be used creatively or physically
Bible	Inspired Word of God	Incomplete, Inadequate book by men
Basis of Ethics	Grounded in God as revealed in Bible Absolute	Grounded in man choices & decisions Relative
Death	Separation of soul/spirit from body to live forever in heaven or hell	Time of merging with the energy force of the universe if enlightened (if not reincarnated)
Satan	Top created angel, real being, not God	Man, his state of unrealized potential
Heaven Hell	Real eternal states of being after death	States of consciousness in this life
Last Things	God-appointed end inaugurated when Christ reigns on earth as king	Human-realized end inaugurated when humankind realizes its inherent divinity

CURE FOR THOSE INVOLVED IN OCCULT OR NEW AGE

Recognize that just because there are nice-sounding words, deep conviction, and even displays of power, that doesn't mean a thing is from God. *"False Christs and false prophets will arise and will show great signs and wonders, so as to mislead, if possible, even the elect. Behold, I have told you in advance."* Matthew 24:24-25

Confess any and all involvement as sin (I John 1:9) and put any access you may have given Satan's forces through your involvement under the blood of Jesus. Take back any openings you may have given demons to work in your life. If anyone in your family has been involved in any of these occult activities (occult, Satanism, secret societies or New Age) put that under the blood of Jesus, too, and take back any access any demons may have tried to claim against you through it.

PRAYER FOR THOSE INVOLVED IN NEW AGE OR OCCULT ACTIVITIES

"Dear heavenly Father, I ask You to reveal to me all the occultic practices, false religions, and false teachers with which I have knowingly or unknowingly been involved."

"Lord, I confess that I have participated in _____. I ask Your forgiveness, and I renounce

_____ as a counterfeit to true Christianity."

MARTIAL ARTS AND THE BELIEVER

While many Christians participate in marital arts, I personally feel they are to be avoided by believers, especially by those who are open to demonic attacks. It is very hard to separate the physical aspect from the Zen Buddhist meditation techniques. These are not just physical gym exercises but actually are seemingly innocuous doorways into non-Christian religions. Taekwondo and martial arts are Zen Buddhist meditation techniques designed to bring a person into the experience of satori, or Buddhist enlightenment. They can be traced to Bodhidharma, a 6th century Buddhist monk who taught his disciples sitting meditation and moving meditation, or the martial arts, to obtain spiritual enlightenment. The sitting meditation commonly done in taekwondo and most martial arts is an essential part of the training, done before and after class to clear the mind of all thought and relax completely, according to the book Official WTF Taekwondo. Synchronized breathing is a key to both Buddhist and Hindu meditation, he said. In contrast, biblical meditation is meditating on God's written Word the Bible, rather than meditating on the empty mind by using breathing and visualization techniques.

The ritualistic patterns of motion in the martial arts are also a concern. Many of the patterns are rooted in semimystical Taoist philosophy and "their deeper meaning is said to be far more important than the mere performance of a gymnastics series of exercises" (quote is by taekwondo author and instructor Eddie Ferrie). We westerners can be naïve about the very subtle influences of martial arts and we lack experience to notice their hidden religious nature.

Some Christians practice the martial arts for exercise, or even as a way of evangelizing, but don't really know what they are getting into. If it works, they don't ask questions about what it means. Eastern religious techniques often are portrayed as neutral so anyone from any religion can use them, but I think this is very deceptive. We can try to ignore the spiritual dimensions, but spirituality is their ultimate purpose historically. The Encyclopedia of New Age Beliefs considers the martial arts as "forms of spiritual education that function as means toward self- realization or self-enlightenment."

Martial arts can be a Trojan Horse in the house of the Lord, eroding the spiritual barriers between Zen Buddhism and the Christian Gospel, and potentially leading vulnerable children and teens into the early stages of Eastern occultism.

It can be difficult emotionally for a person to give up the martial arts, because they may be so involved with them. Rather than considering they may be dangerous they vigorously defend their right to practice them. Personally, I can picture Jesus' exercising, but I can't picture Him involved in the martial arts, can you?

CONCLUSION TO SECTION ON CAUSES OF DEMONIZING

So sometimes we are attacked because of where we live – property we own or where we live. Other times it is because of victories over parents or grandparents – attack us same way. It could be something we did or that happened to us early in life as well. In addition, it could be because of sin in our life. Or we could just be attacked because we are Satan's enemies since we now support God's kingdom. Understanding the direction of the attack can help you know how to defend yourself and have victory over the attack.

IV. CURE FROM DEMONIZING

A. THE SOURCE OF DELIVERANCE

Before anything can be said about how to bring about deliverance, there must be no doubt about whose power is in deliverance. It cannot be done in our own strength; we do not have any power to remove demonizing (Mark 9:14-18). In fact, we can cause more damage than good doing this in our strength and not Jesus' (Acts 19:13-20). Even Michael let God rebuke Satan and wouldn't do it himself (Jude 9). We must be strong in the power God gives us. Not our own. We can only be strong in Jesus' strength and power (Ephesians 6:10-18). We are strong "IN" Jesus (Ephesians 6:10-18), not just "from" Jesus. Strength only comes from a close personal relationship and dependence on Him. This is because Jesus has defeated Satan (Eph. 1:20-22; Philippians 2:9-11; Col. 2:15; Heb. 2:14; I John 3:8; Luke 4:18).

In Jesus we have both **power** (dunamis dunamis - Luke 9:1; 24:49; Acts 1:8; 4:33; 6:8 Ephesians 1:18-23; Hebrews 2:14-15) and **authority** (exousia exousia - Luke 10:1,17-20; Matthew 10:1,8; Mark 3:15; 6:7; I John 4:4). Power comes from the Holy Spirit within (Acts 1:8), authority comes from our relationship as a child of Jesus (John 1:12). A policeman has both authority (badge) and power (gun or club). Both come from a source outside himself, as do ours (Colossians 12:9-10). Satan also has power (Luke 10:19; I Corinthians 15:24; I Peter 3:22) and authority (Luke 4:6; Acts 26:10; I Corinthians 15:24; Ephesians 1:21; 2:2; 3:10; 6:12). Demons have these, also (Revelation 9:3,10,19; Colossians 1:16; 2:10; I Peter 3:22). God's power and authority is superior to that which Satan &

the demons have. Men without Jesus do not have power or authority anywhere near to Satan and his demons, though.

In all areas it is **Jesus' strength**, not ours, that gives us victory (Philippians 4:13). God promises to give us power (II Timothy 1:7; II Thessalonians 3:2-3). God is faithful to keep His promise to strengthen us (Numbers 23:19; Philippians 1:4-6; Hebrews 10:22-23). Our part is to use His strength. We are to fight, but in His strength. We must put on the armor God provides and stand in His strength (Ephesians 6:10-18). We are promised what when we resist Satan in God's strength that Satan will flee (James 4:7; I Peter 5:8-9). Victory is assured when we fight in His might (I Corinthians 15:57; II Corinthians 2:14; I John 5:5). French Painter Emile Ranouf, in a painting called "A Helping Hand," depicted an old man dressed in fisherman's garb, seated in boat with little girl beside him. Both have hands on an oar. He is looking down fondly and admiringly at her. Apparently he has told her that she may assist him in rowing the boat, and she feels she is doing a great share of the task. It is easy to see it is his strong, muscular arm doing the work. That's how it is with us and Jesus! It's all by His grace!

Therefore, we need not fear Satan or his forces (Joshua 1:9; 10:8; 23:9-11; Leviticus 26:8; Exodus 14:13; I Samuel 17:45-47; II Samuel 22:33-35,40-41). They must have God's approval for all they do (Job 1:6-12; 2:1-7; Luke 4:35). God protects His people (Luke 10:19; II Thessalonians 3:3; Revelation 9:4; I Samuel 18:10-11; 19:9-10). Nothing can get us away from God (Romans 8:38; John 10:29). When we ask, God will put a hedge around us or those we are praying for (Job 1:10; 3:23; Isaiah 5:5). God's power is greater than Satan's (Exodus 7:12; 8:18; I Jn 4:4).

NO COMPROMISE WITH DEMONS

Like the boy in the checkout line- the more you give in to demonic demands the harder it will be to really say no and mean it. No one ever 'worked out some sort of deal' with Satan and didn't regret it. It is motivated by fear and just makes things worse, giving the demons even more power in a person's life.

Instead. It's better to have some righteous indignation against what demons are doing.

That is a healthy thing. Righteous indignation is the kind of anger you feel when a bully is hurting a smaller child. It's not a self-centered anger but one that says this isn't right! God gives us it to motivate us to take positive action against a wrong done against us or another.

B. STEPS TO DELIVERANCE

AS JESUS DID IT

Jesus is our **example** in casting out demons. At the start of His ministry, He cast out many demons (Matthew 4:23-24; Mark 1:39,34). In the Gadarenes He cast demons out of two men (Matthew 8:28-34; Mark 5:1-17; Luke 8:20). He cast demons out of the daughter of a Canaanite woman (Matthew 15:21 Mark 7:20), and cured a demonized man (Mark 1:21-28; Luke 4:31-36). He healed a boy with seizures and demons (Matthew 17:14-20). He cast seven demons out of Mary Magdalene as well as out of other women followers (Luke 8:2; Mark 16:9).

How did Jesus cast demons out? Before casting them out He rebuked them (took their power away) (Matthew 17:18; Luke 9:42). Then He "drove" them out (Mark 1:39). He did it verbally (Matthew 8:16), not by a certain ritualistic procedure. He didn't let the demons speak (Mark 1:34; Luke 4:41), expect Legion and that was just to give his name so others would know what was happening (Mark 5:9). He never let them say who He was (Mark 1:25; Luke 4:35; Mark 3:11-12). He told them to "be quiet and come out" (Luke 4:35; Mark 1:25). Other times He told them to "go" (Matthew 8;32). Sometimes He was quite far from the person whom He was delivering (Matthew 15:21-28; Mark 7:24-30). When He cast them out, He forbid them to ever return again (Mark 9:25).

AS THE DISCIPLES DID IT

We have many **examples** of the disciples casting out demons, too. Jesus gave them power and commanded them to use it (Matthew 10:1; Luke 10:17; Mark 6:7; 16:17). They cast out demons as a regular part of their ministry (Mark 9:38; Luke 10:17). Paul cast out demons (Acts 16:16-18; 19:12) and so did Philip (Acts 8:7). When trying to do it in their own strength (without dependence on God) they failed (Mark 9:18, 28-29).

How did the apostles cast demons out? Paul brought deliverance by a word, too (verbally). He said, "In the name of Jesus I command you to come out" (Acts 16:16-18). When God was showing that Paul was His spokesman there was a time when just touching a cloth that Paul had used brought deliverance (Acts 19:12). That was a special event, not a pattern to follow! When directed by God, Paul defeated the demons in Elymas (an unbeliever) by making him blind so he'd stop interfering with God's word (Acts 13:6-12).

AS WE ARE TO DO IT TODAY

When one is surrounded the best thing to do is to attack. That is what God wants us to do, too, when seemingly surrounded by Satan's forces. We are to **follow the example** of the apostles. They did what they did following Jesus' example and, in His power, (Matthew 10:1,8; Mark 3:15; 6:7; Luke 9:1). We, too, are given power over the enemy (Luke 10:19; Matthew 10:1; Zechariah 3:15). We have the authority and power to bind demons and loose oppressed believers (Matthew 16:18-19). This must all be done in the power of Jesus' name (Matthew 8:22; Luke 9:49) for that is the only thing demons will obey. Always refer to His full name: "The Lord Jesus Christ." We, however, must be a clean vessel for Him to fill and use for deliverance (Revelation 12:10-11).

First **pray for God's protection** around us, our families and our properties as we begin (Job 1:10; 3:23; Isaiah 5:5). Ask for protection from the enemy's interference, that all things would be done decently and in order that angels would be present to minister and protect, that the demons would not hide or interfere and that the Holy Spirit would lead and guide in all that will happen. Claim your authority and power over the place, time and people involved. Forbid anything to interfere, distract or embarrass as the session continues. Ask God to take their power and authority away, as Jesus did when He rebuked the demons (Matthew 17:18; Luke 9:42). Seeing God's power over Satan's forces today brings glory to God (Psalm 149:6-9). God promises victory, saying we will see Satan crushed under our feet (Romans 16:20). The very gates of hell cannot prevail against God's work on earth today (Matthew 16:18-19).

Before anything positive can happen, the person must be **willing to submit their whole lives to God** (Romans 12:1-2) and be willing to deal with any sin in their lives (1 John 1:9). There can be no known sin they are holding onto, no immorality or pride. They must be committed to daily Bible reading and prayer as well as regular attendance at a Bible-believing church. If they are not willing to obey and submit to God, they won't find deliverance. Ask them to pray confessing any sin that is still in their life and to reaffirm their total submission to Jesus and their willingness to deal with whatever He shows must be dealt with.

It is not in response to our faith that God delivers, but faith in Him is of the utmost importance. It's not that if we have enough faith good things will happen and if we fall short, they won't. God's deliverance isn't determined by nor limited to our faith. Still, faith in God to be able to deliver and trust in Him to bring to light what is necessary are primary ingredients for God to work.

Now it is time to **start gathering information**. Before a doctor writes a prescription or gives treatment, he first gathers all the facts he can. He will then know by the symptoms and patterns what to prescribe and how to proceed. The same is true in spiritual warfare. These are some of the questions I ask those I am counseling. Other questions might arise depending on their answers.

Can you briefly tell me what some of your earliest memories are? (this can shed light into childhood events, trauma, etc., that may have contributed to the demonizing)

When did your problems and difficulties begin happening? (Going back to the start is very helpful in understanding why they began. If they've always been there then generational spirits can be assumed)

Do you know of any event that may have caused the first one? (this can show an opening that needs to be taken back or a sin that needs to be confessed)

How long have you been a Christian? (Make sure they understand what it means to be a believer and really have trusted

Jesus. Seeing when they became a Christian in relationship to when the demonizing started is helpful as well.)

Does anyone else in your family or any ancestors have/had the same things happening to them? (this shows generational demonizing)

Where are your parents spiritually? (this can show if it is generational as well as how the person was influenced)

Are you married?

Where is your mate at spiritually? (through the sexual union and through soul bonding demons can claim access to the other person)

Have you ever been sexually involved with anyone outside of marriage? (through the sexual union and through soul bonding demons can claim access to the other person)

Is there any sin you are allowing to remain in your life? (God will convict them of this. If they aren't honest not much good will proceed from here.)

Have you experienced any trauma in life? (Abuse, car accidents, extreme fear can break down a person's defenses and take control of their lives out of their hands, thus creating an opening for the demonic.)

Do you have a church you attend? (The Bible commands we are to not forsake the assembling of ourselves. If this command is being broken it is sin and disobedience and must be changed for God to work in their lives. Only in very extreme, rare circumstances is it all right to not be attending a church.)

What denomination is it? (This can tell you something about their beliefs and practices.)

Were you ever involved in occult or demonic activities? (Many people have used Ouija boards of something similar in the past and this is a definite opening to demonizing.)

Do you speak or pray in tongues? (I and many others in spiritual warfare have found that a false tongue, really a demon, is present and entered through one asking for a spirit of tongues)

Did anyone ever lay hands on you to receive the gift of tongues, healing or any other reason? (when someone lays hands on another and prays for them, anything demonic he or she may be open to can be transferred to the person they are praying for)

At this point I may ask them to fill out the list of symptoms of demonizing (page 20) and or the list of sins that lead to demonizing (page 32-33, 37-38) if I feel more detailed information is needed. I may have them fill those papers in before we meet or at the very start. I will use these papers and notes I have taken as I've asked them the questions to guide my praying.

Don't rush this stage, the final product will only be as good as your gathering of this information has been. Like a doctor, the results depend on this part of the process.

Of course, any sins that come up with will have to be dealt with and **confessed** (1 John 1:9). The person themselves must be the one to pray and confess the sin. You can't do it for them. Demons are like rats attracted to garbage, so get rid of the garbage to get rid of the rats.

It is of the utmost importance to make sure that **forgiveness of others** who have hurt them in the past or present, including parents, ex-mates, etc., is dealt with at this time. Ask if there is anyone, they hold anything against, anyone they are bitter towards or don't like to see prosper. You will sense this as they have answered the previous questions but now forgiveness must take place for deliverance to continue. Unforgiven gives demons a solid stronghold from which to work (Ephesians 4:26).

As to forgiveness, what is forgiveness? Forgiveness is not forgetting or letting someone off the hook. Forgiveness is choosing to not desire revenge, to not want to see the other hurt for the hurt they have caused us. When we hurt, we want to hurt back, or see the other hurt for the hurt that caused us. This desire for justice is normal but forgiveness means we don't expect justice, we will take our hurt and deal with it instead of turning it into anger at another.

Remember, anger is a secondary emotion coming from hurt. To forgive means giving up any right you might have to see the other suffer for what they did to you. You can't forget, but whenever the hurt or anger come back, you make that choice again to give up any right to see them suffer. That's how God forgives us - He gives up any right to see us pay for our sin against Him. Therefore, when we forgive, we are being like Him and when we don't, we aren't. If you have trouble forgiving just tell God you are willing but struggling. As God heals the pain you will better be able to forgive.

PRAYER TO FORGIVE OTHERS

Thank You, Jesus, for dying that I might be forgiven. By an act of my will, I now choose to express the desire of my heart and forgive those who have hurt me. (name the people) I release each and every one of these people into the freedom of my forgiveness. In Jesus" name. Amen

Father, I confess that, as a result of being hurt, I have allowed myself to hold anger, resentment and bitterness in my heart against (name). I acknowledge this as sin, and I now repent and turn from this behavior. I ask that You will forgive me and cleanse me. I take back any access this sin has given to any of Satan's demons. In Jesus" name. Amen

When you feel ready to proceed first **explain what will be happening** so they know what to expect. People have all kinds of strange ideas of what „exorcism" is. While this is not exorcism (demons forced out by a religious ritual) but deliverance (free will consent and taking back of access by the person demonized) many may not know the difference. Tell them you will pray and take back access the demons have claimed as well as commanding them to be gone. I explain it like opening a door and allowing someone to enter a room, then realize you shouldn't have done that. You need to close the door so no one else enters, but you also need to command those who already have entered to leave. Confessing the sin and taking back the access closes the door. Rebuking and commanding them to be gone cleans the room. Both steps must be taken, in that order. Remind them there is nothing to fear (Luke 10:17-21) and that fear is one of Satan's biggest tools against them. Tell them to be sensitive to anything God is telling them in their mind or heart. If He brings up sins to confess ask them to interrupt the process so the sin can be dealt with at that time. If God says it needs to be removed then it must be removed to proceed.

As you pray for them start with the **oldest problems and accesses first**. Put any claim they make under the blood of Jesus, forbid them to do any more work against the person, and send them immediately and permanently to where ever Jesus wants them to go. Usually starting with **generational** spirits first is a good idea. Make sure there aren't any of them working and then go from there.

Next pray about **childhood** events and experiences: trauma, rejection, etc. Put them under the blood of Jesus, take back any access demons claim through them and send them to where Jesus would have them go.

Then deal with sins and openings that have come since childhood. Take your time and be thorough. There is no hurry and no rush.

As you proceed be sensitive as to who the **main ruler** (strong man) is. Sometimes it is best to attack him first for he holds the other demons there. Other times he is too entrenched and must be weakened by first casting out the lesser demons, the ones creating the symptoms of sin and difficulties in the person's life. Ask for wisdom and be sensitive as to how God would lead you in this important step.

Usually, it is best to **bind the main ruler first** (Matthew 12:29), then in Jesus' name binds up any and all demons involved (Matthew 16:18-19). Demons never work alone. Search out the "root" spirits (the rulers) and pray against them. Quite often this will be a demon named

„Death" for that is Satan's ultimate plan against all of us. Other powerful rulers may be „Fear, "

„Pride" or similar works. Each name describes the work of the demon. You can know their name by seeing what they do in the person's life. Remember, behind every demonic problem lies a flesh problem. By identifying the flesh problem that is at the root of everything the identity of the main ruler can be discovered. However, that flesh problem must be completely confessed and renounced. Get rid of the garbage and you'll get rid of the rats!

You can **weaken their structure** by breaking up their organization, for they do feed off each other. Break off her children and claim them in the name of Jesus. Take back any access through blood line, name, etc., and set them free. You can separate the power structure in her from that in their mate, parent, or whomever you sense is involved. Just bind the demons into those people and forbid them to bind together or help each other in any way. They are often the same demons who share the person but limiting them to one person helps. Divide and conquer. Forbid any other spirits to come take their place or help from without. Satan's tactic is to isolate us, cut us off from other Christians and God, and then when we are weak work against us. The same strategy works against him, too.

Also be sensitive as you proceed to **sins that the counselee needs to confess**. If God pricks your thoughts go along with this and make sure you stop to deal with any sins that come up. Sins of attitude must be dealt with as well: fear, unforgiven, guilt, pride, revenge, jealousy, etc.

How can you know if the force against you is demonic or not? We are commanded to **"test the spirits"** to see their source (I John 4:1). Challenge them with the deity (I John 4:11), Lordship (I Corinthians 12:3) and blood of Jesus (I John 5:6-7). Be sensitive to the response in the other person or in your own spirit. Angels do not indwell people, nor do they communicate through people as demons do. Remember that demons always lie and deceive, they may even claim to be God or the Holy Spirit. Be sensitive to thoughts put in your mind or the mind of the one you are counseling. If God supplies someone with the gift of discernment as part of their spiritual gift mix (or if you have that yourself) that can be very helpful (Acts 13:9-10; I Corinthians 12:10).

Remember the things covered earlier: we are safe in Jesus and aren't to run from the enemy. We are to use our power and authority. Make sure all opening is confessed and access taken back.

Command the demons to be gone in Jesus' name (Matthew 10:1; Luke 9;49; 10:17; Mark 8:22). Do it in faith in Jesus (Matthew 17:18-27; John 5:4), not fear (Joshua 1:9; 10:8; 23:9-11; Leviticus

26:8; Exodus 14:13; I Samuel 17:45-47; II Samuel 22:33-35,40-41). Be in an attitude of prayer (communication with and sensitive to God - Mark 9:29). Don't be proud, stay humble and submissive to Christ (Luke 10:10; II Peter 2:11; Acts 19:12-16). When cast out commit the demons to Jesus' authority in where He would have them go, that He would carry out His sentence against them (Psalm 149:6-9; Romans 16:20; Job 30:3-8). Remember the "house" must be filled with God's Holy Spirit when the demons are removed or things could be worse than before (Matthew 12:43-45).

Sometimes God may lead you to **lay hands on** the person you are praying for, and on occasion Jesus Himself did this (Luke 4:29; 13:11-23; Matthew 8:15) as did the early church (I Corinthians 1:14f; 12:4; II Corinthians 1:21f; James 5:13-16). Be sensitive to God's leading in this area and do whichever it is He leads you to do. One way is not better than the other. Being obedient to what God would have you do is the determining factor.

Quote Scripture as much as possible (Matthew 4:1-10). God's word is more powerful than and words we may use (Hebrews 4:12) and carry much more weight with Satan's forces. Our authority is God's Word (I Jn. 2:14). Our sword of the Word is our only offensive weapon.

Playing **Christian music** during deliverance or at other times in your home is often very helpful for demons don't like to hear Jesus praised (I Samuel 16:23). There is power in praise (Psalm 22:3), so use praise in your warfare praying. You can praise God in prayer or in song during deliverance or afterwards. Use this whenever attacked.

Do not converse with demons, either by having them give messages to a person's mind or to speak verbally through a person's vocal cords. The object in deliverance is not to get in contact with demons but to remove them. Communication with them makes you a medium and God's words forbids that (Deuteronomy 18:9-13). There are good reasons to not communicate with them. Neither Jesus (Mark 1:25) nor Paul would (Acts 16:17). They are liars and deceivers (John 8:44) and you can't believe what they say. God wants you only to be in touch with Him (Deuteronomy 4:24). Through the Holy Spirit we have access to all truth and power (John 8:31-32; I Corinthians 12:7-11). By communicating with them you give them recognition, allow them to stall, make things much harder on all people involved, and open yourself up to pride. Besides, they are total liars and deceivers so nothing positive will come from it.

What about **when deliverance is slow or not at all**? Remember sometimes God has a greater purpose than casting out every demon as soon as we pray. Sometimes there is delay. Jesus even had times when He had to persevere for a while (Luke 8:31 Greek). Usually, deliverance is a process. It's like peeling the layers off an onion. As new sin is revealed and removed, more ground is taken back from Satan's forces. This gradual process allows the person to better fill the ground which has been reclaimed with God's Holy Spirit and gives him time to grow spiritually (Psalm 59:11; 119:50,67,71) before the next 'layer' is removed. That's why the Jews under Joshua only conquered the Promised Land bit by bit instead of all at once. If they would have driven out the Canaanites immediately then lions would have come in and harmed them. There is a learning process involved that can be used to help others, too (II Corinthians 1:3-4). Other times complete deliverance never comes. Paul's thorn in the flesh is an example (II Corinthians 12:7). Paul testifies God then provides the grace needed to withstand. God wants us to learn to depend on Him (Psalm 119:59,92). Of course, if the opening is allowed to continue then the demonizing will continue, too (Psalm 94:12-16; 81:11-14).

When you start sensing that as much as will take place has taken place you can begin **changing the direction** you are going. Ask the counselee if he has had any thoughts of impressions that he should share. Deal with whatever these may be. Ask if there is anything they would like to talk about or pray about.

Pray again for wisdom, asking God if there is anything else to be dealt with at this time and for His continued leading and guidance. Ask God what else needs to be done. Some time there is lots of spiritual growth and maturity needed. Other times it is consequences of sin that need to be faced. Faith gets tested. Quite often there are other demons or rulers (which are demons, but the leaders) that will need to be dealt with later.

Make sure they understand what has happened and what to expect in the next few hours and days. Doubt, unbelief, guilt are quite common tactics of the enemy. Encourage them to stay faithful, pray, read the Bible, memorize and use verses when attacked and write down any questions they might have. If they don't fill the vacated spaces in their lives then the demons will return in even greater number (Luke 11:24-26; Matthew 12:43-45).

Encourage them to call for prayer whenever needed. That very act on their part can be humbling and work against their pride, thus it can be very freeing. If demons know they will be calling for prayer help they will be more hesitant to attack than if they know the person will try dealing with them alone.

Remind them that this is a **process**, not a once-and-done procedure. It's not that clear cut and dried. Remember Paul's thorn in the flesh? Ultimately God has the final say, not the demons. Remember Job? So, when demons remain after we think they should be gone the first thing we must do is ask God what He is trying to teach us, what He wants to show us. He uses it all for our growth. Do we need to learn perseverance? Patience? Dig deeper for a root sin? Humble ourselves more? Trust? Are we an example to others (as Job was)? The ultimate answer to the questions you is asking lie in God's will, not in a demon's power.

Close with a **prayer of thanksgiving** and praise for what God has done. Ask God to continue the good work He has started in the person. Pray for their protection and growth. Ask for their memories to be healed and the parts that have been emptied to be filled with the Holy Spirit. Forbid any demons to return or others to do the same work. Ask God to bless them and use them for His honor and glory.

TO SUMMARIZE, SUCCESSFUL AND LASTING DELIVERANCE REQUIRES:

1. HUMILITY: no pride in yourself or your own strength (James 4:6-7; 5:16)

2. HONESTY: admit any sin (Psalm 32:5; 139:23-24)

3. CONFESSION: put any and all sin under the blood of Jesus (I John 1:9) Make sure there is no unforgiveness of others (Matthew 6:14-15; 18:21-35)

4. ACCEPT FORGIVENESS: do not carry any guilt around (I John 1:9)

5. REPENTANCE: attitude of willingness to turn from all sin (Amos 3:3; Ezekiel 20:43)

6. RENOUNCE EVIL: verbally reject anything (openings) that have given Satan access, take back that access, and do whatever you must to right any wrongs you have committed (Acts 19:18-19; Matthew 3:7-8)

7. PRAY: ask God to deliver you in Jesus' name (Joel 2:32) Don't forget YOU have the authority to cast demons out in Jesus' name and God expects you to use it.

8. CONTINUAL WARFARE: daily prayer and battle against sin & Satan

C. SPECIFICS ABOUT DELIVERANCE

PHYSICAL HEALING

There is often a strong relationship between **spiritual deliverance and physical healing.** Often physical problems are also gone when the demons leave. That is because the demons were causing the physical problems. Examples of these in the Bible include: crippled limbs (Luke 13:11), Paul's thorn in the flesh (eye disease? - II Corinthians 12:7), muteness (sometimes dumbness, too - Matthew 9:32-33; 12:22; Mark 9:17-18,24-25), blindness (Matthew 12:22), seizures (Mark 1:26; 9:17-18,20,22,25; Matthew 17:15,18; Luke 9:39), deafness (Mark 9:17-18,20,25), sores (skin cancer?) (Job 2:7), boils and other painful afflictions (Psalm 78:49 - the plagues in Egypt were demon-caused), and physical torments of all kinds (Revelation 9:5,10). The Bible states that Satan can cause illness (Job2:7-8), even death (Job 1:19).

Physical healing can be a result of deliverance. If any of the demons were causing physical problems those problems will be resolved when the demons are removed.
Generational spirits can cause the same ailments from generation to generation. Physical problems are usually not God's main concern, rather He is more concerned for the spiritual condition of the heart. We often pray for the symptom (physical problem) to be removed while God wants us to seek Him and what He is trying to teach us through it. Paul's thorn in the flesh is a clear example. It wasn't God's will for that demon to be removed, but for Paul to be spiritually strengthened through the experience.

If a physical problem is present, it can be good to find out when it first started and what else was going on at that time.

Instead of focusing on removing the physical symptom, look for the root cause, be it demonic, spiritual or whatever else it may be.

It must be noted that **not all illness is demonic** in origin. Jesus healed physical ills that weren't demonic (Matthew 4:23-24; 8:16-17 fulfilled Isaiah 53:4; Mark 1:34; Acts 10:34; etc.). The Bible clearly talks about illnesses that are not demonic: severe pain (Matthew 4:24), seizures (Matthew 4:24), paralysis (Matthew 4:24; Acts 8:7), leprosy (Matthew 10:8), blindness (Luke 7:21), crippled limbs (Acts 8:7) and many other various diseases (Matthew 4:24). The fact that some physical ailments are on both lists (like seizures) shows that many ailments may have demonic or natural causes. They could be from one source or the other.

Jesus often cast out demons and cured illness at the same time. Jesus said he would do this (Luke 13:32). He did this at the start of His ministry (Matthew 4:23-24; 8:16; Mark 1:34; Luke 4:41), around Tire and Sidon (Mark 3:10-12; Luke 6:18-19), and in the middle of His ministry (Luke 7:21). Many female followers of Jesus were cured of both (Luke 8:2).

Even more precise are the accounts of when **Jesus both cast out demons and healed illness in a person at the same time** (Mark 6:13; Acts 5:16). Philip did this in Samaria (Acts 8:7) and Paul did it in Ephesus (Acts 19:12).

Thus, it is obvious that **some, but not all illness is demonic**. There is no certain illness that are exclusively demonic, nor others that aren't. Any physical ill can be demonic, but no one ill is always demonic. In our day and age, we err by seeing too little illness as being demonic. Thus, we often miss the cure. How can we tell if an illness or physical problem is demonic or not? Some clues to look for are: medical doctors aren't able to bring relief or cure; there is a pattern of it running in the family;

it seems strange or doesn't follow the regular pattern of symptoms (comes and goes for no particular reason, etc.); or you feel in your spirit that it should be prayed about and looked into as possibly being demonic.

Again, our pattern for bringing about this removal of physical ills by deliverance should **follow Jesus' example**. He rebuked a fever and it left immediately and strength instantly returned (Luke 4:39). On at least one occasion power came from within Jesus to heal (Luke 6:19). He often laid hands on a person to bring both deliverance and healing (Luke 4:40; 13:13; 4:29; Matthew 8:15; Luke 13:1-13).

As to us doing this today, again it must be **done in God's strength and power**. If He chooses to bring healing through deliverance that is His will. We must never demand it or make it dependent on having enough faith. No one today has a gift to heal anyone and everyone. It is right for us to pray for healing when doing deliverance and leave the results to God. It is also necessary to deal with any demons who may be causing the illness (physical or mental, see page 7). Often demons affect our health in indirect ways, such as working in us so we eat or do things that are unhealthy for us in the long run and undermine our health. All of these, too, must be dealt with in Jesus' name (Matthew 10:1). Sometimes God may lead you to **anoint with oil** as a symbol of the Holy Spirit who does the healing (Mark 6:13). Do NOT put any faith in the oil or any ritual in using it, it is simply an audio-visual. For more on healing see pages 116-117

Therefore, be aware that **often illness is demonic**, especially when doctors are unable to bring a cure. Even diseases they can cure can still be demonic, especially if there are other signs of demonizing active in the person's life. Keep this in mind when praying and seeking wisdom. Don't accept any illness as "incurable." Always make sure it isn't demonic (by asking God for wisdom and commanding any demons involved in that ailment to be gone in Jesus' name). Remember, when dealing with emotional and spiritual ills in your warfare praying, don't let out physical ills! Never fear, demons can only cause ills with God's approval (Job 1:6-12).

One word of warning: since demons can cause illness, they can also bring **counterfeit 'healings'** by stopping the physical ills they themselves cause (Matthew 12:24; 24:24; II Thessalonians 2:9; Revelation 16:14). This explains miraculous healings that aren't done in accordance with God's will and Word.

FASTING

Fasting is often **neglected today**, but when done out of a right motive it can be a real help in spiritual warfare. Jesus fasted often (Matthew 4:1-11, etc.). Jesus assumed His disciples would fast (note the "when," not "if" in Matthew 6:16). Fasting is a spiritual exercise distinct from prayer, although often done in connection with prayer. It is still something for us to do today (Matthew 9:15). Usually fasting is done from food (all or a certain food group, like sweets, or a certain meal a day, or no food all day). Sometimes drink is abstained from, other times not. Sometimes sleep (II Corinthians 6:5; 11:27) and/or sex (I Corinthians 7:3-5) are included. Be sensitive to how and when God leads you to fast.

The **motive** in fasting is not to punish self for sin or prove sincerity to God so He will smile with more favor in a certain situation. Hunger pictures humility (Psalm 69:10; Deuteronomy 8:2-3,11-14; Hosea 13:6). Enduring hunger teaches self-discipline and works against pride (Ezra 8:21; Isaiah 58:3). It provides an attitude of submission. Fasting also opens up more time to be available to pray and seek God. It shows a willingness to sacrifice anything to get closer to God. It serves notice to demonic forces that you are serious in your pursuit of God's will and glory (Jeremiah 29:13-14). A side benefit of fasting is that one can learn to depend on God for self-control and thus better control their appetite (I Corinthians 6:12-13; II Peter 2:19). This also helps with self-control over sexual sins as well.

While we usually think of fasting as going without any food, there are various forms fasting can take. Partial fasts can involve eliminating certain foods or meals. Even with a complete elimination of food healthy drinks can be consumed.

Fasting is not a way to force God's hand or get our prayer answered quickly. It must be done for the right motive or there is no benefit (Matthew 6:6-18; Isaiah 58; Luke 8:11-12).

Fasting can provide an attitude of submission (desire to please God and not self). It can free up extra time for prayer. The accompanying hunger can be a reminder to pray without ceasing and the hunger itself can be offered as a sacrificial gift to God.

It is best to begin fasting gradually and not embark on an extended period of fasting the first time. Many good books and articles are available helping one learn what is best to eat before and after a fast. Just remember that the focus is on God, not the faster. The enemy can use it as a source of pride and this negates the whole purpose of fasting.

CHILDREN

As we saw, **children can be demonized**. In fact, there is much more of this going on that we are aware of. The form the demonic attacks take could be anything from causing an infant to scream a lot at night to bed-wetting by an older child or to overt rebellion and disobedience. Anything that seems to defeat you or the child is suspect. God's deliverance is for them, too.

The Bible records demons afflicting children with physical illness (Matthew 17:15; Mark 9:18, 25). They prevent children from being able to control their own emotions (Mark 9:17, 22). They physically try to harm children (Mark 9:20-22). They defile children by satisfying their own evil natures through them (Mark 1:24, 34; 5:9; Luke 4:41). They make them perform or show off (Mark 9:20, 25) and defy the person trying to free the child from their control (Mark 9:19, 23). They may even induce symptoms of death when forced to leave (Mark 9:26-27).

A very, very common pattern is for the **first-born male** to be affect first and most by generational attacks. The first-born Jews were dedicated to God and so Satan tries to attack and claim them first, too. Often it is the first-born male in a family that is attacked spiritually.

Make sure the child knows that he is not the problem but that he has a problem. Often **children are more aware of these things than we think**. They may be so used to hearing voices in their heads, seeing manifestations in their room at night, or being controlled by feelings/emotions beyond their control that they don't realize these are unusual. Spend some unrushed time letting them talk. Ask lots of questions and listen carefully to the answers. Try to put yourself in their place, with their limited vocabulary. Gently probe all areas (voices, manifestations, too-real imaginary friends, etc.). Don't assume things. Take everything, they say seriously. Make notes of things to pray about or talk about later. Be sensitive to God's leading. Go with your impulses and thoughts, they are from God at a time like this. Pray for wisdom from God (James 1) about these things and what the openings may be.

Children are often more sensitive to the spiritual realm. Many have a story from their younger years of seeing an angel. They are also more sensitive to evil. It isn't unusual for a house to have had certain parts (or all) of it opened to demonic forces by things said or done there in the past. If a certain **area of your home** seems to cause problems (especially fear, but it could be anything) go to that area and in Jesus' name takes back any access Satan's forces claim to it. We've used oil to form crosses on the walls, left a light on (symbol of light over darkness) and played Christian music which is something demons hate. Ask your child if there is a certain place in the house where he feels afraid or funny, or where he thinks ghosts or other things may be. They are usually more sensitive to these things than adults.

When too young to understand (below 5 or 6) **children don't even have to be present when you pray for their deliverance**. As a parent you can pray for your children with authority, the same as you pray for yourself. When they are older (about 5 to 10) they should be included for the purpose of educating them about these things. They can pray for themselves, and they can start learning about spiritual warfare, too. Of course, when there is specific sin in their lives they should confess it. The older they are the more responsible they become (especially from about 8 years old on) and the more they should be involved. A lot depends on the openings, too. Free will sin needs their confession while ancestral oppression is something a parent can do for them when they are young. Adopted children especially should have all ancestral openings put under the blood of Jesus. The father as the spiritual leader should pray for the children. Each morning, he should pray specifically for each one by name. If for whatever reason the father isn't filling this role as he should the mother can and should take over.

As for praying for deliverance for children just follow Jesus' example. He administered deliverance to children the same as He did to adults (Mark 7:24-30; 9:14-25). Demons are the same and work the same, so go about it the same.

Pray regularly and specifically for your child. Satan has a plan and purpose for their life. Be sensitive to what it might be and break it in Jesus' name. Some of the time pray out loud with them so they can learn how to pray for themselves and so they know they are committed to God's care and protection. Pray that Jesus be formed in the child (Galatians 4:19), that they be delivered from Satan (Matthew 6:13; Proverbs 11:21), that they will be taught by God and experience His peace (Isaiah 54:13), that they will learn to discern good from evil (Hebrews 5:14; I Peter 3:21), that God's principles will be in their minds and on their hearts (Hebrews 8:10), that they will choose friends who are wise and a good influence (Proverbs 13:20; I Corinthians 5:11), that they will remain sexually pure (Ephesians 5:3,31-33), that they will trust and honor their parents (Ephesians 6:1-3), that they will find as well as be the right mate and that their marriage will last their whole life, and that they will know the career of God's choosing.

> **PRAYER FOR DELIVERANCE OF A SON OR DAUGHTER**
>
> "I humbly bow before you, heavenly Father, to intercede for my child ___. I bring him/her before You in the name of the Lord Jesus Christ. I thank You that You have loved _____ with the love of Calvary. I thank You that You gave him/her to us to love and nurture in Christ. I ask You to forgive us that for all of our failures to guide him/her in the way he/she ought to go. Accepting my position of being "mighty through God to the pulling down of strongholds," I bring all of the work of the Lord Jesus Christ to focus directly against all of Satan's power in _____'s life. I bind up all the powers of darkness set to destroying __ and I loose him/her from their power in the name of the Lord Jesus Christ. I invite the blessed Holy Spirit to move upon ___'s heart and to bring them to you. In my position as mother/father I put all their sin under the blood of the Lord Jesus Christ. I take back any access any of Satan's forces claim through any ancestral openings and I put that under the blood of the Lord Jesus Christ. I plead the blood of the Lord Jesus Christ over their life. I ask that Your Holy Spirit would fill them and ever use them for your honor and glory, so that they would grow up to serve You. In Jesus' name I pray. Amen."

For more information about children and deliverance see page 27.

HUSBAND AND WIFE

It is clear today that a large part of Satan's plan for the downfall of our country starts with a downfall of the family. He works in Christian marriages to undermine them, cause misunderstandings, develop selfish thoughts in the partners, bring focus on the other's weakness', set up little bickering and negative feelings, fuel grudges, keep partners from forgiveness and restoration, builds resentment, inclines each one put their needs first, causing disagreements over money or raising children, brings unfavorable comparing of your mate with others, incites to keep secrets from each other, and just causes drifting apart in general.

Be sensitive to what Satan's plan is for your marriage (how he is working to destroy or neutralize it). Think about lies of his you believe that make his plan work. Put it all under the blood of Jesus.

When one mate is demonized the other must pick up the slack in patience, love, leadership, and prayer. Depend on God's strength to do this. Apply all that has been said about forgiveness, bitterness, anger, pride, etc., to marriage relationships as well.

Keep God's authority pattern: husband as leader and wife submissive (Ephesians 5). Husbands and wives should pray together, out loud, for their marriage and family. The husband should take the lead in this.

When the man or spiritual leader in the family is going away on a trip demons can take that as a weakness and attack that family. The man should pray and declare to all the spirits that he, the high priest in the family, states that when away his wife is in authority. Let them know the children are dedicated to God and Satan's forces do not have permission to disturb them. Reaffirm that any spirits to attack the family still must come through the head of the family, and then forbid any of them to attack you.

PRAYER FOR A MARRIAGE

Loving Heavenly Father, I thank You for Your perfect plan for our marriage. I know that You planned marriage to be beautiful and satisfying, a picture of our relationship with you. I ask that You would do what is needed in and through me to make our marriage all it should be.

Please forgive me for my sins of failure in my marriage. I confess my _____

(confess individually all the sins and shortcomings you are aware of). I ask You to forgive me. I put them under the blood of Jesus and take back any access I have given to any demons through them. Open my eyes to see all areas where I am deceived and help me to apply Your truth to those areas.

I pray for my mate as well and put their sins under the blood of Jesus as well. I intercede for them and ask for your mercy to cover their sins and shortcomings and to take back any access any of Satan's forces claim through them.

Father, I ask that You would fill each of us with Your Holy Spirit. Fill us with the fruit of Your Spirit: love, joy, peace, patience, goodness, kindness, gentleness, meekness, faithfulness and self-control. Heal us from the hurts we have caused ourselves and each other. Give us a spirit of forgiveness for each other. Put Your supernatural love in our hearts and help us to love each other as You love us.

Show me what I need to do to change to correct my hurts and errors

PARENT AND CHILD

Demons often use children to cause problems in the family for the parents or vice versa. For years we have battled demons named "Frustration" and "Misery" whose work was just what their names suggested. They would cause strife among the children, and it would spread to the whole house. Their plan was to make things miserable and they quite often succeeded. We have learned to pray against that at the start of each day and as soon as we sense ourselves feeling it happen. More recently there is a spirit of "Argumentativeness" that rears its ugly head. When we notice a lot of picking at each other in the children we pray against that. We deal with the children, too, but include spiritual warfare also. That really helps improve things! Quite often demons incite children to behavior that will affect others in the family.

We've seen several cases of children being motivated to do things to get into trouble so they would get scolded a lot. That developed an inferiority feeling in them, an image of always being bad or not pleasing their parents. Unless reversed that sets a pattern for life that is all too common! We've also seen several cases of children being afflicted at night (bed-wetting, crying, etc.) to interrupt the parent's sleep and make the parent have a harder time during the day. Impatient parents then scold more and the child also feels **rejected.**

Demons often set up things to cause a long-range cause-effect relationship, like dominoes in a row falling down. David's sin with Bathsheba, for example, was set up many years earlier when he indulged his lust for women (more than one wife). Satan patiently waited for the right time to pull the trap. It's important we raise our children correctly for Jesus and not let any openings develop which Satan can take advantage of.

THE CHURCH'S ROLE

Jesus' promise that Satan and his forces cannot destroy the church are what I base my church ministry on (Matthew 16:18). **Churches have demonic forces assigned to defeat and destroy**

them. As in other cases, there is a ruling spirit (strong man) with other demons under him whose sole purpose it is to undermine a church's ministry (unless that church is already going the way Satan wants it to go). Each church as a whole should be aware of Satan's work against it so they can pray specifically against that. Pray for your church and its community, binding up the powers of any demons assigned to work against it.

Pray especially for your **leaders**, for Satan attacks the leaders first and most since they are so influential in a church (Luke 22:31-32; I Peter 5:1,8). Pray for your church to be protected from false teachers and teachings which are so, so prevalent and subtle today.

Churches are to **discipline** sinning members so they will see the need to repent and also so they will not mislead others. Churches, too, can have openings to demonizing and often it is through those in the Body who are willingly allowing themselves to be demonized and/or are allowing known sin in their lives. This must be put under the blood of Jesus. Discipline means removing them from fellowship in the local church and putting them instead in Satan's kingdom, the world. There they are under his influence (Matthew 18:15-18). In effect it is putting the person in a place to follow their sin without restrictions. This way they will clearly see the consequences of their choice and repent (I Corinthians 5:5 talks about this).

The local Body can be very **helpful in deliverance** from demonizing, too. God puts Christians in a local body to help each other in many ways, and spiritual warfare is certainly one such way. He gives spiritual gifts to some that are quite helpful in spiritual warfare. The purpose of all spiritual gifts is to serve others. God gives a person gifts to use for others in the Body, not for him or herself. Some gifts which are particularly useful in spiritual warfare are:

WISDOM: the special ability to know the mind of God in such a way as to receive insight into how certain knowledge may be best applied to specific needs arising in the Body of Christ. I Corinthians 12:8

DISCERNING OF SPIRITS: the special ability God gives which enables some to know with certainty and assurance whether certain behavior supposed to be of God is in reality divine, human, or Satanic. Acts 5:1-10; 8:23

INTERCESSION: the special ability to pray for extended of time on a regular basis and see frequent and specific answers to prayers to a degree much greater than that which is expected of the average Christian. I Timothy 2:1-2; Colossians 1:9-12; 4:12-13; Acts 12:12; James 5:14-16; Luke 22:41-44

EXORCISM: the special ability to command demons to leave people and have them respond and by Gone. Acts 16:16-19

BEWARE: Satan can counterfeit these gifts and even do miracles today. Make sure you know the source (II Thessalonians 2:8; Matthew 24:24; Revelation 13:13-14; 19:20; Acts 13:8). Demons can speak through people, a kind of demonic 'gift of tongues' (Isaiah 8:19; 29:4; Isaiah 24:8) and they can perform miracles (Matthew 7:22-23). Don't be impressed by something supernatural unless you know the source of the power, for Satan is a GREAT counterfeiter!

III. V. CONTINUING BEYOND DEMONIZING

A. PROBLEM: ONGOING BATTLE

As stated before, deliverance isn't a once-and-done thing. It is a process, like peeling layers off of an onion. Sometimes progress is very slow. It may seem no progress is being made at all. Then, too, it is certainly possible to lose what you have gained (through sin allowing the openings to be used again). Satan's forces don't quit easily, and just because they are defeated or weakened once doesn't mean it is all over. Often the battle gets worse for a while. The more they tried to obey and stay close to God, the more opposition and battles the Jews faced when conquering the land. Paul's thorn in the flesh is an example of this (II Corinthians 12:7-10).

Another example is Nehemiah. When the walls of Jerusalem were in disrepair and no one was making any effort to rebuild them there was calm. But when Nehemiah started encouraging the people to rebuild there was much opposition. Some was external, other internal. Externally Nehemiah faced ridicule (2:19), anger (4:1), criticism (4:2), mockery (4:3), threat of war (4:8), compromise (6:2), and lies being told about him (6:6). The stronger attacks were internal. Satan attacked him within with discouragement (4:10), wanting to quit (4:10), greed (5:1,3,5), and fear (6:10). Nehemiah persevered despite it all and finally the work was completed (6:15) and the enemies of God defeated (6:16).

We, too, will face much opposition, and continuing opposition. When we fight against Satan's kingdom by being true to God's kingdom, we must realize the enemy will fight back. What are we to do about it? Satan's plan is for us to be discouraged, to quit, to not persevere, to stay where we are or to lose ground to him. Here's how to make sure that doesn't happen:

When the Jews crossed the Red Sea God opened the waters and they walked through on dried land, but after they matured in the faith things changed. When they got to the Jordan, they had to rush down the hill and step into the water while it was still there, trusting God would move it when their feet hit the water. He did and again they walked through on dry land. You are no longer at the Red Sea. You've grown beyond that. Now God wants you to commit to obedience no matter what; to step into the rushing water trusting He'll be with you. If you wait for the waters to part first you'll never move. Commit to stop no matter what – even if it kills you. Decide you'd rather be dead than to continue to disobey. Now I don't" think it's a live or death matter, but still you need to be willing to pay any price you may feel will come. I know God will take care of you through it. It will be more of a struggle than you've had with some of the other victories, for God increases the pressure so our faith muscles grown. I like the story of the old lady who was known for her faith. Someone said to her once, "I bet if God told you to run and jump into a wall you'd do it!" The lady said, "Yes, if he told me to do so I would. It's my job to run into the wall and it's His job to take care of the wall."

WHY DOES GOD ALLOW THE BATTLE TO CONTINUE?

That's the age-old question. Why does God allow people to suffer and struggle? How can a God of love allow so much evil to continue? God doesn't defend Himself or explain what He allows. He gives us a free will choice and sin and the resulting evil are the natural consequences or turning from Him. Still, innocent people suffer. We can't try to evaluate God" person and character by these things for He has proven His character and love by leaving heaven, becoming a man, living on earth, then going to cross to take on the punishment for every sin we would ever commit. That proves His love for us beyond a shadow of a doubt. If it weren't for that we would all deserve eternity in hell from this moment on. So, anything less than hell from now on is His grace and mercy. Why He seems to show more to some than others are not up to us to judge. God isn't accountable to us. We cannot stand in judgment of Him until we know all the facts as He knows them and see everything as good or better than He sees it.

Many things seem unfair to little children but they must trust their parents. Getting an injection from a doctor, having a pretty shiny knife taken way, many things seem to a child that a parent doesn't love them but a child doesn't have the perspective to truly view what is happening and we don't have God's perspective on life either. We do know that facing things we don't understand gives us an opportunity to trust. Our faith is stretched and we grow. God is glorified as we see Him deliver and as others watch us patiently trust Him. Spiritual warfare is just one of many forms of suffering God uses for our good and for His glory. That's another reason why deliverance often isn't instantaneous but a drawn-out process.

B. SOLUTION: ONGOING BATTLE

After trying to convince you that the deliverance you've gone through didn't really happen (unbelief), Satan's next weapon is the lie that you won't have victory, you won't change, things won't get better, etc. That's not true! If you follow God's principles you will have continuing progress and victory. How soon and how complete is only up to God.

RETAINING DELIVERANCE:

Put on the whole armor of God (Ephesians 6:10-18)

Confess any sin immediately, but don't dwell on it (I John 1:9)

C.Stay in the Scriptures (Psalm 1:1-3). The Word is a mirror (James 1:22-25) a lamp (Psalm 119:105) a cleanser (Ephesians 5;25-26) a sword (Hebrews 4:12) and food (I Peter 2:2; Matthew 4:4). Use it for all these,

D.Break old patterns, habits, and sins or Satan will return (Matthew 12:43-45: Luke 11:24-26). Fill the void with God's Spirit and His fruit (Galatians 5:9-24; John 15:3). Clean your house of unclean books and things that shouldn't be there (Deuteronomy 14:7-19). Dedicate your home and life to God.

Develop a life of continuous praise & prayer (I Thessalonians 5:17).

F.Stay in close fellowship with other believers (Hebrews 13:5).

G.Commit yourself to totally follow God (Ephesians 6:16).

GROW SPIRITUALLY

We all are either moving ahead or moving back. We cannot be dead still at the same place. If you aren't growing spiritually then you are fading. Continue to grow spiritually. Focus on the basics of the Christian life: prayer, Bible study, fellowship, worship, witnessing, etc. Sometimes growth comes in spurts, other times there doesn't seem to be much outer change (it is during these times that your spiritual roots are going deeper, getting you ready for the next growth spurt). The same is true in nature, there isn't always sustained growth, things grow in spurts.

Do NOT focus on Satan or demons, always thinking about them or fearing what they will do. Do not look for "a demon behind every bush." They love this attention, even if it is negative. It keeps your eyes off Jesus and on them, and that's what they want. It is important to have balance in this area of spiritual warfare. Keep it in balance. It is one of many important spiritual tools for growth. Don't neglect the others for this one.

SUBMIT TO HOLY SPIRIT

Remember, when demons are gone the area must be filled with God's Spirit or it will be an invitation for them to come back -- more and worse than before (Matthew 12:43-45). Casting them out is one thing, keeping them out is another. Close the opening (by confession and covering with the blood of Jesus) and fill the space they occupied in your life with the Holy Spirit.

It isn't my purpose here to go into detail about being filled with the Holy Spirit for many fine books cover that subject quite well. Suffice it to say that immediately at salvation each person receives the Holy Spirit (Ephesians 1:13; I Corinthians 12:13). He never leaves (Ephesians 4:30). Each believer has the Holy Spirit indwelling him, but not each one has the Holy Spirit "filling" (literally "controlling") him (Ephesians 5:18). Allowing Him to fill/control us is a moment-by-moment responsibility. It means we must be 100% yielded to God in all areas of life (I Thessalonians 5:19), not allow any known sin in life (Ephesians 4:30), and to depend on Him and His strength in every area of life (Galatians 5:16). This way there will be no strongholds (openings) reestablished (II Corinthians 10:3-5).

> **PRAYER OF SUBMISSION TO THE HOLY SPIRIT**
>
> "Dear heavenly Father, You have said that rebellion is as the sin of witchcraft and insubordination is as iniquity and idolatry (I Samuel 15:23), I know that in action and attitude I have sinned against You with a rebellious heart. I ask Your forgiveness for my rebellion and pray that by the shed blood of the Lord Jesus Christ all ground gained by evil spirits because of my rebelliousness would be canceled. I pray that You will shed light on all my ways that I may know the full extent of my rebelliousness and choose to adopt a submissive spirit and a servant's heart. In the name of Christ Jesus my Lord. Amen."

WEAR THE ARMOR

Satan does not trouble those who aren't committed believers. They are his subjects (Col. 1:13) and serve him (Eph. 2:2). Only when one wants to turn from that path, having accepted Jesus as his Savior and wanting to make Him Lord of his life, does Satan oppose the person. Satan will not give up one of his subjects easily and will do all he can to gain that person back. He can't take his salvation, but can have him live the same kind of life as before (one of service to Satan and sin). God does not want that for His children, however. He has defeated Satan and has made provision for us to share in that victory. As a good commander He provides the equipment we need to defeat Satan and to protect ourselves (Eph. 6:10-17, II Cor. 10:35, Mt. 12:29). The following is based on Ephesians 6:10-17. Open your Bible as your read the following.

1) <u>Armor Provided</u> Ephesians 6:10-12

"FINALLY" (10): Paul builds to this throughout the whole Epistle.

"BE STRONG" (10): "Be continually strengthened" This is a command, not an option. It is passive, something we receive from outside ourselves. A soldier receives (passive) equipment from his commander, the commander is responsible to provide it, he must use it. The battle is between God & Satan, we are just privates and only get attacked because of joining God's army, it's not our personal battle but us commander who will make sure we can win it.

What makes a soldier strong so he can use his equipment? (1. Proper nourishment (food & drink) - for us the Word of God. (2. Regular exercise to stay fit - not spiritually fat or lazy. (3. Proper rest, meditation, relaxation, worship & praise times.

"IN THE LORD" (10): not "FROM" the Lord for He doesn't just give us a portion of His strength (as great as that would be) to fight in our own strength and to add to our strength. We are actually "IN Christ" (a phrase used over 40 times just in Ephesians). This refers to total dependence, like a baby IN a womb. We are one, we share His foe and His victory. We must stay as close to Christ as possible or we will never have victory.

Picture of Roman soldier

"HIS mighty power" (10): Never look at Satan's power, or your own, just and only at Christ's!

"MIGHTY" (10): The word means a special endowment of power and strength. It is inherent strength, ability, and authority that comes from being "in Christ."

"POWER" (10): This word refers to manifested power, HIS power shown through us. The previous word would be used of the muscular ability a person naturally has, this word of that power shown in use. This power, by the way, comes through the Holy Spirit (Acts 1:8). God is the sovereign general, we are "in Christ," and the Holy Spirit is the power source given to us. What an unbeatable combination!

"PUT ON" (11): This verse tells HOW to be strong in Jesus. This, too, is a command - it is not an option., In the original language this speaks of a once-for-all action. The commander provides the armor, but the soldier must put it on-and then he must NEVER take it off for the warfare is continual. Each morning checks out your armor to make sure it is well maintained, never take it off.

"FULL ARMOR" (11): If missing even just one-piece Satan will attack there.

"TAKE YOUR STAND" (11): This same word is translated "resist" in James 4:7 and I Peter 5:8-9. We are NOT to run, fall back in fear or panic, surrender, sit, or fall asleep. We are to stand alert BEFORE attacked so we are ready to defend ourselves and beat it off.

"DEVIL" (11) "Devil" means "Slanderer," and that is what he does. He slanders God to man (as to Eve in Eden) and man to God (as with Job).

"SCHEMES" (11): The picture behind this word is of a cunning, deceitful animal full of tricks and deceit. Paul commands us to not be ignorant of these tricks and traps (II Corinthians 2:11).

"STRUGGLE" (12): This word-picture of wrestlers shows the life-and-death struggle we are in with Satan. Wrestlers back then tried to pin each other's neck to the ground. This is no innocent misunderstanding or friendly competition!

"NOT AGAINST FLESH & BLOOD" (12): Our main enemy is no other people, or even our own sin nature. We know how those operate from firsthand knowledge. Satan is in another realm that we are often unaware of, and have no idea how to fight.

"RULERS" (12): These are the demons on top of Satan's organizational systems, the generals under him as the commanding officer. They have vast oversight responsibilities, some over geographical areas, others over philosophies or works, etc.

"AUTHORITIES" (12): These very powerful demons are like colonels. They are given authority (thus the name) over certain countries, areas, churches, groups of persons, etc. They don't do the work but, like the Rulers, oversee and coordinate the activity of demons under them. They give power & authority to these lesser demons.

"POWERS OF THIS DARK WORLD" (12): These numerous, workhorse demons' function on the command level, like lieutenants and sergeants. They oversee and work with small forces of demons assigned by 'Authorities' to a certain person, church, cult, location, idea, philosophy, etc. They receive their orders and power through the chain of command above them.

"SPIRITUAL FORCES OF EVIL IN THE HEAVENLY REALMS" (12): These very numerous demons are the daily working demons that carry out the work assigned to them by the above chain of command. These are the privates of Satan's army, the ones we do battle with each day. They are not as smart or clever as the ones higher in the command, they simply carry out orders given them. They have a great variety in their intelligence level, abilities, etc. They each function in one main area of expertise, and are named accordingly (Greed, Listlessness, Self-Destruction, Fear, etc.)

"HEAVENLY REALMS" (12): In the atmosphere is where Satan sets up his kingdom, between this earth and the third heaven where God is. That is why Michael needed to help the other angels get past the Prince of Persia in Daniel (Daniel 10:13). Satan is the "ruler of the kingdom of the air."

2)   **Armor Described** Eph. 6:13-18

BELT OF TRUTH 14 a

"BELT": The belt was the KEY piece of equipment for a soldier because it held his other clothing and equipment in place. Clothing was tucked back out of the way to allow freedom of movement to fight, and it was the belt that gave them freedom. The belt held their valuables and personal possessions, too. It also held the sword, thus the close connection between the truth and God's Word (sword).

"TRUTH": As the belt allowed the soldier's hands freedom, so the truth makes us free. Jesus is the "way, TRUTH and life" (Jn. 14:6) and only in Him ("IN CHRIST") is truth found. He said "I am the truth" (Jn. 14:6; 1:14). When we put on Christ and are strong in Him, we take the truth that comes from Him as revealed in His Word, the Bible (II Tim. 2:15, James 1:18, Ps. 119:41-43). It is through the Holy Spirit that this truth is applied to our hearts and lives, for He is called the "Spirit of Truth" (I Cor. 1:6-15).

By contrast Satan is a liar (Jn. 8:44). He works in deceit and counterfeits to get us to fear and be defeated. He tries to get us to be untruthful (Acts 5:3) and uses any untruth in us to gain access to us. Therefore, we are to "stand firm" against anything not 100% honest and truthful in us or others.

3) <u>Breastplate Of Righteousness</u> 14b

"BREASTPLATE": This vital piece of equipment covered the vulnerable organs of the upper body. Enemy soldiers would grasp each other's left forearms and with the right start stabbing each other in the breastplate. The first one to find or make an opening won!

Satan, too, first attacks our vulnerable areas. He knows where our weak and open spots are. That is why we are defeated over and over by the same besetting sin. Just as a soldier would make sure his breastplate was sound and perfect before the battle began, so we must make sure there are no areas in our life, thoughts, priorities or motives where Satan can defeat us. It doesn't matter how small; he will use it. All openings must be closed and covered with the blood of Jesus.

"RIGHTEOUSNESS": In contrast to our righteousness, which is like "filthy rags", God is pure righteousness (Ps. 48:10; 119:137; 145:17). One of His names is YHWH-TSIDEK ("The LORD Our Righteousness" Jer. 23:6). At the moment of salvation our sins are transferred to Jesus and His perfect righteousness is transferred to us. We must put faith in HIS provision, not our own good works/righteousness. We need to allow His righteousness to shine through us, and to accept His holiness (another word for righteousness) as ours "In Christ". It is in this area we can't have sin or Satan will use that to defeat us.

Note that our back isn't covered, just our front. A soldier of Christ cannot retreat or run but must move ahead in victory!

4) Sandals Of Peace

"FEET": On their feet soldiers wore sandals which were VERY important. They had to be sturdy, dependable and tough. The soldier went everywhere on his feet, and was usually attacked on rough, rocky ground where getting a good footing would be very hard. Failure of his sandals to protect his feet or give him good stability would result in his defeat. Our standing, too, must be sure and ready.

"READINESS": This word has the idea of establishment, a firm foundation.

"PEACE": "Christ is our peace" (Eph. 2:13-14), and we only have peace "in Christ." He provides peace with God (Rom. 5:1) and peace of God (Phil 4:6-9; Rom. 16:20; Prov. 16:7). Jesus is peace

(Jn. 14:27) and we are to live in peace with God, self and others. This is our support, our foundation.

Satan tries to produce turmoil, chaos, and lack of peace in our lives. Then he comes along and offers false peace through drugs, alcohol, sex, compromise, etc.

5) <u>Shield Of Faith</u> 16

"IN ADDITION,": Literally "above all," meaning this is of the greatest importance. Faith, the helmet of salvation, and prayer, the next three, are even more important than the ones already described. The first 3 pieces of equipment are worn as part of the body, affixed to it. They are always to be there. These next ones are to be "taken up" to use when battle was near. The first we receive (passive), these we take up ourselves (active). These are our outer wall of defense.

"SHIELD": The shield was 2 feet by 4 feet. Soldiers would gather behind a wall of shields side-by-side and use it for an outer wall of protection. They would NOT go into battle without a shield!

"FAITH": This is the substance of our shield. We, together with others of like faith, are to throw up a wall against Satan. We can still hear his roaring attacks, but faith keeps us from being defeated by them. It is not just 'faith' that protects, for faith must be in the right object - God.

"FLAMING ARROWS": Burning pitch and arrows tipped with burning pitch would be hurled against soldiers, and only a shield could protect them from it. Satan shoots arrows of pride, temptation, fear, worry, guilt, suffering, etc., at us and only faith in God will get us through those times.

"YOU CAN EXTINGUISH ALL": Some arrows get very close to us (like with Job), but God determines just how close they will fall (also like with Job.) Sometimes it seems like some of them even pierce our shield of faith. However, when that happens, they are no longer Satan's flaming arrows but God's refining and purifying messengers of love, as Paul's thorn in the flesh (see also I Cor. 10:13; Rom. 8:28 etc.) If we keep our shield up the fire refines us. It is only when our faith is down that the fire harms us.

6) Helmet Of Salvation 17a

"HELMET": The helmet protected soldier's heads from the broad sword their enemies carried. This sword was 3 to 4 feet long. The enemy held it with two hands and brought it straight down with all his might right on the soldier's head. Thus, the helmet was very important.

"SALVATION": Our mind is very important, and Satan attacks that in a deadly and vigorous way. Therefore, it is very important to protect our mind: its thoughts, ideas, goals, motives, priorities, values, decisions, etc. (Rom. 12:1-2; James 1:8; II Tim. 2:25-26). This is where Satan attacked Eve (Gen. 3:1-7, II Cor. 11:3) and he attacks us there through our pride, selfishness & self-centeredness, as well as through the influence of the world. It is only through salvation that we can have the "mind of Christ" and thus do His will. Being Christ-like starts in our mind, so it must be protected and filled with God's word (studied and memorized).

7) SWORD OF THE WORD 17b

"SWORD": The only offensive weapon (prayer, next verse, is the other weapon we have but that isn't listed as a weapon the way the sword is in this soldier analogy). All the other pieces of equipment are defensive and for protection. It is only through the offensive weapons, Bible study and prayer, that we can forge ahead and defeat Satan. These weapons don't work until the previous ones are taken care of, though, because if we have a way to be defeated Satan will seize the initiative and we will be driven back instead of driving him back.

"OF THE SPIRIT": ANY weapon used in the flesh will not prosper. Peter used the sword of his flesh and cut Malchus' ear, but on Pentecost he used the sword of the Spirit and thousands of ears were won and opened for Christ. The best defense is a good offense.

"WORD OF GOD": Jesus, the living Word (John 1:1-14), is behind the Bible, the written Word. You need to know God's Word in detail, with much of it memorized, so you can really use this weapon. Jesus won His battles when Satan tempted Him by quoting Scriptures. That is how we are to win, too.

8)   **PRAYER 18**

"AND PRAY": This is our other offensive weapon, equal in importance to knowing God's Word. God doesn't fully pour His Spirit into us in power until we fully pour our spirit out to him in prayer. In our military analogy, communication with the commander is key to receiving orders, help, strength, additional resources, support, etc.

"IN THE SPIRIT": Our prayer must be directed by the Holy Spirit just as our Bible study is ("sword OF THE SPIRIT"). The Holy Spirit directs our praying when we let Him (Rom. 8:26). Prayer in our own strength and wisdom brings no answer (James 4:3). We must be sensitive to the Spirit as He leads us in how to pray and just what to pray for.

"ON ALL OCCASIONS": "Without ceasing." (Prov. 3:5-6). If you feel like it or not, are busy or not, know what to say or not - still pray. Prayer must be consistent and persistent (II Cor. 10:3-5).

PRAYER OF THE ARMOR OF GOD

Heavenly Father, I desire to be obedient by being strong in the Lord and the power of You might. I see that this is Your will and purpose for me. I recognize that it is essential to put on the armor that You have provided, and I do so now with gratitude and praise that You have provided all I need to stand in victory against Satan and his kingdom. Grant me wisdom to discern the tactics and sneakiness of Satan's strategy against me. I delight to take the armor You have provided and by faith to put it on as effective spiritual protection against the spiritual forces of darkness present in the world today.

I confidently take the **belt of truth** that You offer me. I take Him who is the truth as my strength and protection. I reject Satan's lies and deceiving ways to gain advantage against me. Grant me discernment and wisdom to recognize the subtle and sneaky ways in which Satan seeks to cause me to accept his lies as truth. I desire to believe only the truth, to live the truth, to speak the truth, and to know the truth. I worship and praise You that You lead me only in the ways of truth. Thank You that Satan cannot stand against the truth.

Thank You for the **breastplate of righteousness** which you offer me. I eagerly accept it and put it on as my protection. Thank you for reminding me again that all of my righteousness comes from You. I embrace that righteousness which is mine by faith in the Lord Jesus Christ, It is His righteousness that is mine through justification. I reject and repudiate all trust in my own righteousness which is as filthy rags. I ask You to cleanse me of all the times I have counted my own goodness as being acceptable before You. I bring the righteousness of my Lord directly against all of Satan's workings against me. I express my desire to walk in righteousness before God today. By faith I appropriate the righteousness of Christ and invite Him to walk in His holiness in my life today that I might experience His righteousness in total context of ordinary living. I count upon the righteousness of my Lord to be my protection. I know that Satan must retreat from before God's righteousness.

Thank You, Lord, for the sandals of peace You have provided. I desire that my feet should stand on the solid rock of the peace that You have provided.

I claim the peace with God which is mine through justification. I desire the peace of God which touches my emotions and feelings through prayer and sanctification (Philippians 4:6). Thank You that as I walk in obedience to You the God of peace promises to walk with me (Philippians 4:9), I thank you that as the God of peace You are putting Satan under my feet (Romans 16:20). I will share this good news of peace with all others that Your Spirit will bring into my life today. Thank you that You have not given me a spirit of fear but of love and power and a sound mind (II Timothy 1:7). Thank you that Satan cannot stand against Your peace.

Eagerly, Lord, I lift up the **shield of faith** against all the blazing darts that Satan and his hosts fire at me. I recognize that You are my shield and that in Your incarnation and crucifixion You took the arrows of Satan which I deserved. By faith I count upon You to shield me from above and beneath; on my right and my left; in front of me and behind me, that I might be protected, walled in, and encapsulated by You that Satan may gain no way to hurt me or keep me from fulfilling Your will today.

I am willing that any fiery darts of Satan You wish to touch me should do so, but I shall look upon them as refining fires permitted in Your providence and by Your love for my refining and Your glory. Thank You, Lord, that You are a complete and perfect shield and that Satan cannot touch me apart from Your sovereign purpose.

I recognize that my mind is a particular target of Satan's deceiving ways. I take from You the helmet of salvation. I cover my mind and my thoughts with Your salvation. I recognize that the Lord Jesus Christ is my salvation. I fill my head with Him. I invite His mind to be in me. Let me think His thoughts, feel His love and compassion, and discern His will and leading in all things. Let my mind be occupied with the continuing, daily, saving work of my Lord in and through my life. May You meet and defeat all Satanic thoughts in my mind.

With joy I take hold upon the sword of the Spirit, which is the Word of God. I affirm that Your Word is the trustworthy, infallible Word of God. I choose believe it and to live in its truth and power. Grant me the love for Your Word which comes from the Holy Spirit. Forgive and cleanse me from the sin of neglecting Your Word. Create in me a hunger and thirst to study and know Your Word. Enable me to memorize it and to meditate upon its truth. Grant me proficient recall and skill in using Your Word against all of Satan's subtle attacks against me, even as my Lord Jesus Christ used the Word against Satan. Enable me to use Your Word not only to defend me from Satan, but also to claim its promises and to wield the sword strong against Satan to defeat him, to push him back, to take away from him ground he claims, and to win great victories God through Your Word.

Thank You that Satan must retreat from Your Word applied against him.

Thank You, dear Lord, for prayer. Help me to keep this armor well-oiled with prayer. I desire to pray at all times with depth and intensity as the Holy Spirit leads me. I trust the Holy Spirit to enable me and to intercede for me and through me. Grant me great supplication and burden for others in God's family blood-washed saints. Enable me to see their needs and to assist them through prayer as the enemy attacks them. All of these petitions, intercessions, and words of praise I offer up before the true and living God in the name and worthy merit of my Lord Jesus Christ. Amen.

USE THE WORD OF GOD

Knowing and using God's Word, the sword of the Spirit, is key for victory (Joshua 1:8; Psalm 77:12; I Chronicles 28:9; Matthew 22:37-38; I Corinthians 2:16; Philippians 4:8). That's how Jesus defeated Satan (Matthew 4:1-11). Satan tries to plant doubts about God's word in man's mind. This is how he got to Eve. She misquoted God's Word to Satan and when he added to God's Word (making God seem like He was keeping something good from her) she didn't pick it up. Satan was undermining God's Word, and he won! We must be skillful in the use of our sword to win. Below are some verses to memorize and use.

When Jesus was tempted, He quoted Scripture to have victory over Satan's temptations.

Paul says our only offensive weapon is the sword of the Spirit, the Word of God. Psalm 119:9,11 tell us that it's through God's Word that we have victory. When you have these thoughts and attacks use Scripture to have victory. Ask God to give you some verses that will help against these things, write them down and memorize them. Say them over and over when these thoughts attack you. That is the only way to victory, and God guarantees it will work!

Bible Memory Verses

<u>GOD'S LOVE & ACCEPTANCE</u> The LORD is compassionate and gracious, slow to anger, abounding in love. Psalm 103:8

<u>THE BIBLE, GOD'S WORD</u> The Word of God is living and active. Sharper than any double- edged sword, it penetrates even to dividing soul and spirit, joints and marrow; it judges the thoughts and attitudes of the heart. Hebrews 4:12

<u>GOD'S TRUTH FREES</u> "If you hold to my teaching, you are really My disciples. Then you will know the truth, and the truth will set you free." John 8:32

<u>LIVE IN HOLINESS</u> Therefore, I urge you, brothers in view of God's mercy, to offer your bodies as living sacrifices, holy and pleasing to God -- this is your spiritual act of worship. Rom. 12:1

<u>SUBMIT TO GOD, RESIST SATAN</u> God opposes the proud but gives grace to the humble. Submit yourselves, then, to God. Resist the devil, and he will flee from you. Come near to God and He will come near to you. James 4:6-8

<u>GOD IS GREATER THAN SATAN</u> The One who is in you is greater

than the one who is in the world. I John 4:4

GOD WILL MEET ALL OUR NEEDS My God will meet all your needs according to His glorious riches in Christ Jesus. Philippians 4:19

RENEW YOUR MIND WITH CHRIST Do not conform any longer to the pattern of this world, but be transformed by the renewing of your mind. Then you will be able to test and approve what God's will is -- His good, pleasing and perfect will. Romans 12:2

PRAYER The prayer of a righteous man is powerful and effective. James 5:16

AUTHORITY OVER DEMONS Jesus replied: "I saw Satan fall like lightning from heaven. I have given you authority to trample on snakes and scorpions and to overcome all the power of the enemy; nothing will harm you." Luke 10:18-19

RESISTING SATAN Jesus turned and said to Peter, "Get behind me, Satan! You are a stumbling block to me; you do not have in mind the things of God, but the things of men." Matthew 16:23

SIN AS OPENINGS TO DEMONIZING Search me, O God, and know my heart; test me and know my anxious thoughts. See if there is any offensive way in me and lead me in the way everlasting. Psalm 139:23-24

CURSES Christ redeemed us from the curse of the law by becoming a curse for us, for it is written: "Cursed is everyone who is hung on a tree." Galatians 3:13

ANCESTRAL & CHILDHOOD OPENINGS Therefore if anyone is in Christ, He is a new creation; the old has gone, the new has come! II Corinthians 5:17

OCCULT OPENINGS Do not turn to mediums or seek out spiritists, for you will be defiled by them. I am the LORD your God. Leviticus 19:31

NEW AGE OPENINGS Such men (who preach a Jesus other than the Jesus I preached) are false prophets, deceitful workmen, masquerading as apostles of Christ. And no wonder, for Satan himself masquerades as an angel of light. II Corinthians 11:13-15

DELIVERANCE FROM DEMONIZING Dear friends, do not believe every spirit, but test the spirits to see whether they are from God This is how you can recognize the Spirit of God: Every spirit that acknowledges that Jesus Christ has come in the flesh is from God. I John 4:1-2

DELAYED DELIVERANCE The Lord said to me, "My grace is sufficient for you, for my power is made perfect in weakness." ... For when I am weak, then I am strong.   II Corinthians 12:9-10

CONTINUING VICTORY Be self-controlled and alert. Your enemy the devil prowls around like a roaring lion looking for someone to devour. Resist him, standing firm in the faith. I Peter 5:8-9

FOR A COMPLETE LIST OF VERSES FOR ANY NEED SEE APPENDIX 6, pages 95-100.

RESIST, STAND FIRM

KEYS TO FREEDOM & VICTORY

There are 2 keys to attaining and keeping spiritual victory: 1. You have to want it so bad you are willing to pay any price to get it. You must be 100% committed to sticking it out no matter what. 2. The other key is that, as soon as you fail, you get right back up and start again. Don't lay there in defeat but start over. It's taken a lifetime to get into this, it'll take a while to get out. Gradually you will log more and more time 'sober' and less and less 'under the influence.' That's how it works.

PERSEVERE, AS BAD AS IT GETS

Persevere no matter what. God can and will set you free from this. Deliverance is a process He uses to teach us things about Himself and ourselves. He wants us to persevere in faithfulness to Him no matter what for that helps us learn to depend on Him and trust Him. It's also part of the way He works to make us more like Jesus.

I know God is greater and will give the victory. I know the victory comes gradually, as we learn to fight and take back ground that was given to the enemy. When the Jews entered the promised land under Joshua God gave them victory, but one battle at a time, even one generation at a time. He didn't give it all to them at once. He wanted them to learn to fight, to need to keep trusting Him, to develop patience and perseverance. What was true of them physically is true of us spiritually. So don't give up. Persevere. It may be hard to see progress but remember - there is improvement. Look back at your life and you'll see improvement in the past to the present. You certainly wouldn't want to go back! Progress is slow but steady, like the story of the tortoise and the hare. Also be encouraged because it's obvious the enemy is now throwing everything at you he can. That means this is as bad as it gets, this is all he can do. If he could do more he would. While this is bad, knowing it is as bad as it gets and that it will gradually but certainly get better helps. It takes time. God is interested in the process you are going through as you grow, not just the final product. You do the same thing with your children.

We are told over and over again in the Bible to resist Satan (in Jesus' strength), to stand firm and not give in. *"Resist the devil and he will flee from you" (James 4:7-8)* is a promise to claim. The conditions for the promise to work, though, are that we are to *submit to God* (total commitment to God after salvation), *draw near to God* (quality and quantity time in prayer and meditation) and *be pure* (life a holy life, confessing all known sin). The key is keeping our eyes on Jesus.

Be self-controlled and alert. Your enemy the devil prowls around like a roaring lion looking for someone to devout. Resist him, standing firm in the faith. (I Peter 5:8-9). *Alert* means literally to "be sleepless," it implies a purposeful and active state of awareness. It implies being active and watching out for anything that would tone down our alertness (like being seduced by the world's pleasures). *Resist* is a strong word meaning to oppose. We aren't to hide in fear, hoping he'll leave us alone. Each must wage his own fight, you cannot expect a parent, mate, pastor or friend to resist for you. *Stand firm* means to stand solid, hard, unbending in the faith. Jesus prayed Peter would stand when attacked by Satan (Luke 22:32). Satan is like a bully. When he or his forces find someone who will give in, they push them around. Taking a stand may mean a fight for a while, but then the promise comes that he will flee. We are to be courageous and not fearful, taking our stand in the Lord (Joshua 1:9; 10:8; 23:9-11; Leviticus 26:8; Exodus 14:13; I Samuel 17:45-47; II Samuel 22:33-35,40-41).

Since Satan works through getting us to believe his lies, we must really resist and stand fast in this area. By knowing which lies Satan trips you up with you can better be prepared for them. Here are some common ones to look out for.

PRAY

Prayer is powerful (John 14:13-14; 15:7,16; Mark 11:24; 11:22-24; Luke 11:9-10; I John 5:14; Jeremiah 33:3). There should be six parts to your prayer life, all equally well developed. These are:

1.   **CONFESSION** (I John 1:9; Psalm 66:18; 51:1). To confess means to agree with God that the issue at hand is sin (not a mistake, someone else's fault, etc.). Use the lists on page 15-17 to help in this. After you confess your sin make sure you accept God's forgiveness (Daniel 9:9,19; Psalm 130:4; 86:5; 78:30; 99:8; 103:3; Amos 7:2). Only God can forgive sin (Mark 2:7;

11:25; Luke 23:24; 5:24; Matthew 6:14; Colossians 3:13). God doesn't over look sin; he forgives because it was paid for with the blood of Jesus on the cross (Hebrews 9:22; Ephesians 4:32; 1:7; I Peter 2:24; 3:18; Luke 24:46-47; Colossians 1:14; John 19:30). This forgiveness is available to all (Isaiah 53:6; Colossians 2:13; Romans 8:1). When you confess/admit your sin God forgives it. This means He blots it out (Isaiah 43:25; 1:18; 44:22; Acts 3:19; Colossians 2:14; Psalm 32), casts it behind His back (a place He can't see it - Isaiah 38:17; Jeremiah 31:34), forgets it (Hebrews 8:12; 10:17; Isaiah 43:25; Jeremiah 31:34), makes it disappear where it will never be found (Jeremiah 50:20), has it vanish like the morning mist at noon (Isaiah 44:22; John 20:31; Matthew 27:51), and casts it into the deepest part of the sea (Micah 7:19) which will then be gone forever (Revelation 21:1).

2.   **PRAISE** (Psalm 34:1-3; 48:1; Hebrews 13:15). Praise is glorifying God for Who and What He is. It is different than thanking Him for things He has done. We will be praising God for all eternity, so we should start now! God is pleased with our praise (Psalm 22:3; Hebrews 13:5).

The Bible says there is power in praise (Psalm 22:3). Praise can be done by word or song. Make sure you develop a strong praise life (Philippians 4:4; Hebrews 13:15). Read the following passages and turn them into praise prayers: Exodus 15:1-2; Deuteronomy 10:21; 32:3- 4,43; I Samuel 2:1-2; II Samuel 22:4,

50; I Chronicles 16:9,25,31; 29:10-12; II Chronicles 5:12-14; 20:21-22,27; Psalm 8:1-2; 9:1-3; 31:21; 44:8; 40:16; 47:1-3; 68:3-4; 72:18-19; 86:12-13; 104:33; 108:3; 117:1-2; 119:108,175; 138:1-4; 142:7; 149:1,3,6-9; 150:1-6; Isaiah 25:1,9; 38:18-19; 60:18; Daniel 2:20-23; Jeremiah 20:13; Habakkuk 3:17-19; Zechariah 9:9; Luke 1:46-47; Luke 10:21; John 4:23024; Ephesians 1:3; Jude 25; Revelation 4:10-11; 5:5,12-13; 15:3-4.

3.   **THANKSGIVING** (Psalm 116:12; Philippians 4:6; I Thessalonians 5:18). Thanksgiving is thanking God for what He has done, is doing and is going to do in your life (as well as the lives of others). We all appreciate being thanked for things we do, and so does God. Be specific in your thanksgiving. Remember, everything comes from Him and is for our good (Romans 8:28) so we should thank Him for everything!

4.   **INTERCESSION** (Psalm 28:9; James 5:14-20; I Timothy 2:1-4; I Samuel 12:23). Intercession is prayer for others. Often it is good to keep a list of prayer requests so you remember to pray for them and so you can mark down the answer, too. Then thank God for the answer. Remember God answers EVERY prayer. The answer is either yes (now), wait (later) or no (never). Every prayer gets one of these answers. God is able to do anything, but He isn't always willing to do what it is we think He should do to bail us out (Daniel 3:17). Therefore, when you pray for others first be sensitive to how God would have you pray. Don't be so quick to come up with a solution and make that your prayer. God may have another solution (better than ours). Don't pray solutions to God, pray problems and let Him come up with His own solution. You'll find prayers answered more often when you let Him figure out how to

take care of something. Often instead of removing something He gives us grace to endure it (II Corinthians 12:7-10). Include that option in your prayers for others

<u>CONFESSING THE SINS OF ANOTHER</u> Praying for another person is important. Confessing the sins of another person can help free them from demonic oppression. Sin, especially certain sins, is like opening a door for demons to work in a person's life. These sins can be an open invitation. Depression (self-pity), for example, can be almost a „prayer" to Satan because one is so negative and sees everything from a very self-centered viewpoint about how it may affect them. It's almost like they enjoy wallowing in this, so demons just help them move in that direction by putting thoughts in their mind and the person accepts and feeds on these thoughts. When that person tells God they are sorry for opening the door and confess (admit) that as sin, He forgives them and the sin no longer blocks fellowship between the person and God.

However, the door is still open and demons, who can get very technical and never want to give up access they have, will continue to use it. When you enter the picture and put the sins of that person under the blood of Jesus and state that demons can no longer use that sin as an access to the person you are closing the door. If the person hasn't confessed the sin themselves that still blocks their relationship with God, but by interceding for them we can slow down or stop (at least temporarily) the demonic impact so the person can be free from that influence and be better able to turn to God for themselves. Now if they continue in the sin, they keep opening the door. All you can do is keep trying to close it by putting the sin under the blood until the person does so themselves or it becomes evident, they don't want to and won't do it.

5.   **PETITION** (James 4:2; Hebrews 4:15-16; John 15:7). Petition means asking God for things for yourself. This is legitimate.

We shouldn't always pray just for ourselves, nor should we feel unworthy to ever pray for ourselves. Much of what I said under "Intercession" above fits in here. There are some things the Bible says we should ask for: an understanding heart (I Kings 3:7,9), fellowship with other believers (Philemon 4-6), forgiveness (Psalm 25:11,18,20), guidance (Psalm 25:4-5; 27:11), holiness (I Thessalonians 5:23), love (Philippians 1:9-11), mercy (Psalm 6:1-6), power (Ephesians 3:16), spiritual growth (Ephesians 1:17-19) and to know and do God's will (Colossians 4:12). As you pray for yourself think of a Bible promise to claim for it. God promises He will not forget us (Isaiah 49:15), not fail us (Joshua 1:5), will show us what to do (I Samuel 16:3), will help us (Isaiah 41:10) and will strengthen us (Isaiah 41:10).

Remember, it's always good to pray the problem, not the solution. Let God come up with His own solution. Often, we miss it because He answers a different way than we expected. He is God. He can answer any way He wants. Just think of the ultimate result: God being glorified and you growing. Pray for that – God to be glorified in the situation no matter what.

6. **LISTEN** (I Samuel 3:10; Hebrews 1:1-2; 3:15; Psalm 62:5; 46:10) Good communication is a two-way street. Pause a few minutes and listen to God talk to you. You should do that throughout your day. After all, which is more important: you passing on information to God or Him passing on information to you? Be still in your mind, let Him put in thoughts, feelings, ideas, etc., that you need. Be sensitive to His leading. As with any relationship, the better you know the person the better the communication. Good, deep communication is difficult with a stranger, but the more time you spend with a person the better you can 'hear' them, and that's true with God, too. This is an art that takes time to develop, but won't happen if you don't work on

it! For more information on this important art read Appendixes 7 & 8, pages 101-108.

PRAYER FOR SPIRITUAL WARFARE IN GENERAL

"Gracious God, I acknowledge that You are worthy of all honor, glory and praise. I am thankful for the victorious work of Your Son, Jesus Christ at Calvary for me. I apply His victory to my life now as I willingly surrender every area of my life to Your will.

"Thank you for the forgiveness and righteousness that has been given to me as Your adopted child. I trust in Your protection and provision daily. I know that your love for me never ceases. I rejoice in Your victory, my Lord, over all the principalities and powers in the heavenlies. In faith I stand in Your victory and commit myself to live obediently for You, my King.

"I desire that my fellowship with You become greater. Reveal to me those things that grieve You and enables the enemy to secure an advantage in my life. I need the Holy Spirit's powerful ministry in my life; bringing conviction of sin, repentance of heart, strengthening my faith and increasing perseverance in resisting temptation.

"Help me to die to self and walk in the victory of the new creation You have provided for me. Let the fruits of the Spirit flow out of my life so that You will be glorified through my life. Fill me with your love, joy, peace, patience, kindness, goodness, gentleness, faithfulness and self-control.

"Please place your hedge of protection around me, my possession, my family and all my descendants. Protect us from anything the enemy would try to do against us.

"I draw upon those spiritual resources that You have provided me and I attack the strongholds and plans of the enemy that have been put in place against me. I command in the name of Jesus Christ that the enemy must release my mind, will, emotions and body completely. They have been yielded to the Lord and I belong to Him.

"I know that it is Your will that I should stand firm and resist all of the enemy's work against me. Help me to discern the attacks upon my thoughts and emotions. Enable me to stand upon Your Word and resist all the accusations, distortions and condemnations that are hurled against me.

"It is my desire to be transformed through the renewing of my mind, so that I will not compromise with the ways of the world, or yield to the enemy's attacks, but be obedient to Your will. So, give me the mind of Christ in order that I may have His perspective, wisdom, compassion, holiness and truth.

"I draw upon those spiritual resources that You have provided me and I attack the strongholds and plans of the enemy that have been put in place against me. I command in the name of Jesus Christ that the enemy must release my mind, will, emotions and body completely. They have been yielded to the Lord and I belong to Him.

"Lord, enable me to become the person You created me to be. Help me as I pray to be strong in faith. Show me how to apply Your Word in my life each day. I know that I wear the full armor of God when I am committed to and stand firmly upon Your Word. I want You to have the supreme place in my life. Give me a hunger and thirst to know You better, to read Your Word more deeply, to pray more readily and to keep you first in all my thoughts all day long.

"I surrender myself completely to You, Lord. You are always faithful and You extend Your grace to me constantly, even when I do not realize it. I claim Your promise of forgiveness and cleansing in its fullness. In faith, I receive the victory today that you have already put in place for me. I do this in the name of Jesus Christ, my Savior with a grateful heart. AMEN"

HELPING OTHERS

Once you get involved in deliverance, you'll start to see how it can help those around you. You'll want to **share with others** what you've found. That's great! Remember, though, there is a cost of your time (Mark 7:24), energy (Mark 6:31) and patience (Matthew 17:17). Count the cost first (Mark 3:8-15). Getting involved in spiritual warfare for others may bring attacks against you but do not fear such a thing (Matthew 10:24-27). Often the worse part, though, is the criticism and rejection you get from others, believers and unbelievers alike (Matthew 9:32-34); Matthew 10:24-27). Don't fear that, either (Luke 13:31-32).

One danger to watch out for is thoughts popping into your mind of how spiritual you are, or feelings of **pride** because of having power over demons. Others may see you as more spiritual, too. This is a real danger. Jesus makes it clear that being able to administer deliverance is no sign of spirituality or even salvation (Matthew 7:21-23).

Keep in mind, too, that **others minister deliverance in different ways**. I feel strongly that what I have written here is what God has for me according to His Word. However, I am not to judge or reject those who do it differently (Mark 9:38-40).

Follow the steps for deliverance outlined in this book on pages 48-54.

When you find yourself in a situation where you feel God wants you to talk or pray about deliverance just go ahead! **Don't worry about your lack of knowledge or experience** (that's a lie from the demons to silence you). It's God's power and He will give you the right words and wisdom at the right time. Nothing is worse than not doing anything and allowing the demons to continue their work. Just do your best, trusting God for each step of the way.

There is no 'right' or 'wrong' way, no magic formula. God is greater, so just bring His power against the evil forces.

One thing to be careful of, though, is **your own time and schedule**. Don't allow yourself to be a crutch to anyone, for that isn't helping them. Wean them from you and onto God quickly. Don't become too involved with the one you are ministering too. It can become too draining on you and make it hard for you to be objective, plus harder to wean them. At first feeling needed can be very nice, but it is God they should need, not you.

Always **consider the big picture** when praying for deliverance. Keep deliverance in balance. Should they see a counselor? Would a physical from a doctor be helpful? Are they perhaps not giving you the complete, total picture, but just what they want you to know? Do they REALLY want to be free or are they more interested in having your attention? Is there any sin they aren't willing to get rid of?

OUR ROLE IN HELPING OTHERS (What God Expects)

I see myself as a quarterback (football) who throws passes to his receivers. The quarterback must throw the best pass he can – a nice, tight spiral right into the hands of the receiver. But ones the quarterback lets go of the ball it is no longer up to him if it is caught or not. Some receivers drop excellent passes, others make miraculous catches of poorly thrown balls. I used to be very concerned about the results but had to realize that isn't up to me. Now there must almost be callousness over my heart to some extent or I would get burnt out quickly. I give the best advice I can, with God's help, and know that is all God holds me accountable for – but He doesn't hold me accountable to do my best, to throw the best pass I can. If it is caught or not is not up to me but between the persona and God. Many times, I don't if the pass is dropped or caught, but I keep throwing them anyway. And the more one practices the better he gets at it. I keep a list of all the people who wrote me and the emails back and forth. There are hundreds and hundreds of names and almost all have more than one or two emails. Some I've been in touch with for years. They have become a core group to whom I send prayer requests, especially about my India trip. They are the ones I ask to pray for me when special needs come up. They keep me updated, sometimes every few months, and we write more regularly when things get difficult. Jesus spoke to millions, thousands liked what He said, hundreds believed, a dozen gave up everything to follow Him (and one of those turned back), three became His inner core and one His best friend (John). That's about how it goes. In the parable of the Sower and the seed Jesus points out that only about one fourth of the seed sown grows, so if that's true of Jesus I can't expect better! One more factor is that I know I am only the servant and Jesus expects me to be faithful. He doesn't look at numbers.

I throw the best pass I can and then pray for them. For the most part that bit of callous self- protection that all people in the service ministries have to have taken care of it. Now when it's a person I know well, a really bad situation, especially a relative, then it can get to me more. But that motivates me to be the more faithful in prayer and ministry. Even Jesus had Judas.

WHAT YOU CAN DO TO HELP THOSE STRUGGLING:

PRAY continually and regularly for them. Exercise your authority as a believer.

LOVE them unconditionally and let them know that over and over. Unconditional love conveys God's love. That is very, very important to do.

PROTECT them from unwise decisions if you are in a position to do so. Protect them from others, even from themselves.

LOWER your expectations of them. Give them time to understand, grow, act. Be patient, as patient as God has been with you. Don't baby them or keep bailing them out of situations, but accept them as they are and let God work in them at His pace.

IV. IN CLOSING

If you've made it to this point in this handbook you must be serious about learning to win your battles. God's blessing to you! Just remember to be patient with yourself. One doesn't become an experienced, top-notch fighter overnight. It takes time. It takes practice. And it takes failures as well. That's how we all learn. For the Christian, though, none of our failures are fatal, and neither are their final. Victory will come, in this life and the next.

When I first heard the story of the tortoise and the hare as a young boy, I know I found a piece of wisdom I could build on, and that story has helped motivate and shape who I have become. I want to pass it on to you as well. Persevere! Don't quit! Keep going! You don't have to be moving fast. In fact, you probably won't be moving very fast at all. But don't let that bother you. Slow and steady does it. Stay faithful to God. Keep your eyes on Him, not on Satan and his forces. Spend time in the Word and in prayer each day. Fight each battle as it comes. Don't quit, run or give in. When you lose a battle, and you will (we all do) get up and keep going.

Remember, the race is not to the swift but to those who keep on running!

You've a race before you. It's called the Christian life. One of the tools God has provided to help us through to the end is spiritual warfare. Prayer, worship, sharing the gospel, helping others, learning the Word, all these and many more are other tools He has given us as well. Keep all your tools sharp and use the correct one for the job at hand. But when the job is spiritual warfare, make sure you use your weapon to the best of your ability. Each battle will sharpen your skills for the next battle.

It's my prayer that you are found faithful by the One Who has called you and Who works in you to conform you to the image of His Son!

> If you have any questions, comments, suggestions, testimonies or anything you would like to be in contact with me about please feel free to write me a @drjohnsworld on Instagram, TikTok, or Facebook

V. APPENDIX 1

HOW DO WE KNOW GOD EXISTS

"If we have full employment and growth--if we have cities of gold and alabaster--but our children have not learned to walk in goodness, justice and mercy, then the American experiment, no matter how gilded, will have failed. In modernity, nothing has been more consequential, or more public in its consequences, than large segments of American society privately turning away from God, or considering Him irrelevant, or declaring Him dead. Dostoyevsky reminded us in Brothers Karamazov that „if God does not exist, everything is permissible. " We are now seeing „everything. " And much of it is not good to get used to." -- William J. Bennett, The Washington Times Pulpit Helps, March 1996, p. 10.

When people discount the fact that there is a God, the repercussions of that affect every area of their life. Without God there are no moral absolutes, no ultimate accountability, nothing beyond ourselves. Man becomes his own God and anything goes. In fact, many deny the existence of God just so they won't have to be accountable to a higher power or submit to His will. They want to live their own lives the way they want, totally unhindered. They say the idea of „God" is just something emotional cripples use for a crutch to escape reality. Is this so? How can we be sure there is a God? What „proof" do we have that God exists? How can well answer sincere doubters (I Peter 3:15), or still our own unbelief?

No Scientific Proof In the last article we saw proof that the Bible is indeed God's inspired Word. The Bible does claim the existence of God (assumes it, never tries to prove it). Still, to use God to prove the Bible and the Bible to prove God is circular reasoning. What proof is there beyond the Bible? First of all, you can't prove God by a scientific method any more than you can prove Napoleon by the scientific method. Neither can be seen, touched or contacted with our senses. They can't be put under a microscope to be analyzed. They each are accepted on the basis of dependable evidence. There is rational proof for God, though. We do have much dependable evidence, if we choose to accept it.

1. **The Cosmological Argument (Cause & Effect)**

Cause: There must be an uncaused cause or necessary being for each effect. No effect can be produced without a cause. When you see a tennis ball lying on the floor you assume (and rightly so) that someone created it and someone placed it there. It didn't just appear on its own out of nowhere. The same is true of the universe, us, love, hate, etc. -- each of these effects had to have a cause behind it equal to or greater than it.

Motion: If you would see that tennis ball rolling across the floor, you would then assume (and rightly so), that some power outside the ball and greater than it started it moving. The universe is full of motion. Something cannot start and sustain itself. An external agent or force is required. There must be a being that is the ultimate source of all motion.

Interrelationships: Now our tennis balls hang in a large circle by string, each one swinging and hitting the one next to it. The motion keeps going around and around the circle. Each ball is dependent on the others for the system to work. There must be a final being or force who is above these and independent of them to cause it to start. While some evolutionists might have said that the „big bang" caused the motion and interrelationships, this is being less and less accepted as the answer even among atheistic evolutionists.

Perfection: There is a pyramid of beings, from insects to men, in an ever-increasing degree of perfection. There must be a final being who is absolutely perfect, the source of all perfection. This ultimate perfection is the start, not the finish produces, of all else. Things don't build from less to greater, as the second law of thermodynamics states. It says that everything is winding down (entropy) and points back to a starting time. It shows that things now are moving away from perfection, not toward it as evolutionists would say.

2. The Teleological Argument (Order & Design)

Look at your wrist watch. The order and design there causes you to assume that some intelligent being was behind its creation. If God isn't behind everything, then „chance" is. If God didn't create this world, then „chance" did. If God isn't in control of everything, „chance" is. It takes more faith to believe in chance than in God! What „chance" is there of finding a watch just naturally formed of the materials in ground? What chance is there of the Gettysburg Address resulting from an explosion in a print shop? What chance is there that all the universe and life in it would just come about by chance? What chance is there for a liver, or heart, or reproduction system to just come about by chance (and it would have to be completely formed, for a species could not continue if any of these were only partly evolved)? What are the chances of everything working out so perfectly: gravity, the tilt of the earth, freezing temperature of water, rotation of the earth, proportion of water to land, distance from the sun, etc., just working out? All that is in the universe, the human body, or an individual cell tells us there is order and design. The „chance" of it all happening is too great to even be considered! God created nature to show that He exists (Psalm 19:1).

3. **The Anthropological Argument (Moral)**

Suppose our tennis balls, or our wrist watch, all of a sudden developed a moral nature when nothing else around it did, what would this signify? Man, and man alone, has a moral nature. All peoples in all times and places have had moral standards of right and wrong. While they haven't been the same, they have all know there were such standards and that was such a thing as right and wrong (Romans 2:14-15). All people have an innate understanding of these. There is something built into everyone which cries out for justice, for reward for good and punishment for evil. We naturally look forward to a future time when this is so. Where does this come from? Many naturally looks to an afterlife to have these settled. We all know there must be something more to life than existing for one's self then dying and being buried like a dog or a leaf. A restless is built into man showing there must be something more to life, something from without to live for. All of this points to God. All of this also shows there is a God who built it into all men. Where else could it have come from? How could something like love and hate evolve? If so, why just in man? These strong emotions had to be created be a greater being than man, then passed on to man. They couldn't come from „chance."

4 . **The Ontological Argument**

Man everywhere and in all time has naturally known there is a power greater than and outside himself that he has worshipped. Satan usually counterfeited and took the worship, but it is naturally in man to believe God and seek Him. Those today who deny God's existence often has to shout so loud and long that one wonders if it isn't the voices inside they are fighting against. When the infidel Robert G. Ingersoll was delivering his lectures against Christ and the Bible, his oratorical ability usually assured him of a large crowd. One night after an inflammatory speech in which he severely attacked man's faith in the Savior, he dramatically took out his watch and said, "I'll give God a chance to prove that He exists and is almighty. I challenge Him to strike me dead within 5 minutes!" First there was silence, then people became uneasy. Some left the hall, unable to take the nervous strain of the occasion, and one woman fainted. At the end of the allocated time, the atheist exclaimed derisively, "See! There is no God. I am still very much alive!" After the lecture a young fellow said to a Christian lady, "Well, Ingersoll certainly proved something tonight!" Her reply was memorable. "Yes, he did," she said. "He demonstrated that even the most defiant sinner cannot exhaust the patience of the Lord in just 5 minutes!" Another man added, " As I was coming downtown today, a belligerent little fellow came running out of an alley, daring me to hit him. Do you suppose I actually struck him, just because he challenged me to do so? In the same way, our Lord will not strike everyone dead who defies Him. We should be thankful that in this age He is still operating in grace and desires to show His love rather than His wrath." (Romans 9:22)

5. Subjective Inner Awareness

Inside each one of God's people there is an inner voice that says "Yes!" when the question of God's existence comes up. Demons try to flash thoughts of doubt through our mind, but whenever those questions pop up realize it isn't our minds but Satan's trick to take away our peace. When a Christian praises God in song or worship or prayer, something inside says "YES!" When we talk to others about Jesus there is that "YES!" in our spirit. When we heard a godly speaker or read a special passage in the Bible the "YES!" is clearly there. That is God's Spirit confirming the truth of God's existence (Galatians 4:6).

6. Why Does Man Deny The Existence Of God?

Man doesn't want to be accountable to God. Man is basically self-centered and prideful, and like Satan, wants to be independent of God. Man wants to be his or her own God with no other higher power to be accountable to. Thus, man must convince himself that there is no God in order to accomplish this. The fact of the matter is that God does exist and will reveal Himself to any and all who are open to seriously seek Him (Heb. 11:6).

7. **Answering Doubters**

There is no answer for those who aren't open to consider the possibility of a God. Arguments won't force anyone to believe something they don't want to believe. But for serious seekers the above answers should help. Actually, against this evidence it is up to them to prove to you that there is no God. They are going against the majority opinion for all the ages. Point out to them that if they are right and you are wrong, you have not lost anything, for you believe has at least given you a more peaceful and humane existence. But if you are right and they are wrong, then not only is their quality of life in this existence at stake, but so is their eternal destiny. Are they so sure there is no God they that they are willing to bet eternity in hell on it if they are wrong?

8. **So What?**

This is more than an academic exercise for us Christians, too. Have you ever thought how your life would be different if there was no God? What if this life was all there was, everything happened by chance, and there was no God (and therefore no Jesus or Bible)? Thinking about this for even a short time should help us feel compassion for those who face life this way, and also cause us to thank and praise God all the more for His existence and his so clearly revealing Himself to us! That is certainly reason to thank and praise Him!

VI. APPENDIX 2

HOW DO WE KNOW THE BIBLE IS GOD"S WORD?

Roy Whetstine purchased a stone "from an amateur collector at an Arizona mineral show for $10,000," according to Newsweek, Nov. 24, 1986. It has since been "valued at as high as $2.28 million" and declared to be the world's largest sapphire.

Western-world Christians have in their possession a precious gem of far greater value which many treat just as cheaply. They fail to avail themselves of the joy such wealth could bring them, fail to share it with their own families, and even fail to carry it with them to the house of God. They leave it lying wherever it happened to be the last time the furniture was dusted under newspapers and magazines. If it were stolen, they probably would not miss it for a month.

There are multitudes in many parts of the world who would gladly give a month's salary, go for days without food, and walk great distances to get one copy of the Bible to share with their entire fellowship. Let's not be too quick to cast aspersions upon the intelligence of the amateur gem collector. Often, we are just as bad in attributing the true worth to the Bible.

1. **God Reveals Himself**

God has revealed Himself to man in a general way in nature (Romans 1; Psalm 19) but in a very specific way in the Bible. The Bible (which means "book" in Greek) is composed of 66 books: 39 in the Old Testament and 27 in the New Testament. The Old Testament focuses on the Jews and the law. The New Testament focuses on Jesus and grace.

2. Possible & Necessary

While some doubt God could or would reveal Himself to man, it is entirely possible that God would reach out and contact man in this way. Since He is sovereign, He can certainly do this if He so chose. Not only is this possible, it is also necessary, for if God had not contacted man, then man would not know God. Thus, a revelation from God, like the Bible, is possible and necessary.

3. Inspiration

The Bible claims to be God's Word (II Tim. 3:16-17; II Peter 1:19-21). Jesus considered and spoke of the Old Testament as inspired by God (Mt. 22:29; 24:37; Mk. 7:13; Lk. 24:44). "**Inspiration**," meaning "God-breathed" in Greek, refers to God working through the 40 men who wrote the Bible (over 1500 years) to ensure that what they wrote is without error. Without taking away their individual personality and its contributions to their writing, God showed them what to include, what to omit, and made sure all was accurate. God **revealed** some parts of the Bible, things man wouldn't have known on their own (creation, Revelation, etc.). Now God **illuminates** the Bible for us, showing us the truth of His Word as we read it.

4. Multiple Author Theory

It isn't uncommon today to hear someone say that Genesis is composed of material from 5 different writers or that two men wrote Isaiah. That isn't true. It just undermines inspiration, and makes the books younger than they really were. Thus, prophecies in the books can be said to be written after the event. This takes away from the greatness of the Bible. Liberal scholars for years said Daniel had to have been written after the fantastic events described in it, for they could not have been prophesied. The discovery of the Dead Sea Scrolls has contradicted this. It isn't surprising that, despite the discovery in 1947, Daniel still hasn't been released to the public! Scientific study shows the books weren't written by different authors.

Researchers in Israel, after subjecting the first five books of the Bible to exhaustive computer analysis, came to a different conclusion than expected. The Torah, or Books of Moses, had long been assumed by skeptics to be the work of multiple authors. But Scripture scholar Moshe Katz and computer expert Menachem Wiener of the Israel Institute of Technology analyzed the book's material through sophisticated computer analysis. They discovered an intricate pattern of significant words concealed in the canon, spelled by letters separated at fixed intervals. Mr. Katz says that the statistical possibilities of such patterns happening by chance would be one to three million. The material suggests a single, inspired author -- in fact it could not have been put together by human capabilities at all. Adds Mr. Wiener, "So we need a non-rational explanation. And ours is that the (Torah) was written by God through the hand of Moses."

5. **Old Testament Manuscripts**

Some are quick to point out that no Old Testament manuscripts from before the Massoretic text in AD 900 exist, and that leaves open the possibility of errors in transcribing the Bible from generation to generation. The truth is, though, that the Jews were very careful in copying the Bible. They would count each letter in each line, even in each column, total them up, and make sure every letter was exact. If not, the whole page would be burned. Also, comparing the Massoretic text with translations in Latin, Greek, Syrian, etc., which have been passed down from generation to generation in their own countries and languages, and which have not been influenced by other translations, show that they all say the same thing. This shows there haven't been errors from when they were originally translated hundreds and hundreds of years earlier.

Archaeological discoveries are disproving those who question the Bible's accuracy and supporting its inspiration. A recent archaeological report in the science magazine Discovery contained amazing findings about the Old Testament. Before the discovery of the Dead Sea Scrolls in 1947, the oldest Hebrew manuscripts dated about AD 900. The Dead Sea Scrolls, in startling agreement with the Masoretic text, dated to about 150 BC. Whole or parts of almost every Old Testament book are present. When these are compared to the Masoretic text over 1,000 years later, they are both the same! Perhaps one word per large document differs, and these are small things like spelling changes (like „honor" for „honor"). None affect the meaning of the passages they are in.

There is also the Septuagint (LXX), a Greek translation of the Hebrew Old Testament, made in Egypt in 200 BC. It, too, agrees with the other translations and manuscripts. Remember, these all were passed down over hundreds of years, in different parts of the world, without being compared to each other until recently. Yet all say the same thing!

Now archaeologists have discovered a pair of tiny silver scrolls that date back to about 600 BC! While digging at the site of a 5th-century church in Jerusalem, researchers found a Roman legionnaires' cemetery. Exploring still deeper, they found a small burial cave containing the scrolls. Very carefully, less than a hundredth of an inch at a time, the scrolls were unrolled. On each of them appeared an excerpt from the book of Numbers that included the word Jehovah. These scrolls date back to the days before the exile to Babylon, earlier than liberal scholars said Pentateuch was written.

6. **New Testament Manuscripts**

There are many more New Testament manuscripts than Old. There are about 4,000 manuscripts of the New Testament available to use today. The earliest ones date back to the time of contemporaries of Jesus (early 100"s). Excellent manuscripts date from the 300"s. (For more information about this see # 14 in "18 Reasons from Outside the Bible Proving It Is God's Word" later in this paper). In addition, there are hundreds of Bible verses quoted by early writers, and these helps support the other manuscripts. As with the Old Testament, the New Testament was translated into many other languages (Syriac, Egyptian, Latin, etc.). They also were copied and passed on for hundreds of years without comparison to others, and when recently compared all support each other. There are minor changes (spelling, punctuation, etc.) but nothing that affects any doctrine.

7. **The Canon**

The term „canon" is given to the collection of 66 books in our Bible. How do we know the right books were included? Could some uninspired books have been included and/or some inspired ones left out? Again, if it is possible and necessary for God to reach out to man and let His will be known, that it is also possible and necessary that He could make sure the right books are included, and that they come down accurately to us today.

The New Testament canon developed over many years and much prayer. In various locations many godly men found certain books to be helpful and used of God above other

books. Gradually the same group was used in many places and in a series of meetings and councils, after much prayer and seeking God's leading, it was affirmed that the 27 books we have today were the ones God wanted in the New Testament. By comparing them to the books not included one can easily see a big difference in literary style, spiritual value and historical accuracy.

8. Chapters And Verses

When originally written, the Bible didn't have chapters or

verses. Chapters were formed by Stephen Langton in 1228 and verses by Robert Stephanus in 1551. These were added to make it easier to find and identify places in the Bible. Because they were added by men, they aren't always 100% accurate in where they are placed.

9. Errors And Contradictions

Some say the Bible has contradictions. It is way beyond the scope of this article to consider each one, but there are well-written books available that consider each seeming contradiction and clearly explain how these passages do not contradict..

10. Reasons From Outside The Bible Proving It Is God's Word

Anyone can write a book and claim that it is from God. Thus, to really pin down the authority of the Bible we need to look at supporting evidence from outside the Bible. These are given below:

1. The Bible is theocentric (God-centered), not anthropocentric (man-centered). If man wrote the Bible, he would be the leading character. In the Bible God is sovereign and absolute authority (I Chronicles 29:11; Isaiah 43:7). Man's highest good is submission to His will. The purpose of all we do is for His glory (Revelation 4:11). All other 'holy' books focus on man and build up man, not God.

2. The Bible is **monotheistic** (one God), not polytheistic (more than one God). 'Scholars' say that man started with many gods and eventually evolved to having just one. The Bible, at the

beginning of man, says there was just one. If man were writing the Bible he would have one God evolve out of many. Even the fact that the Jews were worshipping the golden calf and other gods at the time the first commandment was written (which say God was the only god, Exodus 20:1-6) show that even they believed there was more than one God.

3. The fact of the **Trinity** helps prove man didn't write the Bible. Would natural man write about something that he could not understand, something with no parallel or analogy in nature? No finite mind has ever comprehended how 3 separate persons could form one essence/substance. If man wrote the Bible he would NOT write about a Triune God.

4. If man wrote the Bible, would he say that the world was **created** from nothing (Hebrews 11:3)? Nothing is a state man has never known. He would come up with some rational explanation, as evolutionists try to do today.

5. If man wrote the Bible, would he say his basic nature is evil and **sinful** (Romans 3:23)? Would man say there was nothing he could do but accept God's cure for sin (Ephesians 2:8-9). Every religion man has developed or 'holy' book man has written has something man must do to earn/deserve removal of sin, but not the Bible.

6. The **extent of revelation** in the Bible shows it is beyond what man could or would write. How could man write of things beyond his own senses and experiences? Yet the Bible speaks authoritatively about heaven, hell and eternity without hesitation (I Corinthians 2:9-12; II Corinthians 5:8; Luke 16:19; Revelation 19:20-21).

7. If man wrote the Bible, its **ethics** would be based on individual, relative decisions (Judges 17:6) rather than absolutes.

Because man is a child of wrath (Ephesians 2:3) by nature his ethics would be corrupt (as they are today apart from the Bible) and would end in chaos. One example: the Bible tells us to use things (I Cor. 7:31) and love people (Rom. 12:10). Man's ethics are the opposite.

8. It is humanly impossible for **44 authors** over a period of **1500 years** unknown to each other and from vastly different backgrounds and cultures to arrive at 66 books so internally systematic and consistent as the Bible. It would be like 44 men each tossing a stone on a pile over 1500 years and the finished product being a modern hospital. There must have been one Author behind it all.

9. The fantastic number of **fulfilled prophecies** in the Bible show that it is no book authored by mere man. Experts in probability give these statistics concerning the following prophecies:

    ✧ prophecies against Tire in Ezekiel 26:3-4,7-8,12,14,21 coming true: 1 in 7.5×10^7

    ✧ prophecies against Samaria in Hosea 13:16 & Micah 1:6 come true: 1 in 4×10^4

    ✧ prophecies against Gaza & Ashkelon in Amos 1:8, Jer 47:5, Zeph 2:4-7: 1 in 1.2×10^4

    ✧ prophecies against Moab & Ammon in Ezek 25:3-4, Jer 48:47; 49:6: 1 in 10^3

    ✧ prophecies against Edom in Isa 34:6-15, Jer 49:17-18; Ezek 25:13-14; 35:5-7: 1 in 10^4

    ✧ prophecies against Babylon in Isa 13:19-22; 14:23; Jer 51:26,43: 1 in 5×10^9

    ✧ prophecies about Jerusalem in Jeremiah 31:38-40: 1 in 8

x 10^{10}

- prophecies about Palestine in Lev 26:31-33; Ezek 36:33-35: 1 in 2 x 10^5
- prophecies about Petra & Edom in Isa 34:6-18; Ezek 25:13-14; 35:5-7:1 in 2 x 10^5
- prophecies about Thebes & Memphis in Ezek 30:13-15: 1 in 10^3
- prophecies about Nineveh in Nahum 1:8,10; 2:6; 3:10,13,19: 1 in 10^2

The probability of these 11 prophecies coming true is 1 in 5.76 x 10^{59}! This is almost impossible to visualize. Suppose this number were silver dollars. There would be enough to fill 10^{28} suns! Or think of it like this. In the universe there are about 2 trillion galaxies, each containing about 100 million stars. From our 5 x 10^{59} we could make all of the stars in all of the galaxies 2 x 10^5 times! Only one silver dollar in all of these stands for the chance a writer could have guessed all these prophecies correctly! Even more astounding is the fact that these are only 11 prophecies. There are literally hundreds and hundreds of others which have already come true. (For more information about this see "Evidence That Demands a Verdict" by Josh McDowell).

1. The exceptional **literary value** of the Bible cannot be attributed to the natural ability of human writers. How could such unlearned men write such a surpassing piece of literary genius beyond their own ability? The Bible far exceeds the intellectual and moral qualifications of other books being written in its time such as the Talmud (Jewish), Apocrypha (Christian) and Koran (Islamic). The living quality of the words, reaching to all ages and social positions of people for century after century show its uniqueness. The Bible is deep enough

for the most gifted scholar to spend a lifetime in one small part of it and never get out all there is, but also simple enough for a young child to read and understand. One of the greatest truths expressed is just 7 monosyllables, each 3 letters or less: "You in me and I in you" (John 14:20). The Bible stories are never hurried or cramped, neither are they drawn out and boring. The Bible does not gloss over the sins of its heroes, neither does it overemphasize them. The values and opinions of the writers are not the focus, just there.

2. Another proof for the Bible not being written by man is its **enduring freshness**. Voltaire said 150 years ago: "Within 100 years the Bible will be obsolete." It has not happened; in fact, his home now houses a Bible society! The Bible never grows old. No other book in the world not only invites but sustains a ceaseless re-reading. Other books come and go, but the Bible has remained for thousands of years. It remains a fresh, up-to-date book, not an old book.

3. If man wrote the Bible, would he say to further spiritual ends by love & reliance on divine **power** or by political force? The Inquisition and Crusades in Christianity as well as the history of Islam, Shintoism, Nazism, etc., all show man used political force to spread their beliefs. The Bible commands to do it in a way that is not natural for man, the opposite way.

4. No human **scientist** has been able to avoid being obsolete in a later time. Science is always changing but the Bible is scientifically infallible in all ages. The Bible spoke accurately of scientific truth thousands of years before man 'discovered' them, while the very writers often believed the opposite of what they were writing. For example, the Bible says the life of the flesh is in the blood (Leviticus 17:11) yet until recent times doctors bled people to cure them. The Bible says the physical

world is basically non-physical in its ultimate essence (Hebrews 11:3; Colossians 1:16-17), something no human writer could or would have guessed at. The Bible has always said the earth was round (Isaiah 40:22), rotates (Job 38:12,14), has gravity (Job 26:7), and the whole solar system orbits in the universe (Psalm 19:16). Man believed the moon was greater than the earth for many centuries but the Bible says opposite (Genesis 1:16). Even atomic energy and its results is found in II Peter 3:10-12 (the Greek word means to ""loosen"" or "set free" as what happens when atoms are released). The laws of thermodynamics are there, too: #1 (Genesis 2:1-2; Hebrews 4:3,10) and # 2 (Psalm 102:25-27; Hebrews 1:10-12; Romans 8:20-22). There are hundreds of other examples, too.

5. The number and accuracy of the **ancient manuscripts** of the Bible that have come down to us today show God's work in giving and keeping the Bible for us. Of Caesar's "Gallic Wars" we have only 9 manuscripts, the oldest 900 years after the original. Of the "History of Thucydides" and "History of Herodotus" we have only 8 manuscripts each, from 1300 years after they happened. Yet of the Old Testament we have 1,700 manuscripts, the oldest 100 years after the original. The variation percentage between them is one minor difference every 2,000 words! Evidence for the New Testament is even greater: 13,000 manuscripts with the oldest portion 10 years after the original and the variation percentage being only one minor difference every 200,000 words! Manuscripts have come down in many different languages and large portions come to us quoted in the works of hundreds of authors. The recent discover of the Dead Sea Scrolls pushed back the date of the earliest Old Testament manuscripts 1,000

years, yet there was no difference between them later manuscripts.

6. The study of **archaeology** continues to prove there are no historical inaccuracies in the Bible. William F. Albright, one of the greatest archaeologists ever, said, "The Bible's incredible historical memory has been many times validated by the process of discovery. No archaeological discovery has contradicted a Biblical reference." For many years scholars thought the Bible in error about the Hittites for no trace of that vast and great civilization had ever been found. In recent years, though, much has been found about them, again validating the truth of the Bible.

7. The preservation and regathering of the **nation Israel** after 2,000 years is proof of the greatness of the Bible. It has never happened, nor was it ever thought possible to happen, for a group of people to survive 2,000 without a homeland yet stay a separate cultural unity. That has happened with the Jews. Where are the Ammonites? Philistines? Hittites? Not only that, but the Jews are now back in their homeland, truly a sociological miracle!

8. The **inner testimony of the Holy Spirit** inside His people gives us assurance that the Bible is true. He gives us peace and assurance within that the Bible indeed is God's book.

9. The **life and resurrection of Jesus** also give validity to the Bible. If everything about Him, His deity and His resurrection is true, then the Bible is true. If it is not true the Bible cannot be from God. This will be considered in the next article about the deity of Jesus.

BIBLE: A MIRACLE BOOK

1. It is miraculous in its origin -- coming to us by divine

inspiration.

2. It is miraculous in its durability -- outlasting the opposition of its critics and surviving the attempts of its enemies to exterminate it.

3. It is miraculous in its results -- transforming the lives of those who read and believe it.

4. It is miraculous in its harmony -- agreeing in all its parts, even though written over a period of 1600 years by about 40 different authors.

5. It is miraculous in its message -- telling of many occasions when God supernaturally intervened in the affairs of men to accomplish his redemptive purposes.

6. It is miraculous in its preservation -- maintaining its accuracy and reliability down through the centuries.

Yes, the Bible is God's Miracle Book!

If you are cold, let it WARM you,

If you are asleep, let it WAKE you,

If you are a backslider, let it WARN you, if you are defiled, let it WASH you.

If you are disobedient, let it WHIP you.

If you are uncertain, let it WITNESS to you. If you are unsaved, let it WIN you.

THEN WHY DOESN"T EVERYONE BELIEVE? If there is this great body of evidence, why do so many deny the Bible as being God's Word? Let me answer that with a story. Many years ago, while on a visit to England, a wealthy man was fascinated by a powerful microscope. Looking through its lens to study crystals and the petals of flowers, he was amazed at their beauty and detail. he bought one and took it home. He thoroughly enjoyed using it until one day he examined some food he was planning to eat for dinner. He discovered tiny living creatures were crawling in it. He was especially fond of this food and didn't know what to do. Finally, he concluded there was only one way out of this dilemma: he smashed the microscope to pieces. That is what man tries to do to the Bible when it shows up his sin. Like bugs under a rock run from the light when the rock is turned over, so man in sin runs from the light of God's truth about him. That is what many do with the Bible because it reveals their sin. What a privilege we have in owning and reading God's written message to mankind!

VII. APPENDIX 3

HOW DO WE KNOW JESUS IS GOD?

Did Jesus really live? Was there REALLY a historical person by the name of Jesus, from Nazareth, who lived in Palestine early in the first century AD? Can you prove it?

JESUS THE MAN There is so much historical proof, in the Bible and by secular historians alive at the time, that no one doubts that Jesus lived as a man. It's a proven historical reality. Ralph Waldo Emerson has said, "The name of Jesus is not so much written as plowed into the history of the world." Was there really a person named Jesus? It's not even questioned.

JESUS THE GOD However, was this human Jesus also God? Was He divine? That's where many people, not wanting to admit to any God to whom they are accountable, deny Jesus is God. Still, there is proof, abundant proof, that Jesus is God. Let's look at some of it.

I. **JESUS CLAIMED TO BE GOD**

Some try to say Jesus never claimed to be God, but that just isn't true. *"Before Abraham was, I Am" (John 8:58) "Father, glorify me with the glory which I had with You before the world was." John 17:5 "I and the father are One."* John 10:30 He accepted worship as if He were God. He claimed to be able to forgive sin (Mark 2:5). Look at the following list:

Claimed Equality with God Matt. 28:19; John 5:17-18; 12:45; 13:20; 14:1, 9

Claimed Oneness with God Matt 4:7; Luke 4:12; 8:39; John 10:30, 36-38; 17:11, 21-22; 20:28

Claimed To Be Sent by God Jn 4:34; 5:37; 7:16-29; 8:16; 9:4; 11:42; 14:24; 16:28; 17:18,23

Claimed To Be the Son of God Matt 16:17; 22:42-45; Mark 12:35-37; 14:61-62; Luke 20:41; John 9:35-37; 22:69-70 ("Son" does not mean He is inferior to His "Father" but of the same substance, equal in right and position. God is called the ETERNAL Father, thus Jesus the eternal Son. Thus, they both always existed. It's not that the Father came first! This Father-Son reference is just to show family closeness and equality. Reading in inferiority for the Son is way beyond the limits of legitimate interpretation.

Claimed To Be From Heaven John 6:33, 35, 51

Claimed Attributes of God John 8:42; 16:15

Omniscience Matt 11:21-22; Luke 10:13

Omnipresence Matt 18:20; 28:20

Omnipotence Mark 14:61-63; Luke 22:69-70; John 2:19, 10:18; 11:25-27

Forgive sin Mark 2:5,9,10; Luke 5:20-21; 7:48-49

Divine Authority Matt 7:21-23; 28:18

Honor John 5:22-23

Pre-Existence John 8:58; 17:5; 1:1f

LORD, LUNATIC or LIAR Many people try to write Jesus off as just a nice man, a good teacher, a fine example. That could have been if it weren't for His claims of deity. When someone goes around saying He is God, can forgive sin, and accepting worship as God, then those who would follow Him must deal with these claims. While claiming to be humble, Jesus said over and over He was God. There are only three possibilities, and a good teacher isn't one of them: LORD: He could be right and really God. LUNATIC: He could be deluded, mixed up mentally, or demonized and really think He is God but be mistaken. LIAR: He could know He isn't God but just be trying to deceive people. You see, either He is God or He isn't. If He is then He is much more than just a good teacher, He is Lord. If He isn't, then He cannot be a good teacher for He is either a lunatic or liar and no matter which not worthy of being followed, for what about Him can really be trusted? Lord, Lunatic or Liar -- which do you say He is?

II. **PROOF HE WAS GOD**

Not only did Jesus' claim to be God, but there is abundant proof that His claims were true. Consider there:

A. **Proof From Reason**

For one thing, His character coincided with His claims. When some goofball claims to be God, his character doesn't agree with the claims. But Jesus lived a sinless, perfect, other-centered life. Even Pilate recognized this (Mt. 27:54).

For another thing, Jesus demonstrated a power over natural forces. Nature responded to His every word: storms, water to wine, fish and bread multiply, even demons submit.

Also, He shows the Creator's power over sickness, making the lame to walk, dumb to speak, blind to see, and bringing people back to life.

Finally, others felt He was God. Those who knew Him, lived with Him day in and out for 3 years, called Him Lord, Son of God, Father, Master, etc. Even his enemies, who had spies investigating His every action looking for a slip, could find nothing imperfect about Him.

Certainly, there is proof from reason that Jesus is God. There is more proof, too:

B. **Proof From Fulfilled Prophecy**

Old Testament prophecies were all fulfilled, in Jesus Christ and Him only. Here is a partial list of the prophecy and fulfillment.

1. Born of the seed of woman: Gen 3:15; Gal 4:4, Matt. 1:20

2. Born of a virgin: Isaiah 7:14; Matthew 1;18,24,25; Lk 1:26-35

3. Son of God: Ps 2:7 (I Chron 17:11-14; II Sam 7:12-16), Mt 3:17; 16:16 (Mk 9:7; Lk 9:35)

4. Seed of Abraham Genesis 22:18 (12:2-3); Matthew 1:1; Gal 3:16

5. Son of Isaac: Genesis 21:12; Lk 3:23,34 (Mt 1:2)

6. Son of Jacob: Num. 24:17 (Gen 35:10-12); Lk 3:23,34 (Mt 1:2; Lk 1:33)

7. Tribe of Judah: Genesis 49:10; Lk 3:23,33 (Mt 1:2; Heb 7:14)

8. Family line of Jesse: Isaiah 11:1, 10; Luke 3:23,32 (Mt 1:6)

9. House of David: Jeremiah 23:5 (II Sam 7:12-16; Ps 132:11); Lk 3:23,31 (Mt 1:1; 9:27)

10. Born at Bethlehem: Micah 5:2; Matthew 2:1 (Jn 7:42, Mt 2:4-8; Lk 2:4-7)

11. Presented with gifts: Psalm 72:10 (Isaiah 60:6); Matthew 2:1,11

12. Herod kills children: Jeremiah 31:15; Matthew 2:16

13. His pre-existence: Micah 5:2 (Isa 9:6-7; Ps 102:25); Col 1:17 (Jn 1:1-2; 8:58; Rev 1:17)

14. He shall be called Lord: Psalm 110:1 (Jere 23:6); Luke 2:11; 20:41-44

15. Shall be Immanuel (God With Us): Isaiah 7:14; Matthew 1:23; Luke 7:16

16. Shall be a prophet: Deut 18:18; Matthew 21:11 (Luke 7:16; Jn 4:19; 6:14; 7:40)

17. He shall be a priest: Psalm 110:4; Hebrews 3:1; 5:5-6

18. He shall be a judge: Isaiah 33:22; John 5:30; II Timothy 4:1

19. He shall be a king: Psalm 2:6 (Zech. 9:9; Jer 23:5); Matthew 27:37; 21:5 (John 18:33-38)

20. Special anointing of the Holy Spirit: Isaiah 11:2; Matthew 3:16-17; 12:17-21 (Mk 1:10-11)

21. His zeal for God: Psalm 69:9; John 2:15-17

22. Preceded by messenger: Isaiah 40:3; Matthew 3:1-2; 3:3; 11:10

23. Ministry to begin in Galilee: Isaiah 9:1; Matthew 4:12,13,17

24. Ministry of miracles: Isaiah 35:5, 6a; 32:3,4; Matthew 9:32,33,35; 11:4-6 (John 5:5-9)

25. Teacher of parables: Psalm 78:2; Matthew 13:34

26. He was to enter the temple: Malachi 3:1; Matthew 21:12

27. He was to enter Jerusalem on a donkey: Zechariah 9:9; Luke 19:35,36,37a (Mt 21:6-11)

28. "Stone of Stumbling" to the Jews: Psalm 118:22 (Isa 8:14; 28:16); I Peter 2:7 (Rom 9:32-33

29. "Light" to Gentiles: Isaiah 60:3; 49:6; Acts 13:47,48a; 26:23; 28:28

30. Betrayed by a friend: Psalm 41:9; 55:12-14; Matthew 10:4; 26:49-50; Jn 13:21

31. Sold for 30 pieces of silver: Zechariah 11:12; Matthew 26:15; 27:3

32. Money to be thrown in God's house: Zechariah 11:13b; Matthew 27:5a

33. Price given for potter's field: Zechariah 11:13b; Matthew 27:7

34. Forsaken by His disciples: Zechariah 13:7; Mark 14:50 (Mt 26:31; Mk 14:27)

35. Accused by false witnesses: Psalm 35:11; Matthew 26:59-61

36. Dumb before accusers: Isaiah 53:7; Matthew 27:12-19

37. Wounded and bruised: Isaiah 53:5 (Zech 13:6); Matthew 27:26

38. Smitten and spit upon: Isaiah 50:6 (Micah 5:1); Matthew 26:67 (Luke 22:63)

39. Mocked: Psalm 22: 7,8; Matthew 27:31

40. Fell under the cross: Psalm 109:24-25; John 19:17; Luke 23:26; Mt 27:31-32

41. Hands and feet pierced: Psalm 22:16 (Zech 12:10); Luke 23:33 (John 20:25)

42. Crucified with thieves: Isaiah 53:12; Matthew 27:38 (Mk 15:27,28)

43. Made intercession for His persecutors: Isaiah 53:12; Luke 23:34

44. Rejected by His own people: Isaiah 53:3 (Ps 69:8; 118:22); John 7:5,48; 1:11 (Mt 21:42,43)

45. Hated without a cause: Psalm 69:4 (Isa 49:7); John 15:25

46. Friends stood afar off: Psalm 38:11; Luke 23:49 (Mk 15:40; Mt 27:55-56)

47. People shook their heads: Psalm 109:25; 22:7; Matthew 27:39

48. Stared upon: Psalm 22:17; Luke 23:35

49. Garments parted and lots cast: Psalm 22:18; John 19:23-24

50. To suffer thirst: Psalm 69:21; 22:15; John 19:28

51. Gall and vinegar offered Him: Psalm 69:21; Matthew 27:34

52. His forsaken cry: Psalm 22:1; Matthew 26:46

53. Committed Himself to God: Psalm 31:5; Luke 23:46

54. Bones not broken: Psalm 34:20; John 19:33

55. Heartbroken: Psalm 22:14; John 19:34

56. His side pierced: Zech 12:10; John 19:34

57. Darkness over the land: Amos 8:9; Matthew 27:45

58. Buried in rich man's tomb: Isaiah 53:9; Matthew 27:57-60

59. Resurrection: Psalm 16:10; 30:3; 41:10; 118:17 (Hosea 6:2); Acts 2:31(Lk 24:46; Mk 16:16)

60. Ascension: Psalm 68:18a; Acts 1:9

61. Seated at right hand of God: Psalm 110:1; Heb. 1:3 (Mk 16:19; Acts 2:34,35)

Note: no one else in history has ever come close to fulfilling even a few of these. No one ever can, since all Jewish records of lineage were destroyed with Jerusalem in 70 AD.

Note also: the probability of just 1 through 8 coming true would be 1 in 10 with 16 0's. (If each chance is a silver dollar and they were laid down side-by-side on state of Texas they would cover whole state 2 foot deep! One is marked, all others not. Blindfold a man and let him walk anywhere, the chance he'd pick right one is the same as first 8 prophecies just happening!

III. PROOF FROM THE RESURRECTION

Another line of reasoning deals with the resurrection. It's quite a claim to say one is going to come back to life, and then to have it claimed to have happened! If Jesus really did come back to life, this alone would prove His deity. If not, He can make no claims of deity. What about the resurrection?

If Jesus didn't come back to life, how are we to explain the empty tomb? Well, some say the disciples stole His body to make it look like He came back to life. But then how do we explain His 10 appearances to a total of over 500 people? Also, if they knew He didn't come back to life, where did they get the courage to all of a sudden be willing to die for Him?

OK, others say, it was His enemies who stole the body. That still doesn't explain His many appearances. Also, when people started thinking He was alive the enemies would have produced the body to prove He wasn't alive, and they never even tried to do so.

Finally, some say Jesus never died, that He just swooned and then revived. Think about what that means, though. First, He was pronounced dead by experienced Roman executioners, then a sword shoved in His side up into His heart. He was wrapped cocoon-like, head to foot (no way to breathe), covered with 100 pounds of spices, sealed in a dark, damp tomb for 3 days. Somehow, He would have to revive, slip out of his wrappings (the Greek says they were undisturbed, like a cocoon after the butterfly leaves), with hands and feet ruined by nails He'd have to move a thousand-pound stone uphill from the inside (no handholds), overpower many Roman soldiers, and travel many miles to Emmaus where He'd convince everyone that He has a glorious, superior, eternal body!

There are just too many proofs to the resurrection to doubt it. He appeared 10 times to 500 witnesses. Without the resurrection being real, would could account for the spread of the early church, the conversion of Paul and millions of others, the willing martyrdom of so many? How would the Lord's Supper have gotten started (why worship the body and blood of a dead person)? Why even bother with baptism, which is a picture of Jesus dying and coming back to life? There is no reason staunch Jews would change their day of worship from Saturday to Sunday unless something really momentous, something greater than the creation of the world (which is what the 7th day celebrates) really happened. Then, too, there is the whole Easter celebration of the resurrection. Why would that have started and continued if people then knew He didn't arise?

Also, there is external proof of Jesus. Many secular historians recorded what they heard about Jesus and the claims of His followers to have come back to life. Pliny the Younger wrote to the emperor Trajan in 112 about these things. Tactius, a very anti-

Christian historian, recorded what was believed and happening. Thallus, another historian, wrote about the resurrection but personally disbelieved it. So did Josephus, a famous Jewish historian of the time period. Since these men didn't personally believe, but honestly recorded the facts of history, we know they weren't part of any plot nor did they have any personal gain in recording these things. Obviously, the belief in the resurrection of Jesus in the first century was well accepted and well recorded.

One final interesting fact is that Tiberius Caesar, the Roman emperor, obviously heard about the claims of Jesus" resurrection and the impact it was having in his empire, for he had a marker erected in the Nazareth cemetery (probably because he heard that Jesus of Nazareth arose but didn't learn that it was in Jerusalem) saying that anyone robbing a grave would be put to death. While none of these alone can prove the resurrection, all of them together do add up!

The resurrection of Jesus Christ is the cornerstone of the Christian faith. Without it the believer has no hope for this life or for the life to come. The apostle Paul wrote, "And if Christ be not raised, your faith is vain" (1 Cor. 15:17). Our belief in this great teaching is not based upon some religious feeling or upon an unfounded idea about what may have happened in the past. Nor are we talking about an isolated rumor, but about a historical fact with solid evidence to support it.

In the early part of this century, a group of lawyers met in England to discuss the biblical accounts of Jesus' resurrection. They wanted to see if sufficient information was available to make a case that would hold up in an English court of law. When their study was completed, they published the results of their investigation. They concluded that Christ's resurrection was one of the most well- established facts of history!

In his little book, Countdown, G. B. Hardy has given us some thought-provoking questions about the resurrection. "There are but two essential requirements: 1. Has anyone cheated death and proved it? 2. Is it available to me? Here is the complete record: Confucius' tomb -- occupied. Buddha's tomb -- occupied. Mohammed's tomb -- occupied. Jesus' tomb -- empty! Argue as you will, there is no point in following a loser."

The resurrection of Jesus Christ is a reality. Countless changed lives testify that it's a fact -- not a fable!

IV. PROOF FROM FULFILLED EXPECTATIONS

Let's look at this important subject from another angle. You know, if God became man, there are certain things you would expect. For example, IF GOD BECAME MAN, THEN YOU WOULD EXPECT HIM TO:

1. **Have an unusual entrance into life.** What entrance could be more unusual than to be born of a virgin? This is fully attested to by Bible writers as well as early church leaders. Why would someone make up such a preposterous beginning if they wanted to get people to believe and follow them? Unless this was true it wouldn't be claimed!

2. **He without sin.** Jesus claimed to be without sin (John 8:46). Those who lived with Him as well as His enemies all attested to this.

3. **Manifest the supernatural in the form of miracles.** Jesus claimed to be able to do miracles and many claimed to have witnessed them. The Bible (Matthew, Mark, Luke, John, peter, Jude) and early church writings all affirm these claims.

4. **Have an acute sense of difference from others.** Jesus saw Himself as unique, different. Others saw Him that way, too. Even

those who didn't follow Him attest to that: the Koran, Roman and Jewish writers and leaders, and historians and scholars throughout the centuries.

5. **Speak the greatest words ever spoken.** Jesus said: "My words will not pass away" (Mt. 324:35). Roman officers: "Never a man spoke this way" (John 7:46). He is more quoted by secular teachers and philosophers than anyone else ever.

6. **Have a lasting and universal influence.** Historians agree Jesus is the most influential life who ever lived on this planet.

7. **Satisfy the spiritual hunger in man.** These needs were met individually in Matthew, Peter, Nicodemus, Zachaeus, the woman at the well, and millions of others from then to today.

8. **Exercise power over death.** He claimed to conquer death. He brought back to life a widow's only son at Nain, the Centurion"s servant and Lazarus. He Himself came back to life.

CONCLUSION

If Jesus were not God, then He deserved an Oscar! Two infidels once sat on a railroad train, discussing the life of Christ. One of them said, "I think an interesting romance could be written about him." The other replied, "and you are just the man to write it. Tear down the prevailing sentiment about His divinity, and paint Him as a man - a man among men." The suggestion was acted upon and the romance written. The man who made the suggestion was Colonel Ingersoll, the noted atheist. The writer was General Lew Wallace, and the book was called "Ben Hur." In the process of constructing the life of Christ, Gen. Wallace found himself facing the greatest life ever lived on earth. The more he studied, the more he was convinced Christ was more than man. Until one day, he was forced to cry, 'Verily, this was the Son of God!"

VIII. APPENDIX 4

HOW CAN I BE SURE I AM A CHRISTIAN?

When a baby is born everyone checks immediately to make sure it is alive and healthy. There are certain signs that show life: movement, crying, pulse, etc. The same is true spiritually. There are certain spiritual „signs" that show us that we have been born into God's family. I John lists 5 of these:

1. **BELIEF IN JESUS AS SAVIOR AND LORD**

   1 John 5:1 Everyone who believes that Jesus is the Christ is born of God, and everyone who loves the father loves his child as well. A sign of spiritual life is a deep awareness that Jesus is God and Savior, that He is the One who provides salvation and it isn't anything we do or deserve.

2. **STRONG DESIRE TO OVERCOME SIN IN LIFE**

   1 John 5:18 We know that anyone born of God does not continue to sin; the one who was born of God keeps him safe, and the evil one cannot harm him. Along with new birth comes a different attitude to sin. We now know it is wrong and have a strong desire to stop. While we may struggle with certain sins, there should be a slow but steady progress in godliness. Gradually we become more and more like Jesus in what we think and do.

3. **DOING WHAT GOD CONSIDERS RIGHT**

   1 John 2:29 If you know that he is righteous, you know that everyone who does what is right has been born of him. A baby doesn't know just how to live the moment it is born, and neither do we who are born spiritually. It is a learning process, it takes growth. Growth is a sign of life. God says that those who are alive spiritually will grow spiritually. *"GROW in the grace and knowledge of our Lord and Savior Jesus Christ".* II Peter 3:18 *"Brothers, I could not address you as spiritual but as worldly -- mere infants in Christ. I gave you milk, not solid food, for you were not yet ready for it. Indeed, you are still not ready. You are still worldly. For since there is jealousy and quarreling among you, are you not worldly? Are you not acting like mere men?"* I Corinthians 3:1-3

4. **LOVE FOR OTHER BELIEVERS**

1 John 3:14 **We know that we have passed from death to life, because we love our brothers. Anyone who does not love remains in death.** There will be a natural bond between those are in God's family. We have the most important things in life in common.

Usually there is instant rapport. We have a desire to spend time with and get to know other Christians. That is a joy and encouragement, for we are likeminded.

5. **VICTORY OVER WORLDLY WAYS**

1 John 5:4 **for everyone born of God overcomes the world. This is the victory that has overcome the world, even our faith.** While victory over sin often comes slowly and gradually, as Christians we know that we have within us a Power greater than that which is in the world and we can experience God giving us victory over things that used to defeat us.

IX. APPENDIX 5

HOW CAN I BE SURE I STILL AM A CHRISTIAN?

When first born babies are very susceptible to disease and illness so they must be protected from these. They are very vulnerable. Until they grow and become stronger, they are in danger of things that won't be nearly as hard to fight off later on. When someone is a new believer there is danger, they will start to doubt their salvation or fear they have lost it. Thus, it is important to make sure young Christians are protected from the diseases of doubt and fear.

DISEASE OF DOUBT

It's not unusual for Satan to put doubt into a person's mind right after they become a Christian. Did it „work"? Did they „do it" right? There is no requirement to meet so there is nothing that can be done wrong. Salvation is simply a heart attitude of believing that Jesus is God who paid for your sins on the cross. If you believe that you are saved.

Rom 3:28 For we maintain that a man is justified by faith apart from observing the law.

John 3:16 "For God so loved the world that he gave his one and only Son, that whoever believes in him shall not perish but have eternal life.

Eph 2:8-9 For it is by grace you have been saved, through faith-- and this not from yourselves, it is the gift of God-- not by works, so that no one can boast.

If you aren't sure when you accepted Jesus as Savior and for that reason wonder if you really did, just take a moment right now to pray and ask Him to forgive your sins and live in you. You will know for sure that He has done that now if not before, so you never will have need to wonder or worry. Write down today's date so you can always go back to this time and remember that you really did put your faith in Him.

DISEASE OF FEAR

If getting a person to doubt their salvation doesn't work Satan will try to have you believe that you have somehow lost your salvation. That will take away your peace and joy and replace it with fear. Believing you can loose your salvation will cause you to try to do all you can to not lose it. Thus, instead of the Christian life being one of security and assurance in what Christ has done, the emphasis focuses to what you do or don't do. Fear of doing something that will cause you to lose your salvation becomes the primary motivating force in your Christian life. How could a family operate if everyone had to be nice to the others for fear they would be kicked out of the family?

God wants us to know for sure that there is nothing we can do to lose our salvation. He wants us to be assured of His love forever. He wants us to serve Him our love for Him, not because we are afraid, He will send us to hell!

WE ARE UNDER GRACE, NOT LAW, so there is nothing we can do to lose salvation. Rom 6:14 *For sin shall not be your master, because you are not under law, but under grace.*

GOD IS FAITHFUL to His promise to save us if we believe. Even if we become unfaithful, He still keeps His promise to us. 2 Timothy 2:11-13 *Here is a trustworthy saying: If we died with him, we will also live with him; if we endure, we will also reign with him. If we disown him, he will also disown us; if we are faithless, he will remain faithful, for he cannot disown himself.*

GOD PROTECTS US when we are weak and faltering. When we sin and drift, He does not cast us aside. *Matthew 12:20 A bruised reed he will not break, and a smoldering wick he will not snuff out, till he leads justice to victory. Psalms 37:24 though he stumbles, he will not fall, for the LORD upholds him with his hand.*

GOD WILL NEVER HOLD OUR SINS AGAINST US for they were all paid for on the cross. Thus, there is no sin that will ever be charged to us. *Romans 4:6-8 David says the same thing when he speaks of the blessedness of the man to whom God credits righteousness apart from works: "Blessed are they whose transgressions are forgiven, whose sins are covered. Blessed is the man whose sin the Lord will never count against him."*

SALVATION CANNOT BE RETURNED, AND SATAN CANNOT TAKE US FROM GOD There is nothing that can come between us and God, not even we ourselves. *John 10:28-29 I give them eternal life, and they shall never perish; no one can snatch them out of my hand. My Father, who has given them to me, is greater than all; no one can snatch them out of my Father's hand. Romans 8:37-39 No, in all these things we are more than conquerors through him who loved us. For I am convinced that neither death nor life, neither angels nor demons, neither the present nor the future, nor any powers, neither height nor depth, nor anything else in all creation, will be able to separate us from the love of God that is in Christ Jesus our Lord.*

So, any time you feel one of these diseases trying to hit you and take your joy and strength, remember you have no reason to doubt your salvation and you have no reason to fear losing your salvation.

X. APPENDIX 6

TOPICAL INDEX

Abortion is murder: Exodus 21:22-25; Psalm 139:13-15; Romans 14:22-23; Jeremiah 1:5; Genesis 2:7; 9:6

Adversaries Will Be Defeated: Deuteronomy 32:43; Philippians 1:28; Deuteronomy 33:27

Angelic Intervention promised: II Kings 6:17; Psalm 34:6-7; Psalm 91:11; Daniel 6:22; 10:5-14; Acts 12:15

Angels, creation of: Colossians 1:16; Job 38:6-7; Jude 6; Hebrews 12:11

Angels, ministry to believers today: Hebrews 1:14; Acts 12:7; 27:23-24; I Corinthians 4:9; I Timothy 5:21; Luke 15:10; 16:22; Acts 8:26; Jude 9

Angels, nature of: Hebrews 1:14; Mark 12:25; Luke 20:36; Psalm 8:4-5; II Peter 2:11

Annihilation at death doesn't happen: Matthew 17:1-3; 22:32; John 11:25; Genesis 35:18; II Corinthians 5:8; Philippians 1:21-23; John 3:36; Luke 23:43

Assurance of salvation: John 3:16; 5:24; 6:37, 44; 10:28-29; Romans 8:1, I 29-39; Ephesians 1:13-14; Colossians 1:12-14; I Peter 1:3-4; I John 2:1-2; I John 5:13

Assured Of Eventual Triumph Over Our Adversaries: Acts 2:39

Atonement for sin: Exodus 12:13; Matthew 26:28; 28:5-7; Luke 24:39; John 1:29; 19:33; Romans 5:6-8; Ephesians 1:7; Colossians 1:20

Believe, what does that mean? Ephesians 2:8-9; John 1:12; I

Corinthians 15:1; Colossians 2:6; II Thessalonians 2:10

Bible, importance of studying it: Luke 6:40; John 5:39; Acts 20:32; Ephesians 6:17; II Timothy 2:15; James 1:21-22; I Peter 2:2; II Peter 1:2

Bible, inspired Word of God: II Timothy 3:16; II Peter 1:19-20; I Corinthians 2:13; II Peter 3:15; Hebrews 1:1; 2:3; 4:12; I Peter 1:10-12, 25; II Samuel 23:1-2; Matthew 24:35; John 10:35; 17:17

Bible, reliable & trustworthy: John 19:35; I John 1:1; II Peter 1:16; Luke 1:1-4; Acts 2:22

Comfort Promised: Psalm 23:4; Lamentations 3:22-23; Matthew 5:4; 11:28-30; John 14:16, 18; John 14:16, 18; Romans 15:4; II Corinthians 1:3-4; II Thessalonians 2:16-17

Confession Means Cleansing & Forgiveness: I John 1:8-9; Thessalonians 5:23-24; I Timothy 4:5; Luke 11:13; II Timothy 2:21; Jude 1; Romans 8:33-39; Titus 3:4-5

Conscience used by God: Acts 24:16; Romans 14:14, 23; II Timothy 1:5; Titus 1:15; Matthew 6:22-23; Romans 1:14-15; 9:1; I Corinthians 10:27-29

Courage promised: Proverbs 38:1; I Corinthians 16:13; II Timothy 1:7

Creation is by God: Genesis 1:1, 26-27; Nehemiah 9:6; Psalm 24:1; 8:3; Exodus 20:11; ISamuel 2:8; Psalm 33:6; 146:6; Isaiah 40:12; Jeremiah 51:15; Acts 14:15; Ephesians 3:9

Creation shows God: Romans 1:19-20; Psalm 19:1-2

Death no fear to believers: Psalm 23:4; 49:15; 116:15; John 14:1-3, 6, -19, 27

Demons, activity of: Daniel 10:10-14; Revelation 16:13-16; 12:3-4; Ephesians 6:11-12; Matthew 4:24; 9:33; Luke 3:11, 16; Mark

5:13; Colossians 2:15; I Timothy 4:1

Demons, possession & deliverance: Matthew 4:1-11; 17:19-21; 18:20; 28:18-20; Mark 5:9; Luke 8:30; 10:17; 18:1; John 14:14; 15:7; Ephesians 5:18-20; 6:10-18; Colossians 1:20; 3:16- 17; II Timothy 3:16-17; Hebrews 4:12; James 5:14-16; I John 1:9; 4:1-8

Depression Defeated: Psalm 42:11; Isaiah 26:3; Philippians 2:5; 4:8; Nehemiah 8:10-11; Psalm 51:12; 1 Peter 5:7; Isaiah 26:3

Don't judge others: Romans 14:3-13; 2:1-6; I Corinthians 2:14-15; 4:5; but do evaluate/discern: Matthew 18:15-18; 6:2, 5, 16; 7:1-12, 16-17; I Corinthians 5:12-13; John 7:24; Luke 12:57;

Eternal life: Mark 12:25; Luke 16:19-31; Jn 11:25-26; I Thes 4:16-18; James 2:26; I Jn 5:11-13

Everything Will Work Out Right in the End: Romans 8:28

Evil and suffering, why exist: John 9:1-3; II Peter 3:9; Revelation 21:1-8; Romans 8:28

Faith, what does it mean: Psalm 118:8; Proverbs 3:5; Isaiah 26:3; Mark 11:22; John 3:16-17; Romans 5:1; 4:3-5; Galatians 2:16; Ephesians 2:8-9

False Teachers: Matthew 7:13-27; Jeremiah 23:16, 32; Deuteronomy 18:20-22; Matthew 24:4-5; 11, 24; II Pet 2:1-3

Fear of Death gone for believers: Psalm 23:4; 49:15; 116:15; John 14:1-3, 6, -19, 27

Fear, promises to claim: Proverbs 3:25; Isaiah 14:3; Psalm 34:4; Joshua 1:9; 10:8; 23:9-11; Leviticus 26:8; Exodus 14:13; I Samuel 17:45-47; II Samuel 22:33-35, 40-41

Fear, The Believer Has Nothing to Fear: Proverbs 3:25; Isaiah 14:3; Psalm 34:4; Joshua 1:9; 10:8; 23:9-11; Leviticus 26:8; Exodus 14:13; I Samuel 17:45-47; II Samuel 22:33-35, 40-41

Forgiveness, receiving from God I John 1:9; Psalm 19:12; 139:23-24; 32:1-5; Psalm 103; Isaiah 1:18; 43:25; Romans 4:7-8; Hebrews 8:12; I John 2:12

Forgiving others: Matthew 6:12-15; 18:23-27; 18:35; Ephesians 4:32; Mark 11:25-26; Colossians 3:13; Proverbs 24:17-19; Romans 2:23-24

Free will of man: Proverbs 1:23; Isaiah 31:6; Ezekiel 14:6; 18:32; Matthew 18:3; John 6:29; 19:1; I John 3:23

Freedom from law, legalism: law a unit, go by all of it or none (Matthew 5:19); law given only to Israel (Leviticus 26:46; Romans 2:14; 9:4); law fulfilled by Christ (Galatians 3:13); law done away with (Romans 6:15)

God Hears & Answers Prayer: Matthew 7:7; Luke 11:9; Jeremiah 33:3

God Is Always with Us: Matthew 28:20; Hebrews 13:5; Matthew 18:20; John 14:16, 21; Revelations 3:20

God judge those who have never heard? Romans 1:18-25; 2:1, 14-16; Acts 14:15-17; Hebrews 11:6

God Promises His Care & Protection: Deuteronomy 33:27; Genesis 17:1; Jer. 23:24; 32:7

God Promises To Fight For Us: I Samuel 14:47; Jeremiah 1:8

God Will Help Us Carry Our Burdens: Nehemiah 4:10; Matthew 11:30; Psalm 55:22

God Will Meet All Your Needs: Philippians 4:19: Psalm 84:11; Romans 8:32; I Samuel 12:24

God, a Trinity: Matthew 28:19; 3:16-17; Genesis 1:26; 11:7

God, above & separate from creation: John 4:24; Hebrews 1:3

God, creator: Genesis 1:1, 26-27; Nehemiah 9:6; Psalm 24:1; 8:3;

Exodus 20:11; I Samuel 2:8; Psalm 33:6; 146:6; Isaiah 40:12; Jeremiah 51:15; Acts 14:15; Ephesians 3:9

God, existence: Genesis 1:1-3; Romans 1:20

God, grace: Romans 3:242; 11:5; Ephesians 2:8; II Peter 3:18; Genesis 6:8; Psalm 51:1; John 1:16; Romans 5:2; II Corinthians 12:9; Hebrews 4:16

God, holy: Exodus 15:11; Leviticus 19:2; Habakkuk 1:13; Revelation 4:8

God, personality: personal (John 4:24; Hebrews 1:3); Remembers (Isaiah 43:25; Jeremiah 31:20; Hosea 8:13); Speaks ((Exodus 3:12; Matthew 3:17; Luke 17:6); Knows (Jeremiah 29:11; II Timothy 2:19; I John 3:20)

God, seen in creation, nature: Romans 1:19-20; Psalm 19:1-2

God, sovereign: Exodus 18:11; 15:18; Matthew 6:10, 13; 11:25; Deuteronomy 4:39; I Chronicles 29:11; Daniel 6:26; John 7:17; Ephesians 1:11; I Tim 2:4; 6:15; Rev 19:6

Guidance Is Promised: Psalm 32:8; Isaiah 30:21; 58:11; Luke 1:79; John 15:13

Heaven: Matthew 22:30; Luke 20:34-38; 23:43; Revelation 7:9; 8:1; I Corinthians 13:12; 15:42; Philippians 1:23; I John 3:2; II chronicles 2:6; Mark 16:19; Deuteronomy 26:15; Job 3:17; Psalm 17:15; 73:24; Matthew 3:17; 5:3; Luke 16:19-31; 12:32; John 14:1-3; I Thessalonians 4:17

Hell & punishment are real: Revelation 20;15; 14:9-11; Matthew 5:22; 8:11-12; 13:42, 50; 22:13; Mark 9:44-48; Luke 3:17

Holy Spirit indwells believers: I Corinthians 1:21; 5:5; I John 2:20, 27; John 3:3-8; 7:37-39;

14:16-17; Romans 5:5; 8:9; I Cor 2:12; 6:17-19; 12:13; John 7:37-39

Holy Spirit: John 14:16-17, 26; 15:26; 20:22; 16:8-14; I Corinthians 2:10-15; Matthew 1:18; 3:11, 16-17; 10:20; Isaiah 63:10; Acts 5:3-4; Ephesians 4:30; Acts 8:29; 13:2; Luke 12:12; John 16:7-18

Homosexuality is sin: Romans 1:26-32; I Corinthians 6:9-10; Leviticus 20:13; Genesis 2:18-22; I Timothy 1:8-10

Hope in Jesus: Psalm 31:24; 71:5; 62:5-8

Hypocrisy doesn't invalidate Christianity: Matthew 23:23-36; Isaiah 29:13; Matthew 7;23; Proverbs 26:23-26; Titus 1:16; I John 1:8, 10

Israel, God's special protection of: Isaiah 11:11-14; 19:19-25; Genesis 12:3; Jeremiah 48:12-15; Ezekiel 29:9-10; 35:1-5

Jesus Greater than Demons, Satan: Mark 1:21-28; 5:1-20; 7:24-30; 9:20-27; 2 Corinthians 12:7-10; Hebrews 2:14-15; Luke 9:1-2; Luke 10:17-20; Revelation 12:7-11; Revelation 20:7-15; Mark 1:21-28; Mark 5:1-20; Mark 7:24-30; Mark 9:20-27

Jesus Is Constantly Praying & Interceding on Our Behalf: I John 2:1; Hebrews 7:25

Jesus, Deity of: John 1:1, 34; 5:17-23; 10:30, 36-38; 12:45; 13:20, 45; 14:1, 9; 17:11, 21-22; 20:24-31; Ephesians 1:20-23; Philippians 2:6-10; Hebrews 1:18; Matthew 1:23; 3:17; 8:29

Jesus, fully human: Galatians 4:4; Luke 2:52; 19:10; I John 1:1; Matthew 26:12; 4:2; Hebrews 4:15

Jesus, the only way to God: John 14:6; 8:24; 3:16-18; 10:30; Matthew 26:63-64; Acts 4:12; Galatians 1:8; I Corinthians 3:11; I John 2:23; Luke 10:16

Jesus" resurrection, physical & literal: Luke 24:39-44; John 20:27-28; Mark 16:14; I Corinthians 15:15

Jews, God's chosen people: Deuteronomy 14:2; 7:6-7; 10:14-15; Ezekiel 22:17-22

Jews, God's special protection of: Isaiah 11:11-14; 19:19-25; Genesis 12:3; Jeremiah 48:12-15; Ezekiel 29:9-10; 35:1-5

Law, legalism – believers free from: law a unit, go by all of it or none (Matthew 5:19); law given only to Israel (Leviticus 26:46; Romans 2:14; 9:4); law fulfilled by Christ (Galatians 3:13); law done away with (Romans 6:15)

Life after death: Matthew 17:1-3; 22:32; John 11:25; Genesis 35:18; II Corinthians 5:8; Philippians 1:21-23; John 3:36; Luke 23:43

Life, only God can create: Jeremiah 10:16; Col 1:16-17; Job 33:4; Gen 1:26; Ps 8:6

Light: John 3:16-21; 8:12; 12:46; 1 John 1:5-7

Marriage, believers only marry other believers: II Corinthians 6:14-18

Materialism, attitude to money, accumulating money, uses of money, etc.: see verses at end of this booklet

Materialism, attitude to: Proverbs 30:8-9; 10:15; 28:22; Matthew 19:23-24; II Corinthians 9:8; II Thessalonians 3:10; Ecclesiastes 10:19; Acts 8:20; Jere3miah 9:23-24; Mark 8:36-37

Miracles really happened: Matthew 8:14-15, 26-27; 9:2, 6-7, 27-30; Mark 1:32-34; John 2:1-11; 6:10-14; John 10:24-25; 20:30-31; 3:2

Money, attitude to: Proverbs 30:8-9; 10:15; 28:22; Matthew 19:23-24; II Corinthians 9:8; II Thessalonians 3:10; Ecclesiastes 10:19; Acts 8:20; Jere3miah 9:23-24; Mark 8:36-37

Money, materialism, attitude to money, accumulating money, uses of money, etc.: see verses at end of this booklet

Motives matter to God: James 4:2-3; Proverbs 16:2; 1 Corinthians 4:5; Hebrews 4:12-13

Nature shows God: Romans 1:19-20; Psalm 19:1-2

No Need To Worry: Matthew 6:25,34; I Peter 5:7; Isaiah 40:11; Matthew 5:38-39; Psalm 37:1-9; Jude 24

Occult, spiritism wrong: Leviticus 19:31; 20:6-7, 27; Exodus 20:27; 22:18; Deuteronomy 18:10-12; I chronicles 10:13-14; Isaiah 8:19-20; Galatians 5:20; Revelation 21:8

Peace Is Available No Matter What: John 14:27; Romans 5:1; Colossians 1:20; Isaiah 26:3; Philippians 4:6-7; Matthew 11:28-30; II Timothy 1:7

Peace Promised: Philippians 4:6-7; Isaiah 26:3; Romans 15:13; Psalm 85:8; 29:11; Ephesians 2:14-15; Isaiah 53:5; Colossians 1:20; John 14:27; Romans 5:1; John 16:33; Galatians 5:22-24; Philippians 4:7

Prayer, promises: Matthew 18:19; 21:22; Mark 11:24; Isaiah 65:24; Jeremiah 33:3; Matthew 7:7-8; John 14:13; I Thessalonians 5:17; Ephesians 8:18; Hebrews 4:16; Philippians 4:6-7; I Timothy 2:1

Resurrection of Christians: Psalm 49:15; 16:9-10; Luke 14:14; II Corinthians 4:14; Job 14:12-15; 19:25-27; John 5:28-29; Acts 24:15; I Corinthians 15; Philippians 3:20-21; I Thessalonians 4:16-18; John 11:23-26

Resurrection of Jesus, physical & literal: Luke 24:39-44; John 20:27-28; Mark 16:14; I Corinthians 15:15; I Corinthians 15:1-19; Matthew 27:62-66; 28:1-17; Mark 16:9-14; John 20:19-31

Salvation by faith only is too easy: Matthew 19:16-26; Ephesians 2:8-9; John 20:31

Salvation only through Jesus John 14:6; 8:24; 3:16-18; 10:30; Matthew 26:63-64; Acts 4:12; Galatians 1:8; I Corinthians 3:11; I John 2:23; Luke 10:16

Salvation, a free gift: Romans 6:23; Ephesians 2:8-9; John 1:12-

13

Salvation, Atonement for sin: Exodus 12:13; Matthew 26: 28; 28:5-7; Luke 24:39; John 1:29;19:33; Romans 5:6-8; Ephesians 1:7; Colossians 1:20

Salvation, available for whoever comes: Ezekiel 33:11; Romans 10:13; I Timothy 2:4; II Peter 3:9; Matthew 12:50; 18:4; 10:32

Salvation, can't be lost: John 3:16-18, 36; 5:24; 6:37-40; 10:27-30; 20:30-31; Romans 8:14-16, 28, 37-39; 14:8; II Corinthians 1:21-22; Ephesians 1:13-14; 3:12; Hebrews 6:4-6; 2 Timothy 2:11-12; Matthew 12:20; Psalm 37:24; Romans 4:6-8; 8:37-39

Salvation, man can't save self: Psalm 49:7; Luke 11:24-26; I Peter 1:18-19; II Peter 2:20-22

Salvation, man's need of: Isaiah 64:6; Romans 5:12; Hebrews 9:27; I John 1:10

Salvation, not earned by good works: Ephesians 2:8-9; Romans 3:20, 27; 4:4-5; 5:8; 6:232; 11:6; Galatians 3:11; James 2:10; I Peter 2:24; Titus 3:5

Salvation, not everyone will get to heaven: Matthew 25:46; Luke 16:19-31; John 3:18, 36; 5:28-29; 6:37-40; I John 3:10; Revelation 20:10-15

Salvation, provided by Jesus: John 3:15-18, 36; 14:7; 10:10; Isaiah 53:5-6; I John 4:10; 5:12; Romans 5:6-8; I Peter 2:24; 1:18-19; II Corinthians 5:21; I John 5:11-13; Acts 4:12; Eph. 1:7

Salvation, received by faith: Romans 10:13; John 5:24; Acts 17:31; Galatians 3:22; 5:6; John 3:16

Satan, defeated Colossians 2:15; Psalm 3:4; Psalm 6:8-10; 72:12-14; 82:1-7

Satan, defeating: Matthew 4:1-11; John 15:7; 17:15; Ephesians

6:10-18; II Thessalonians 3:3; James 4:7; I Peter 5:8-9; I John 4:4; 5:18; Romans 8:28; II Cor 2:7; Jude 8-9

Satan, fall of: Ezekiel 28:11-19; Isaiah 14:12-20; I Tim 3:6

Satan, nature of: Ezekiel 28:12-14; Ephesians 6:11-12; Job 1:12; John 8:44; I John 3:8; I Peter 5:8; Revelation 12:10; II Thessalonians 3:3

Sex, outside marriage forbidden: Matthew 5:27-32; 19:9; I Corinthians 6:9-10, 18-20; Hebrews 13:4; Exodus 20;14; Deuteronomy 5:18; 24:1-4; Luke 18:20; James 2:11; II Peter 2:14; I Corinthians 5:9; Ephesians 5:3; Leviticus 20:10; I Thessalonians 4:3

Sex, to show love in marriage: Genesis 3:16; 18:12; 26:8-9; 2:23-25; Deuteronomy 24:5; 34:7; Proverbs 5:15-19; Song of Solomon 7:6-10; Hebrews 13:4; I Corinthians 7:3-4

Sexual Temptation, victory over 2 Corinthians 5:17; Psalm 51:10-12; Romans 12:1; James 4:6-8; I John 4:4; Philippians 4:19; Matthew 16:23; Psalm 139:23-24; 2 Corinthians 5:17; 2 Corinthians 12:9-10; 1 Peter 5:8-9; Job 31:1; Matthew 5:27-28.

Sin defined: Romans 3:23; 14:23; Galatians 5:19-21; James 4:17; I John 3:4

Sin paid for by Jesus: Exodus 12:13; Matthew 26:28; 28:5-7; Luke 24:39; John 1:29; 19:33; Romans 5:6-8; Ephesians 1:7; Colossians 1:20

Sinfulness of man: Mark 10:18; Isaiah 53:5-6; 59:1-2; Rom 3:10-12, 23; 6:23; James 2:10; I John 1:8-10; 3:4; 5:17

Sins of believers, forever gone: John 3:18, 36; II Thessalonians 1:7-9; Romans 8:1; II Peter 3:9-14; Revelation 20:11-15

Sorrow, God Will Help In Your Sorrow: Proverbs 10:22; Isaiah 53:4; John 16:22; II Corinthians 6:10; I Thessalonians 4:13;

Revelation 21:4

Soul sleep wrong: Matthew 17:1-3; 22:32; John 11:25; Genesis 35:18; II Corinthians 5:8; Philippians 1:21-23; John 3:36; Luke 23:43

Spiritism, occult wrong: Leviticus 19:31; 20:6-7, 27; Exodus 20:27; 22:18; Deuteronomy 18:10-12; I chronicles 10:13-14; Isaiah 8:19-20; Galatians 5:20; Revelation 21:8

Spiritual warfare promises, memory verses: see verses at end of this booklet

Suffering and Evil, why exist John 9:1-3; II Peter 3:9; Revelation 21:1-8; Romans 8:28

Suffering, attitude to: Philippians 1:29; 3:10; I Peter 2:19-21; 5:10; John 15:2; 13:7; Hebrews 12:7; 11:25; Revelation 3:19; Romans 8:18, 28; II timothy 2:12; I Peter 4:12-19; Hebrews 2:10; 5:8; II Corinthians 4:17; Matthew 5:45

Suffering, reasons for: Job 1 – 2; Hebrews 5:8; II Corinthians 12:7; I Peter 1:7-8; John 16:33; II Corinthians 4:8-11; 1:3-24; II Timothy 2:10-13

Thoughts, Rejecting Wrong Thoughts: II Corinthians 10:5; Psalm 139:23-24; 141:3-4; Isaiah 26:3-4; Romans 12:2; Ephesians 4:22-24; Philippians 3:18-21

Trials Are Allowed To Bring Spiritual Growth: Psalm 119:67,71,75; 94:12; Isa. 48:10; Rom. 5:3

Trinity: Matthew 28:19; 3:16-17; Genesis 1:26; 11:7

Truth: Psalm 51:6; 25:5; John 14:6; 16:13; 1:17; 8:44; 14:17; 17:17; Matthew 5:33-37; John 8:31-36; Ephesians 4:25

Victory in spiritual warfare: Hebrews 2:14-15; Luke 9:1-2; 10:17-20; Revelation 12:7-11; 20:7-15; Matthew 25:41

Victory Is Guaranteed Us: I Corinthians 15:57; Romans 8:37; I

Chronicles 29:11; I John 5:4, 18; II Chronicles 32:8; Revelation 3:5; 21:7

Victory Promised:: I Corinthians 15:57; I Chronicles 29:11; Proverbs 21:31; I John 5:4, 18; Rev. 12:11; 15:2; Romans 8:37; II Corinthians 2:14; John 16:33

We will never Be Separated From God: Romans 8:35-39; John 10:27-29; 3:36; 5:24

Wisdom Is Promised Those Who Ask: James 1:5; 3:15-17; Luke 16:8; 21:15; I Cor. 2:5; 3:19

Word of God's Power: Ephesians 6:17; Hebrews 4:12; Isaiah 55:11; 59:21; Psalm 119:81, 105, 11-112; Proverbs 30:5; Lamentations 2:17; 3:37; Matthew 24:35; John 5:24; 8:51; 15:7; Romans 10:17

You Won't Ever Face Anything You Can't Handle With God's Help: I Corinthians 10:13

XI. APPENDIX 7

LISTENING TO GOD

"What Does God's Voice Sound Like?"

In the dome of St. Paul's Cathedral there is what is known as the "Whispering Gallery." Through the peculiar construction of the dome a whisper by a person at one side travels round and can be distinctly heard by another person standing at the other.

An even more remarkable whispering gallery is that known as the "Ear of Dionysius" at Syracuse in Sicily. This is a vast cave, which externally bears a resemblance to a human ear. Entering by a low doorway, the visitor finds himself in a huge cavern. High up, concealed in the roof, is a chamber, which can only be entered by a concealed path at the top. The faintest whisper uttered below is distinctly heard by those concealed above. In this chamber the tyrant Dionysius used to sit listening to his slaves working or to his captives imprisoned below. All their plots against him were thus, to them, mysteriously discovered and circumvented. From this historical fact the cave has received the name of the "Ear of Dionysius."

We, too, can learn to hear everything God says – if we know how to listen.

We saw last week that God really does speak to us today. He desires communication with us and we desire communication with Him. We saw that hearing from God is probable, possible and even very necessary.

Then we saw examples of those whom God spoke to in the Old Testament. These include Moses, Samuel, David and the prophets. In the New Testament we see Him speaking to Jesus quite often, to Paul on the road to Damascus and to many others.

We also looked at some of the ways God speaks to man. Some of the means God used to communicate to men in the past but which He no longer uses include audible voice (although there may be some times He still speaks audibly to people today), angels, dreams, visions, casting lots and the Urim an Thummim. We observed more closely some of the ways God spoke in the past and still speaks today. He speaks through nature, other people, circumstances and experiences, prayer, the written Word, the Holy Spirit and our conscience.

Thus, we have established that God wants to speak to us and in deed does. Now we want to look at how He speaks and what He says.

I hope you've been learning to listen to Him this past week. Have you taken time to let Him speak and to sit and listen? Have you become more aware of when and how He speaks to you? I hope so. The whole purpose of these messages is for you to take this information and apply it to your own lives during the coming week.

I. **WHAT DOES GOD"S VOICE SOUND LIKE?**

Out of the several ways God uses to communicate His messages to us today, we will be focusing on His speaking to us by the Holy Spirit. He speaks to us today and we can hear His voice. It's not a sound, it's a voice. It's not something you hear with your ears but in your mind. Once you learn to recognize and respond to this voice you'll recognize it often.

There is an old story about two men walking down a busy, loud New York City Street.

Horns honked, engines roared, PA systems blasted advertisements. All of a sudden one of the men, who had been an outdoorsman all his life, stopped and said, "What's that?" The other man couldn't imagine what he was talking about with all the noise and confusion all around.

The first man went over to the side of a building and picked up a cricket he had heard. The friend was amazed that the outdoorsman had even heard it, but his ears were attuned to that sound and could pick it out of the din around them. That's how our spiritual hearing needs to be. We need to be able to pick God's voice out of all the other voices clamoring for our attention. Hopefully this message will help you to be able to do that.

First we'll look at what God's voice sounds like, and then we'll talk about some of the things He says. The first clue we have to what God's voice sounds like is in I Kings 19 where we see it is a still, small voice – a gentle whisper.

Kings 19:11-13 The LORD said, "Go out and stand on the mountain in the presence of the LORD, for the LORD is about to pass by." Then a great and powerful wind tore the mountains apart and shattered the rocks before the LORD, but the LORD was not in the wind. After the wind there was an earthquake, but the LORD was not in the earthquake. After the earthquake came a fire, but the LORD was not in the fire. And after the fire came a gentle whisper. When Elijah heard it, he pulled his cloak over his face and went out and stood at the mouth of the cave. Then a voice said to him, "What are you doing here, Elijah?"

In the still, small voice of God we are given a message that bears the stamp of His personality quite clearly and in a way, we will learn to recognize.

There is a speaker system at the Ontario Motor Speedway in California that has an output of 30,800 watts connected to 355 speakers and able to communicate to 230,000 people above the noise of the car races. God could outdo that, but instead chooses to speak quietly. Therefore, if we want to hear Him, we can't wait for Him to shout over the noise in our life but we need to learn to be quiet and listen for His still, quiet voice.

I remember several years ago I was marrying a couple that I had known for a long time and had been coming to church and Bible studies for quite some time. They had some major

„issues" it seemed that had worked through, but the day before the wedding the groom did something that was part of his old pattern. I clearly heard God's voice in my spirit telling me not to marry them, so I didn't. The bride and both families really put a lot of pressure on me to go ahead with the wedding but I knew that God had spoken.

Dr. Martin Lloyd-Jones writes: "God sometimes answers directly in our spirit. The prophet said, „I will watch and see what He will say in me. " God speaks to me by speaking in

me. He can so lie something upon the mind that we are certain of the answer. He can impress something upon our spirits in an unmistakable manner. We find ourselves unable to get away from an impression that is on our mind or heart; we try to rid ourselves of it, but back it comes."

Remember, this is not verbal voice, a sensation or an emotional experience. In fact, it can be very easy to overlook His voice or just think it's a thought of our own.

Try an experiment: Be as still and silent as you possibly can for the next 30 seconds or so. Listen as intently as you can, noticing the sounds you hear. How many sounds? What are they? --Close your eyes and begin to listen. Pause: Did you hear 1 sound-- 2? 3? 4? 5? Did you hear the ticking of the clock? Heater noise? Birds? Traffic? Voices? Your own breath? Your heartbeat? Ringing in your ears?

We are seldom still enough to hear the subtle sounds. Most of us suffer from a steady dose of noise pollution: TV, radio, conversation. Constant sound bombards us until the naturalness of silence sounds foreign, unnatural, threatening, and we'll do just about anything to cover it up. In a significant way, we are in fact addicted to noise. The constant blaring of the TV is for many an electronic companion whose presence we take for granted; Mazak fills the elevator; we jump in the car and switch on the radio to fill the uncomfortable void; even a lapse in social conversation is viewed with alarm, and someone has to rescue the moment by talking. Even in church, if a few moments of silence are called for in worship, most church members have this internal response: "When will this be over?"

We need to learn to hear God's still voice as He speaks to us. I can think back on times He told me to talk to someone about Him and I didn't. Those still haunt me. Better memories are the times when God put it on my heart to speak to someone and I obeyed.

Writer Charles Swindoll once found himself with too many commitments in too few days. He got nervous and tense about it. "I was snapping at my wife and our children, choking down my food at mealtimes, and feeling irritated at those unexpected interruptions through the day," he recalled in his book *Stress Fractures*. "Before long, things around our home started reflecting the patter of my hurry-up style. It was become unbearable."

Martin Luther wrote: "If the Holy Spirit should come when these thoughts are in your mind and begin to preach to your heart, giving you rich and enlightened thoughts, then give Him the honor, let your preconceived ideas go, be quiet and listen to Him Who can talk better than you; and note what He proclaims and write it down."

James Dobson has given some of the best practical advice I have ever heard on how someone who really wants the will of God and who has a basically correct understanding of it should proceed. Describing how he does it himself, he says, "I get down on my knees and say,

„Lord, I need to know what you want me to do, and I am listening. Please speak to me through my friends, books, magazines I pick up and read, and through circumstances."

Often God's still, small voice takes the form of thoughts that are our thoughts, though they are not from us.

When God speaks in your heart it doesn't matter where your mind has been going; He blocks and overrides all circuits. You are captivated by His voice speaking to you. He commands your undivided attention. There is absolute certainty in what He says. What He says is right. His word has perfect balance and proportion. Everything He shows us fits together seamlessly. The word He gives us is complete. Everything He says compliments everything He's been showing us.

It's true that Satan can counterfeit this, but that just proves that God does speak to us in this way. A little later we'll have a whole message on how to tell God's voice from Satan's counterfeit leading.

When I study, when I prepare sermons and lessons, I try to be very aware of the rich and enlightening thoughts that God sends me by means of His Spirit. When I counsel, I always try to be sensitive to His leading and direction. When we are involved in spiritual warfare it is essential to be in tune to hear what thoughts God gives me.

Often this still, small voice speaks rich and enlightening thoughts by causing a burning within my heart.

The disciples who talked with Jesus on the road to Emmaus that first Resurrection Sunday experienced this. Luke 24:32 says, "They asked each other, „were not our hearts burning within us while he talked with us on the road and opened the Scriptures to us?

Psalm 39:1-3 talks about this as well. "My heart grew hot within me, and as I meditated, the fire burned."

One of the more familiar quotes about this comes from the journal of John Wesley for May 14, 1738. "In the evening, I went very unwillingly to a society in Aldersgate-Street, where one was reading Luther's preface to the Epistle to the Romans. About a quarter before nine, while he was describing the change which God works in the heart through faith in Christ, I felt my heart strangely warmed. I felt I did trust in Christ, Christ alone for salvation: And an assurance was given me, that he had taken away my sins, even mine, and saved me from the law of sin and death."

Haven't you found yourself moved by something you sense in your spirit? Perhaps it happens during a song or sermon, when listening to a testimony or out in nature? This stirring is God speaking to our hearts through His Holy Spirit, putting His fire within us to highlight something of importance.

Charles Stanley writes: "As you pray and read, trust the Holy Spirit to quicken your spirit to His truth. You may feel this as warmth inside, or you may feel a great sense of absoluteness about a particular verse. Sometimes the words on the page of your Bible may seem to stand out to you as if they were written in bold headlines. Sometimes you may not be able to get away from a particular passage. It comes repeatedly to your mind, and you can't seem to shake it from memory."

So, we see that this still, small voice speaks rich and enlightening thoughts by causing a burning within our hearts. How He speaks is by a gentle, quiet whisper. Where He speaks is to our thoughts and to our hearts. He touches our rational mental capacity (enlightened thoughts) as well as our emotional feelings (burning hearts).

II. **WHAT DOES GOD'S VOICE SAY?**

Hopefully that makes hearing God's voice a little clearer, but there is one more part I want to add which can be very helpful. What does His voice say? What can we expect to hear from God? What sort of things does He communicate to those who are listening?

To Ezekiel God complained that "these people have ears to hear but they never hear, eyes to see but they never see" (12:2). Jesus repeated this complaint several times as well.

We saw last time the many different people that God spoke to in the Old Testament.

Often, He spoke to them many times. We see throughout the Bible phrases like "the voice of the Lord" (14 times), "the voice of God" (3 times), "the Lord spoke" (24 times), "God spoke" (6 times), and "the word of the Lord came to…" (99 times). There is no way of knowing how many times this was a verbal voice and how many times it was God's still, small voice speaking rich thoughts to their mind or heart (or both). If it was verbal or not, however, the result was still the same – God spoke to them and they heard Him.

When we look at these occurrences, we see they can be grouped into five areas of revelation. God spoke conviction, information, encouragement, enablement in ministry, and revelation of Himself.

For most of us, the first time we heard God speak to us He was convicting us of sin, showing us our need of salvation. Jesus said, "When the Holy Spirit comes, He will convict the world of guilt in regard to sin and righteousness and judgment: in regard to sin, because men do not believe in me" (John 16: A7-11). I Thessalonians 1:4-5 says the gospel comes to us with the Holy Spirit and with deep conviction.

Of course, we all know that how we respond that that conviction is a free will choice each will need to make.

In the 1640s George Fox, founder of the Friends or Quaker movement, wandered the fields and lanes of the English countryside, seeking someone who could show him the way to peace with God. He finally became convinced that "there was none among them all that could speak to my condition. And when all my hopes in them and in all men were gone, so that I had nothing outwardly to help me, nor could I tell what to do; then, oh! Then I heard a voice which said, „here is one, even Jesus Christ, that can speak to thy condition"; and when I heard it, my heart did leap for joy. Then the Lord did let me see why there was none upon the earth that could speak to my condition, namely, that I might give him all the glory."

One way in which God speaks to us is to show us the sin in our life. He does this before salvation so we will see our need of Him. He also does this in the lives of those who have freely received His free gift of salvation. He shows us sin so we can confess and remove it.

Charles Stanley wrote: "As we read God's Word, we nearly always come to what I call a Gulp point". Something we read challenges us to change something in our lives, to gulp and say, "Wow! That really hit me. I need to do something about that." Sometimes it's a conviction about sin in our lives. Sometimes it's a correction in the way we have been taught or the way in which we act toward others. Sometimes it's a clear call to engage in a new discipline or area of ministry.

The problem is that we have a tendency to only listen to what we want to hear. A doctor can give us good advice about diet changes or needed exercise, but it's very easy to ignore his counsel if it means changes, we don't want to make.

I've learned to recognize God's Spirit when He convicts me of sin. He warns me ahead of time through my conscience. He also censures me after I have sinned. While we may not want to hear these things from Him, we can thank Him for faithfully bringing sin to our attention. Suppose He didn't?

A second type of content God speaks to us is information and guidance.

Jesus said, "But when He, the Spirit of truth, comes, He will guide you into all truth. He will not speak on His own; He will speak only what He hears, and He will tell you what is yet to come" (John 16:13).

The Bible abounds with examples of this. Paul said the Holy Spirit warned him of what was to come when he went to Jerusalem (Acts 20:22-23). He reminded the church in Corinth that they had the "mind of Christ" (2:16). Joseph heard of Pharaoh's dream and God told Him the contents and their meaning. Daniel heard Nebuchadnezzar's dream and God gave him the interpretation. Jacob (Genesis 46:2) and Samuel (2 Samuel 23:2) both said God spoke His guidance to them. Simeon was moved by the Spirit to find Jesus with His parents in the temple (Luke 2:25-28). Several times the Bible tells us that God guided Him by directing His spirit (Mark 2:8; John 13:21). God spoke to Ananias and told him to go to blind Paul (Acts 9:11-15).

An analogy I like which explains this is the shepherd-sheep illustration. He said that His sheep hear His voice and follow Him (John 10:4, 16, 27). Jesus" definition of a disciple is one who follows Him, who hears His voice and responds.

St. Augustine tells of a time God's voice guided him. "I heard from a neighboring house a voice, as of a boy or girl, I know not, changing, and oft repeating, „Take up and read. Take up and read. " I could remember no child's game with these words. So, checking the torrent of my tears, I arose; interpreting it to be no other than a command from God, to open the book, and read the first chapter I should find." Thus, he came upon Romans 13:13-14 which led to his salvation and transformation.

That's why it's so important to be listening to God and letting Him guide and direct.

A very remarkable illustration of this concerns Peter Marshall, the Scot who in the middle of the twentieth century became one of America's most widely acclaimed ministers. Through his outstanding qualities as a man and a minister, he brought the office of the chaplain of the United States Senate to a new level of prominence.

Back in Britain, on one foggy, pitch-black Northumberland night, he was taking a shortcut across the moors in an area where there was a deep, deserted limestone quarry. As he plodded blindly forward, an urgent voice called out, "Peter!" He stopped and answered: "Yes, who is it? What do you want?" But there was no response.

Thinking he was mistaken, he took a few more steps. The voice came again, even more urgently, "Peter!" At this he stopped again and, trying to peer into the darkness, stumbled forward and fell to his knees. Putting down his hand to brace himself, he found nothing there. As he felt around in a semicircle, he discovered that he was right on the brink of the abandoned quarry, where one step more would certainly have killed him.

It's not just the big things, but little things He leads us with as well. Many times, I've not been able to find my keys or something I've misplaced. After frantically looking everywhere I finally stop and pray, and then soon after that their location pops right into my mind!

Charles Stanley adds excellent counsel to this. "In the Old Testament when men such as King David inquired of the Lord, the question was nearly always put to the Lord in such a way that the answer was yes or no. I believe this is the foremost way that the

Holy Spirit speaks to us hour by hour as we walk through our particular set of circumstances. We can never ask too many times of the Holy Spirit, „Should I do this – yes or no? " We will sense in our spirits His word of reply to us. Generally, it will be a sense of enthusiasm and eager desire marked with great joy and freedom, or it will be a sense of foreboding, danger, caution, or need for silence. I find that it is much easier to receive the direction of the Holy Spirit by asking for yes-or-no counsel than to say to Him in general terms, „What do you want me to do? "''

So, when we talk about the content of what God speaks, we find He speaks conviction, information and guidance, and also encouragement.

God doesn't just speak information to us; quite often He speaks words of encouragement, peace, comfort and strength. "Peace, I leave with you; My peace I give you. I do not give to you as the world gives. Do not let your hearts be troubled and do not be afraid" (John 14:27). "And the peace of God, which transcends all understanding, will guard your

hearts and your minds in Christ Jesus" (Philippians 4:6-7).

God has given me encouragement and peace about our church. Despite the numbers and financial difficulties, I know He wants me to persevere here.

So, God speaks conviction, information and encouragement to us. He also tells us how to carry on the responsibilities and ministries He has given us.

His voice calls people into ministry (I Timothy 1:12; 2:6-7) and then tells those whom He has called what to say. Moses is an example of this (Exodus 4:10-12). I'm sure you've noticed times when you were talking to someone about spiritual things and all of a sudden, the right thoughts came to you and you were able to explain something in a way you never thought you could.

When I teach and preach, I depend on God to give me the right things to say. That's why I always pray before I start, asking Him to give me His words to speak and that everyone would hear Him and not me. I need to listen to Him and you need to be hearing from Him as you hear me.

The final form His communication may take is that of revelation of Himself. Often it will just seem to „hit" us how wonderful, powerful or majestic God is. This is Him revealing Himself to us by His Holy Spirit. He does this so we will respond in praise and worship.

That happens to me when I listen to my son Dan plays the piano or when I listen to Southern Gospel Music.

Sometimes we can be so overwhelmed with God's love in our soul that we find ourselves enraptured in an immense feeling of being loved deeply, of God telling us how much He loves us. Our natural response is to worship, to love Him back.

So we've seen this morning that God speaks to us in a gentle whisper. When He does, He speaks rich and enlightening thoughts to our minds. Or He may cause a warm burning in our hearts as He speaks to our emotions and feelings.

The content which He communicates to us consists of conviction, information and guidance, encouragement and peace, enablement in ministry, and a revelation of Himself to cause us to worship Him.

In which of these areas has He been speaking to you during the last week? In which is He speaking to you now? Where do you need to hear Him speaking in the coming week?

Now that you know a little better what God's voices sound like and the kinds of things He talks about, make sure you are listening for them this week. Many people like to write down these things so they remember and follow through with them.

Make sure you are always listening, for God will be speaking. He will speak to you this week; will you hear Him?

I'd like to close with a story I shared on a Wednesday evening several years ago. It's a great example of listening to God speak.

XII. APPENDIX 8

LISTENING TO GOD

"How Can I Tell the Voice is God's and Not Satan's?"

Impersonators make good money entertaining and impressing audiences with their ability to look and/or sound like someone famous. They can make good money cashing in on someone else's fame and good name.

Satan does the same thing. He pretends to be God speaking to man – but not just for entertainment and amusement. The results are deadly if we listen to the wrong voice.

In World War II the Japanese found ways to broadcast on American airwaves to soldiers, giving commands and orders to deceive and defeat our troops. Soldiers had to make sure they were taking orders from the right source. As God's soldiers in a deadly war with Satan, we must make sure that we are hearing from Him and not our enemy. Sometimes that isn't so easy.

I. **WHAT VOICES DO I HEAR?**

There are actually three counterfeits „voices" that can confuse or mislead us. The first is the voice of the flesh. As Paul says in Romans 8:5-8, the flesh is, in essence, the part of us that tends to sin. It is in opposition to the Spirit in us and leads us to disobedience of God (James 1:13-14). The desires of the flesh can be strong, especially if they have been given free rein in the past.

By knowing what God's Word says and by listening to the convicting voice of the Spirit within, we can learn to recognize this voice for the self-centered temptation it is.

A second „voice" is the voice of the world. The world system, with its values and goals, can have a strong appeal to our sin nature (flesh). John warns us not to the system around us that is not based on love of God and His Word (I John 2:15-17). Its „voice" comes to us through what we see, hear and read in our daily lives. It can come through others, the media, or our own envy of those who seem better off than we are. Inputs from the world around us can be very persuasive, effecting how we think and therefore behave. They can sound very appealing, so we need to carefully study God's will as revealed in the Bible and be sensitive to the Spirit" promptings and warnings. When the voice of the world lines up with the voice of the flesh, the temptation can be very strong.

The most dangerous voice, however, because it is most subtle, is the voice of Satan. Ananias obviously listened to Satan's voice instead of God's when saying he was donating all he received for the sale of his land when it was, in fact, only part of the amount (Acts 5:3).

Satan does communicate with man. He did so with Jesus when He was tempted after forty days in the wilderness (Matthew 4). Paul says Satan sows' deception in the hearts of people (2 Corinthians 11:3).

Jesus says that everything Satan says is a lie, for that is his nature. "You are of your father the devil, and you want to do the desires of your father. He was a murderer from the beginning, and does not stand in the truth, because there is no truth in him. Whenever he speaks a lie, he speaks from his own nature; for he is a liar, and the father of lies" John 8:44.

The Bible doesn't give details about just how Satan does this, but we do know he can put thoughts into a person's mind. "But turning around and seeing His disciples, He rebuked Peter, and said, "Get behind Me, Satan; for you are not setting your mind on God's interests, but man's" Mark 8:33.

In addition, Satan can take thoughts out of a mind. "When anyone hears the word of the kingdom, and does not understand it, the evil one comes and snatches away what has been sown in his heart. This is the one on whom seed was sown beside the road" Matthew 13:19.

As with Adam and Eve, Satan's communication with man is always deceitful and destructive. He can make suggestions about how we may meet a legitimate need on our own without waiting for God's provision. He can put thoughts of guilt and failure into our minds. He can provide excuses to justify a sinful course we are taking. He can undermine God's goodness and the Bible's authority.

Satan is willing to speak as much as a man is willing to listen. He uses various forms of the occult to communicate with man, such as tarot cards, Ouija boards, séances, and other means. He can and will speak directly to a person much as the Holy Spirit does. "Be self- controlled and alert. Your enemy the devil prowls around like a roaring lion looking for someone to devour" (1 Peter 5:8). Because Satan is the most dangerous of the counterfeit voices we hear, we will focus on him for this message.

Satan is a counterfeiter. He tries to counterfeit all God does for His people. Judas heard Satan's voice and betrayed Jesus (Matthew 26:14-16). Peter heard Satan's voice and did not believe the voice of Jesus (Mark 8:31-33). A leper was healed by Jesus and told not to tell anyone who did it but he heard Satan's voice and disobeyed (Mark 1:40-45).

While we know Satan is limited to one place at a time, we must recognize that he does his work thorough demons. It is highly unlikely that Satan will ever speak to us directly, but by assigning certain demons to harass and impact us the result is the same. Thus, when we say that „Satan speaks to us" we are really recognizing that all demonic forces work together for Satan.

David's thought to take a census of the people was demon-inspired (1 Chronicles 21:1ff; 2 Samuel 24:1ff). Saul's jealousy and anger at David was as well (1 Samuel 16:14-23).

Ananias and Sapphira's greed were demon stimulated as well (Acts 5:3). When God didn't speak to Saul, he went to a medium to connect with a supernatural power (1 Samuel 28:4-7). For this reason, John warns, "Do not believe every spirit, but test the spirits to see whether they are from God, because many false prophets have gone out into the world."

Therefore, it is essential to make sure you can tell Satan's voice from God's voice. Let's look at how to do that.

II. **HOW CAN I TELL THE VOICE IS GOD"S AND NOT SATAN"S?**

The first way we can tell the difference between God's voice and Satan's voice is that <u>God convicts while Satan condemns</u>. When God speaks to us about sin, we feel guilty and sinful but still loved. When it is Satan condemning us, we don't feel loved but rejected and hopeless.

Jesus forgives and restores, as with the woman taken in adultery. Jesus straightened up and asked her, "Woman, where are they? Has no one condemned you?" "No one, sir," she said. "Then neither do I condemn you," Jesus declared. "Go now and leave your life of sin" (John 8:10-11).

By contrast Satan accuses and focuses on our guilt. That's why he's called the „accuser of our brothers" (Revelation 12:10).

God will expose the sin and focus on it, but only for the purpose of us confessing and removing it. He offers hope of restoration. He doesn't emphasize our guilt, failure and unworthiness in that area and as a person in general, but Satan does.

When Jesus convicts, we know specifically what He is talking about and what to do about it. When it comes from Satan, we just have a nagging sense of unspecified guilt and failure to discourage and defeat us. Or Satan will point to past sins which have been confessed and forgiven and try to get us to feel miserable about them, ignoring the fact that God has forgotten them.

So, God convicts but Satan condemns.

A second way of telling the difference is to remember that <u>God clarifies but Satan confuses</u>. When God speaks to us it is to clearly show us sin in its true, deadly light. The pleasure and deception is removed and the awful deadliness is revealed. Satan, however, tries to perplex us with worldly logic and explanations. He feeds us excuses, justifications, thoughts of how it is another's fault and general confusion over it (James 3:15). When God speaks there is a sense that everything is under control (1 Corinthians 14:32). Satan's purpose is to ensnare and take captive (2 Timothy 2:24-26).

God's voice brings peace (Philippians 4:7) but Satan's voice brings uncertainty for what he tells us conflicts with what the Spirit is also telling us. Thus, we feel perplexed.

If the voice you are hearing brings a nagging, gnawing feeling of frustration in your spirit, it's not from God. God brings a deep calmness in your spirit.

Thus, God convicts while Satan condemns. God clarifies while Satan confuses. There's another way to tell the difference: <u>God confirms while Satan contradicts</u>. When it's God's voice speaking to us we know it lines up with the Bible and advice Godly believers would give us. It passes Paul's test of making sure everything is true, noble, right, pure, lovely and admirable (Philippians 4:8-9). However, when Satan speaks his words don't agree with the Bible or advice of mature Christians. When we desire it so much, we ignore the warnings in our spirit we are headed to sin.

So, God convicts while Satan condemns, God clarifies while Satan confuses, and God confirms while Satan contradicts.

Further, <u>God chooses while Satan captures</u>. God's voice brings us freedom, there are no strings attached. "You shall know the truth and the truth shall set you free." Following Satan's voice brings bondage, we are trapped and taken prisoner (2 Timothy 2:26).

Satan says, "Do your own thing, do what you want to do." God says, "Consider the effects of your behavior on others. Live a selfless, self-giving life." Satan says, "Live for the moment." God says, "Live with an eye on eternity." Satan says "Don't concern yourself with what others say." God says, "Receive godly counsel." Satan says, "You're as mature as you ever need to be. You're grown up." God says, "Continue to grow and mature and to become more and more like Jesus." In all these Satan's advice, while appealing to our flesh, leads to bondage and defeat. God's will, instead, brings freedom and life.

God convicts while Satan condemns, God clarifies while Satan confuses, and God confirms while Satan contradicts. God chooses while Satan captures.

In addition, <u>God constrains but Satan constricts</u>. God draws us by His love and gives us a desire to want to live for Him. "For Christ's love compels us" (2 Corinthians 5:14). Moving from sin to following God is like taking a shower when we are really dirty because we know how good we'll feel afterwards. Satan's communication does not bring that. It constricts, limits, makes us feel dirtier and ineffective. We feel discouraged and hopeless.

Satan is like the salesman trying to force us to make a decision we aren't quite sure of, telling us if we don't buy now it'll be too late. God respects our free will and doesn't force us. He gives us time to think the alternatives through. When we feel forced, pushed or in a hurry we can know Satan is speaking, not God. God is never in a hurry

So, in summary we see that God convicts while Satan condemns, God clarifies while Satan confuses, and God confirms while Satan contradicts. God chooses while Satan captures. God constrains but Satan constricts.

The way to tell Satan's voice from God's voice is to run what you hear through the following test:

1. **Is it consistent with the word of God?** Does this solution fit the principles that are in the Bible? Does it violate anything in the Bible? Would Jesus, do it?

2. **Is it a wise decision**? In your own heart and mind is it the type of solution that Jesus Christ himself would agree with? Would Jesus implement this solution himself?

3. **Are you confident in asking God to enable you to achieve this solution**? Can you look upon this solution as one that God would send into your life?

4. **Do you feel that it is a God given solution**? Deep within your heart do you feel or sense that this solution is the will of God?

5. **Does this solution fit a child of God**? From all that you know about God, does this solution or this answer fit a person that truly loves, believes, and trusts God?

6. **Does the solution fit God's overall plan for your life**? Does this solution fit in with God's guidance and direction of your life?

7. **Does this solution honor God**? Does it bring glory and praise to Almighty God?

Have you been able to recognize any of these traits of Satan's voice in communication you have been hearing? Make sure you don't follow anything that doesn't come from God!

Are you now better able to discern God's voice from Satan's voice? If you really want to hear from God only and not be deceived, He'll make sure you have the discernment you need. Just ask Him.

XIII. APPENDIX 9

DOES GOD WANT US TO SPEAK IN TONGUES TODAY?

BAPTISM IN THE SPIRIT, SECOND BLESSING, TONGUES & SUCH MATTERS

What a land-mine this subject is! It gets so divisive. I'm sure God hates to see that among His children. I don't write this to be divisive, but God does require each of us to come to our own conclusions on this matter, based on the Bible. I don't try to explain how or why others feel led as they do, I don't in any way judge or condemn them, I only know how God is leading me from His Word. I have thoroughly studied this whole issue with as open a heart as possible, even wishing there were some higher form of spirituality and victory that would take me to a higher plane. Still, I feel totally convinced God is showing me through His Word that these things are not for me nor the people I shepherd. What is happening in Pentecostal and Charismatic circles I do not know. I only know how He leads me.

The Bible teaches that each believer is **filled with the Holy Spirit** at the moment of salvation (I Cor 10:1ff; 12:3; 6:19; Eph. 4:5; Rom. 5:5). One cannot be saved without the Holy Spirit indwelling them (John 7:37-39; 14:16-17; I Cor 6:19-20). From there on it is not a matter of getting more of the Holy Spirit but of the Holy Spirit getting more of us! As we totally submit and live a holy life He fills and works through us.

Then what about Acts 2, 8, 10 and 19, when the Holy Spirit came on those who were already believers? **Acts 2** is a one-time, non-repeatable experience (not even repeated in Acts 8, 10 or 19). Just like the Second Person of the Trinity made a unique, one-time entrance into the world through a virgin in a stable, so the Third Person made His entrance in a unique, one-time way. When Jesus came back to earth after the resurrection to the apostles, Paul or John on Patmos, He never repeated the virgin-in-a- stable entrance. Acts 2, also, is non-repeatable.

Acts 2 is a transition, from Old Testament law when the Holy Spirit only indwelt some believers sometimes, to New Testament grace, when the Holy Spirit indwells all believers for their whole life. The apostles had already accepted Jesus" claims and were saved in the old dispensation, then when the new dispensation started and the Spirit came, they naturally would be the first to receive Him in that way. That is non- repeatable, too. In **Acts 8** we see this same truth applied to half Jews and half Gentiles, in **Acts 10** to Gentiles in Palestine, and in **Acts 19** to Gentiles outside of Palestine. They were similar to Acts 2 to show that Jews and Gentiles were now equal in the same Body, that the same thing happened to each. Each one showed the changeover from Old Testament law to New Testament grace. There had to be a definite time of change, showing the transfer had been made and those believers accepted. Still, what happened was different enough to show that it wasn't Acts 2 repeated again. Those were the only times anything even resembling Acts 2 happened in Acts, and it only happened once for each new group as the gospel spread from Jerusalem. All others received the Holy Spirit immediately at salvation.

Tongues is not proof of Spirit baptism. Many received the Holy Spirit but not tongues: 3,000 on the Day of Pentecost (Acts 2:38-41), early church believers (Acts 4:31), Samaritans (Acts 8:14-17), Paul (Acts 9:17-18), John the Baptist (Luke 1:15-16),

Jesus (Lk. 3:21-22; 4:1,14,18,21) and many others (Acts 4:8,31; 6:5; 7:55; 11:24; 13:9,52). Speaking in tongues is never mentioned in the leadership qualities in Titus or I Timothy. The Bible makes it clear that obedience is the proof of the Holy Spirit's indwelling, not tongues (Eph 5:18f).

Tongues in Acts and Corinth were the same. The same Greek word („glossa" meaning „tongue, to speak, language") is always used of known foreign languages and is used in both Acts (2:6-11, etc.) and Corinth (I Cor 14:21; 12:10). In Acts is it obvious that the listeners heard known languages spoken by those who had no previous knowledge of the language. There is no indication that what Corinth experienced was different. It is only the church at Corinth that is mentioned as using tongues, and then many corrections were needed because it was a very carnal church (I Cor. 3:1-3).

The purpose of tongues was to show Jews that God's judgment was on them. They were to spread God's message to Gentiles but failed. God would show He was judging them for that by bringing His word to them by Gentiles in Gentile languages. This was prophesied in Isa. 28:9-12; 33:19f; Duet 28:49; and Jer 5:15. Paul said tongues fulfilled those prophecies (I Cor 14:21-22). When the Jews didn't heed this sign and repent, God's judgment came upon them in 70 ADS when Jerusalem was destroyed. After 70 AD there is no instance of tongues being used in the early church. Signs are placed before what they are to mark, not after! Paul said (I Cor. 13:8-12) that tongues "will be stilled." The Greek word, „pauo, " is in the middle voice; they will stop by themselves and not start again. History records only a very few, very isolated, very minor outbreak of tongues from Acts to the present. These groups were often heretical in some or all of their other beliefs. Obviously, tongues did stop. There is nothing to indicate that they would ever begin again, for their purpose has been fulfilled. When Joel 2 talks about the Holy Spirit coming back after the Tribulation, there is no mention of tongues!

Then what about those with the gift of interpretation? First, the Greek word for this refers to someone who interprets known languages, like from Spanish to German. The use of foreign languages was to show God's judgment to the Jews present. The content of the message was God's good news, which the Jews should have been spreading. Since speaking in an unknown language would mean nothing to Gentiles present, Paul said there had to be an interpreter present when the gift was used (I Cor 14:26-28). This was necessary for the weak and immature Corinthian believers (14:20-22) who were ignorant of God's truth (12:13). It was to be kept to a minimum (14:6-12) because it was an inferior gift (I Cor. 14:4). Paul himself only used his ability to speak in unknown languages in Jewish synagogues, not Jewish services (14:39).

Applying these criteria to tongues today (known foreign language, showing God's judgment on the Jews, used only with Jews present, seen as a lesser/minor gift whose use was to be kept to a minimum, etc.) shows that what is happening today is different from what happened back then.

Tongues are not a heavenly language. The Greek word makes it clear they are a KNOWN language (Acts 2:6-11; I Cor 14:21; 12:10). This is different than the

„groanings" of Romans 8:26 for those are clearly said to be unutterable (not able to be spoken). The "tongues of angels" (I Cor. 13:1) is a hyperbole (overemphasis to make a point) like "faith to move mountains." Besides, when angels spoke in the Bible, it was always in the known language of those to whom they were speaking.

Tongues are not a private prayer language. All spiritual gifts are given for the sake of others, not the one having the gift (I Cor 12:7, 12f; 14:19,27), that's why an interpreter had to always be present in Corinth (I Cor 14:26-28). Every time the gift of tongues was given in the Bible it was given to a group, not an individual. It was always used in a group, too, no instance of private use is recorded. The tongue is to be controlled by the speaker, not beyond his control (I Cor. 14:28-33). Plus, tongues were to be a sign to unbelievers, not believers (I Cor 14:22). Jesus Himself warned about praying words we don't understand (Mt 6:7). Paul said he always understood what he said when he prayed, even in tongues (I Cor 14:15). When asked how to pray Jesus gave the Lord's Prayer, not tongues.

Dangers of speaking in tongues today. Paul warns about Satan's ability to counterfeit this (I Cor 12:2-3) as he has in other religions and cults today. Tongues is said to be an inferior gift because it is self-centered (I Cor 14:4) and leads to emphasis being put on emotions which can lead people astray (II Cor 6:11-12; Rom 16:17-18). We are told to pray with understanding (I Cor 14:13-17) and control our spiritual gift (I Cor 14:28-40). God arbitrarily chooses which gifts to give to whom (I Cor 12:7,11,18,28). We are told to not seek any particular gift (I Cor 12:31; 14:1-4). Tongues speaking can become a substitute for spirituality (I Cor 14:26-28). Worse of all, it can produce a false security by those who put faith in it as proof that God loves and accepts them. Most who practice tongues-speaking do not believe in eternal security of salvation, so their speaking in tongues becomes their proof of acceptance by God. Our faith must be in Jesus" work on the cross, not in our ability to speak in „tongues. " Those without the gift can feel pressured to fit in with the rest of the group.

XIV. APPENDIX 10

IS IT GOD"S WILL FOR EVERYONE TO BE HEALED TODAY?

There are those today who believe that Jesus not only paid for sin on the cross, but that He also paid for our sickness. They say that each is received by faith, if you have enough faith to receive it. Loss of faith, then, causes the loss of these benefits of faith. They claim some are especially gifted in healing and can heal those who come to them. They say God did miracles in the Bible and he is still a miracle-working God today.

What about this? Is this true? This is not just one peripheral issue, but stands very central in our salvation and Christian life. Is God's sovereignty or man's free will the final and ultimate deciding factor? It must be God's sovereignty. The motive for living for Jesus should not be fear of losing our salvation. The goal of living for Jesus should not be a problem free life. Pain and suffering aren't to be faced by whipping up enough faith so that God removes it (or living with the feelings of failure and guilt if it isn't removed and we believe that is our fault by not having enough faith). What about these claims of „faith healers"? What does the Bible say?

IS THE GIFT OF HEALING FOR TODAY? While it's true that Jesus and the Apostles healed, it was done as a sign to authenticate that they were from God (Mt 12:39). This was God's way having people listen to them instead of all the counterfeits around. When they were fully authenticated, there was no longer any reason for the sign. In AD 35 all were healed but by AD 60 some were not (Epaphroditus, Paul's thorn in the flesh). Then by AD 67 very few were being healed (Trophimus was left at Miletus sick, Timothy's stomach was unhealed, etc.). Jerusalem, the scene of many early miracles, had not one miracle done in it after Stephen was stoned. The people had the evidence but rejected it. James, the oldest book in the Bible, says that if someone is sick, we are to pray for them (James 5:14).

SHOULD WE SEE MIRACLES TODAY LIKE IN BIBLE TIMES? Actually, if you list all the miracles in the Bible, you will find almost all of them fit three time periods. They aren't evenly spread out throughout history but cluster in the times of Moses/Joshua, Elijah/Elisha and Jesus/apostles. In each of these times a new mess had developed so God sent a new message through a new messenger whom He authenticated by miracles ("signs"). One more time of miracles is coming, called the Tribulation.

IS FAITH A PREREQUISITE FOR HEALING? Jesus didn't make faith a requirement for healing. Many that He healed didn't have faith. The impotent man at the pool didn't even know who He was. The man with the withered hand and the man with dropsy were healed as a sign to religious leaders who were present, they didn't ask to be healed. The cripple that Peter and Paul healed outside the temple didn't exercise any faith. Of course, the demoniacs who were delivered and those brought back from the dead didn't exercise faith. Then there are others who had strong faith but weren't healed: Stephen, Paul, Timothy, Job, David, Elisha, etc.

IS „HEALING" TODAY THE SAME AS IN BIBLE TIMES? Today's „healers" must meet the same characteristics of Jesus and the apostles to claim they are doing what was done then. Jesus and the apostles healed with a word or touch wherever and whenever.

There was no special place or time, no chants or music, no gimmicks, nothing. Do today's faith healers walk down the hall in a hospital and empty every room? That's how Jesus and Peter did it. Also, Bible miracles were done instantly, not gradually or slowly. There was no healing to „claim" or lose. Healing was then done totally, not partially, and it was never lost. Everyone was healed. There was no screening done. 100% of every one, no matter the need, was healed. Organic diseases were healed: limbs grew back instantly, strong enough to walk on, eyes were open, leprosy instantly gone and healthy flesh gown. Then, too, the dead were raised. Today's faith healing doesn't nearly meet these characteristics.

DOES GOD NOT HEAL? Yes, a sovereign God can always heal. He is always able to heal, but He is not always willing. Healing isn't guaranteed. Healing isn't based on our having enough faith. Miracles by Jesus and the apostles were done as a sign to authenticate the One who could heal an unseen soul. God can and does heal, but He doesn't gift others to do it, nor does He say that is the recommended norm for His people.

WHAT ARE WE TO DO WHEN SICK? When we are sick it's good to first make sure it isn't for sin or disobedience. If there is sin that God is using the sickness to point out, confess it and God will forgive and then use that illness for good (Romans 8:28). It's fine to pray, asking God to heal if that is His will. We are to submit to His will; not demand He do what we want. Ask Him to use the pain and suffering for His glory (that we and others can see His Greatness through His provision and peace) and our growth (make us trust Him more and become more like Jesus). Use the best available resources: diet, rest, exercise and medical help. Realize that all healing does ultimately come from God. Leave the results to His will, though.

Granted, this whole subject of faith and healing can be a confusing and guilt- producing area. Specific verses can be found to seemingly support most any view. However, an overview of the Bible and it's teaching about these things definitely seems to substantiate the above view of healing. Always remember, our faith must be in Jesus. HE is the object of our faith, never a human person or group. Put faith in Jesus, not faith in your faith! HE is the one we are to look to and glorify. Always keep your eyes on Him. Trust and serve Him no matter what.

ALPHABETICAL INDEX OF SUBJECTS COVERED

Abuse and demonizing 26 Actions of Satan 8-9 Adoption & demonizing 26-27 After deliverance 62-76

Ancestors' sins 23-24 Angels and believers 6 Angels our helpers 5 Anger 18, 29-30

Anointing with oil 22, 23, 56, 58

Apologetics 79-81 Armor, wear it 64-72 Authority and power 47 Believers and angels 6

Believers can be demonized 13-14 Believers, demons work against 11 Believers, Satan's work against 9-10 Belt of truth 66-67

Bible and deliverance 68, 70-72 Bible verses for all occasions 95-100

Bible, How We know Is God's Word 82-86 Breastplate of righteousness 67

Causes of demonizing 21 Character of demons 10 Character of Satan 8-9

Characteristics of demonizing 13-20 Childhood access broken 27 Children and demonizing 57-58 Children and parents 60

Christian, how to know for sure 92 Church and deliverance 60-61 Church discipline 60

Communication, None with Demons 53 Compulsive thoughts 16 Confessing the sins of another 74 Confession of sin 34-36, 73 Conversing with Demons is Out 53 Counsel to others 76-77 Counterfeit Healings 56

Creation of angels 5 Creation of demons 10 Curses 25-26 Cutting 18-19

Darkness, Satan behind 12 Death, Satan's goal for us 12 Deception and truth 16 Deliverance by Jesus 47 Deliverance doesn't come 53 Deliverance slow 53

Deliverance today 49-54

Deliverance ongoing 62-76 Demonic influence of the mind 14-15

Demonized people, how responsible? 19 Demonized who may be 37-38 Demonizing defined 13

Demonizing of believers 13-14 Demonizing openings 22-46 Demonizing evidence of (list) 20 Demons, enemy soldiers 10-12 Description of demonizing 14-20 Deuteronomy 18:9-13 39 Discerning of spirits 61 Disciples and deliverance 48 Discipline, church 60

Duties of angels 6 Duties of demons 11

Emotions and demonizing 13 Ephesians 6:10-18 64-70

Eternal security 93-94

Evidence of demonizing (list) 20 Existence of Satan 7

Exorcism, sp gift 61

Faith, shield of 67-68 Fasting 56-57

Fear 17-18

Forgive others 50-51 Forgiveness of sins 34-36 Fortress illustration 21

Freemasonry 41-42

Generational openings/sins 23-24 God our commander 5

God How We Know He Exists 79-81 God's voice from Satan's voice 109-112 God's voice, how to hear 101-108

Healing and deliverance 55-56 Healing for all today? 116-117 Healings, Counterfeit 56 Helmet of salvation 68

Helping others 76-77 Holy Spirit, submit to 64 Home demonized 22

Humanism 43 Husband and wife 59

Idolatry based sins 30

Illness and demonizing 55-56 Illness, Mental 9, 17

Immorality based sins 25, 31

Intercession 74 Intercession, sp gift 61

James 4:7-8 78

Jesus and deliverance 48

Jesus, How We Know He Is God 87-91 Jesus, source of deliverance 47

Karate's influence 46

Listening to God 75, 101-108

Lists of sins, openings 20, 32-33

Marriage 59

Martial Arts 46

Masonic Lodge 41-42

Mediums 72

Memory verses 71-72

Mental illness 17

Mind and demonizing 14-15

Ministering Deliverance to Others 76-77

Names of Satan 8-9 Nature of angels 5 Necromancy 39

New Age 43-45

No Deliverance 53

Obsessive thoughts 16 Occult and demonizing 39-46 Occult and the Bible 39

Oil, anointing with 22, 23, 56, 58

Ongoing battle 62-76

Openings for demonizing 22-46 Openings common sins 32-33 Organization of angels 6

Organization of demons 10 Others, helping 76-77

Pantheism 43, 45 Parent and child 60 Parent's sins 23-24

Persevere no matter what 72-73 Personality of angels 5 Personality of demons 11 Physical healing 55-56

Poor self-image sins 32 Power and authority 47 Power of demons 10 Power of Jesus 47 Power of Satan 7 Praise to God 73-74

Prayer and deliverance 72-76 Prayer and the armor 69-70 Prayer, how to 72-76

Pride 2,7,8,10,24,32,41,52

Promises of victory 29 Property an opening 22-23 Purpose of what Satan does 9

Rebellion and demonizing 26-27 Rejection and demonizing 26 Removal of sin access 34-36 Resist and stand firm 72 Responsibility of the demonized 19 Retaining deliverance 63

Salvation, can't be lost 93-94 Salvation, how to be sure 92 Salvation, need of 3

Sandals of peace 67

Satan, enemy commander 7

Satan's voice from God's voice 109-112 Satan's work 8-10

Satanism 42-43

Schizophrenia 17

Scripture and deliverance 68, 70-72 Scripture for all occasions 95-100 Secret societies 41-42

Security of salvation 93-94 Self-image sins 32

Self-mutilation 18-19

Sexual sin & demonizing 25, 31 Shield of faith 67-68

Shriners 41-42

Sin openings for demonizing 25-46 Sin recovery from 36

Sin list of common 32-33 Soul ties and demonizing 27 Source of deliverance 47 Spiritual blindness 12

Spiritual gifts and deliverance 60-61 Spiritual gifts, tongues 113-115 Spiritual growth 63-64

Spiritual warfare, why do it? 4 Steps to deliverance 48-54 Submit to Holy Spirit 64 Suicide 18-19

Sword of the Word 68

Talk, Not with Demons 53 Test the Spirits 52, 72, 110 Thanksgiving in prayer 74

Thoughts and demonizing 14-15 Tongues, for us today? 113-115 Topical index 95-100

Truth and deception 16

Victory promised 29

War, believer in spiritual war 2 Who may be demonized 37-38 Why spiritual warfare? 4

Wife and husband 59 Wisdom, sp gift of 61 Witchcraft 24, 25, 39 Word of God 68, 70-72

Yoga's influence 46

As an author, Pastor Edward Johnson is seasoned with humor, compassion, revelatory insight, and personal candor, Edward translates hard-hitting spiritual insights into everyday language that empowers individuals to activate purpose and maximize potential. Edward has released several powerful books: Demonic Warfare, How to defeat your mind, 7 Steps to healing from trauma and soul wounds, and Spiritual Warfare.

Reach out to Pastor Johnson at @drjohnsworld

on Instagram, Facebook, and TikTok.

Milton Keynes UK
Ingram Content Group UK Ltd.
UKHW021247021124
450426UK00008B/59

9 798330 291809